Competition
VERSUS
Monopoly

Competition
VERSUS
Monopoly
Combines Policy in Perspective

Donald Armstrong
Edited by Walter Block

THE FRASER INSTITUTE
1982

Canadian Cataloguing in Publication Data

Armstrong, Donald E. (Donald Eugene), 1925-
    Competition versus monopoly

    Bibliography: p.
    Includes index.
    ISBN 0-88975-047-5

    1. Competition. 2. Monopolies. 3. Industrial laws
and legislation — Canada. 4. Canada. Combines
Investigation Act. I. Block, Walter, 1941-
II. Fraser Institute (Vancouver, B.C.) III. Title.
HD41.A75   338.6′048   C82-091050-3

Printed in Canada.

". . .in my country, some 25 years ago you could make a long-distance call on our privately-owned telephone system from San Francisco to New York for $28. For that same amount of money you could send 1,376 letters. Today, you can make the same telephone call for $2.50 and for that amount you can send only 41 letters. So the government is investigating the Bell System."

Ronald Reagan
Governor of California

Table of Contents

TOM SMITH
AND HIS INCREDIBLE BREAD MACHINE

by R.W. Grant

This is a legend of success and plunder
And a man, Tom Smith, who squelched world
    hunger.
Now, Smith, an inventor, had specialized
In toys. So, people were surprised
When they found that he instead
Of making toys, was BAKING BREAD!

The way to make bread he'd conceived
Cost less than people could believe.
And not just make it! This device
Could, in addition, wrap and slice!
The price per loaf, one loaf or many:
The miniscule sum of under a penny.

Can you imagine what this meant?
Can you comprehend the consequent?
The first time yet the world well fed!
And all because of Tom Smith's bread.

A citation from the President
For Smith's amazing bread.
This and other honors too
Were heaped upon his head.

But isn't it a wondrous thing
How quickly fame is flown?
Smith, the hero of today —
Tomorrow, scarcely known.

Yes, the fickle years passed by;
Smith was a millionaire,
But Smith himself was now forgot —
Though bread was everywhere.
People, asked from where it came,
Would very seldom know.
They would simply eat and ask,
"Was not it always so?"

However, Smith cared not a bit,
For millions ate his bread,
And "Everything is fine," thought he,
"I am rich and they are fed!"

Everything was fine, he thought?
He reckoned not with fate.

Note the sequence of events
Starting on the date
On which the business tax went up.
Then, to a slight extent,
The price on every loaf rose too:
Up to one full cent!

"What's going on?" the public cried,
"He's guilty of pure plunder.
He has no right to get so rich
On other people's hunger!"

(A prize cartoon depicted Smith
With fat and drooping jowls
Snatching bread from hungry babes
Indifferent to their howls!)

Well, since the Public does come first,
It could not be denied
That in matters such as this,
The Public must decide.
So, antitrust now took a hand.
Of course, it was appalled
At what it found was going on.
The "bread trust," it was called.

Now this was getting serious.
So Smith felt that he must
Have a friendly interview
With the men in antitrust.
So, hat in hand, he went to them.
They'd surely been misled;
No rule of law had he defied.
But then their lawyer said:

"The rule of law, in complex times,
Has proved itself deficient.
We much prefer the rule of men!
It's vastly more efficient.

Now, let me state the present rules,"
The lawyer then went on,
"These very simple guidelines
You can rely upon:
You're gouging on your prices if
You charge more than the rest.
But it's unfair competition
If you think you can charge less.

"A second point that we would make
To help avoid confusion:
Don't try to charge the same amount:
That would be collusion!
You must compete. But not too much,
For if you do, you see,
Then the market would be yours —
And that's monopoly!"

Price too high? Or price too low?
Now, which charge did they make?
Well, they weren't loath to charging both
With Public Good at stake!

In fact, they went one better —
They charged "monopoly!"
No muss, no fuss, oh woe is us,
Egad, they charged all three!

"Five years in jail," the judge then said.
"You're lucky it's not worse.
Robber Barons must be taught
Society Comes First!"

Now, bread is baked by government.
And as might be expected,
Everything is well controlled;
The public well protected.

True, loaves cost a dollar each.
But our leaders do their best.
The selling price is half a cent.
(Taxes pay the rest!)

Preface

I   Introduction

In April 1981, Consumer and Corporate Affairs Minister André Ouellet released "A Framework for Discussion," introducing his proposals for amending the *Combines Investigation Act*.

The importance of this document, together with the legislation proposed in the Spring of 1982, can hardly be overestimated for the Canadian economy. The *Combines Investigation Act* (CIA) strikes at the very heart of our industrial structure, affecting firms in every sector of the economy. The new rules it would put in place, if enacted into law, will have a profound effect upon our entire society, well into the twenty-first century. All the more unfortunate, then, that the new competition bill bodes well to follow in the footsteps of its predecessors, Bill C-256 and Bill C-13, and will likely be based as they were on theories of competition that are increasingly being called into question by economists.

There are two theories, or world-views, contending for supremacy in the economic sub-specialty called industrial organization. Each tries to explain the phenomena of competition — the encouragement of which is the presumed basis of anti-combines policy.

Structuralism

The first is called structuralism, and takes as its main point of departure the number of firms in an industry. That is, for the structuralist view, the more firms there are in an industry, the more competitive it is. The ideal, or "perfect competition," is obtained when there are an infinite number of firms in the industry. What matters is not how firms act, or what they do — a mere nose count can determine the degree of competition in existence.

Farming is often taken by the structuralists as a prime example of the closest real world approximation to the perfectly competitive model. There are thousands and thousands of "competitors." There is a homogeneous product — this is important so that large numbers can "compete" against each other; if farm produce was heterogeneous, there would be too few farmers producing each item for "perfection" to be reached. Ironically, however, there is virtually no *feeling* of rivalrous competition between farmers. Apart from co-operatives and farmers' associations, each farmer virtually ignores all the others, especially as individual competitors.

But this is the issue upon which most anti-combines conspiracy trials turn. In structuralist terms, ignoring competitors is good (perfectly competitive) and watching them is bad (monopolistic or oligopolistic). Scathingly remarks Professor Don Armstrong, the author of this book:

> This is hardly a conclusion that could be based on competition in love, war, sports or any other field of human endeavour. Any boxer who climbed into the ring intent on being so perfectly competitive that he ignored his rival would have that particular idea knocked out of his head soon enough. I count myself lucky that I did my boxing before I did my economics. Fortunately, it never crossed my mind that I would be more competitive in the ring if I just minded my own business; otherwise I might have qualified for the 'Perfectly Competitive Boxing Citation' (usually awarded posthumously).

Behaviourism

The second theory is called behaviourism, and as its name implies, it is concerned with how business firms *act*. Of crucial importance for this view is that new entry into the industry not be artificially blocked by government restrictions. (Entry restrictions include legislatively imposed tariffs, regulations, marketing boards, permits, licences, or bylaws which specifically prohibit competition, such as those which protect the newly-created Canada Post Corporation from alternative mail delivery firms.) As long as there are no legal barriers to entry, reasons the behaviourist view, high prices and profits in any sector of the economy will tend to be eroded by the emergence of competitors anxious to share in the great rewards.

Other basic elements of the behaviourist view of competition are the importance of offer improvement, rivalry, innovativeness, and an emphasis on continuous change in a dynamic economy. Because behaviourists must be concerned with what managers actually do, their models of the firm and the market are likely to be much more realistic than the conventional price theory models of the structuralists.

The number of firms as an indication of competitiveness is rejected outright. There may be only two or three large firms in an industry, indicating a very highly concentrated structure. And yet they may compete like cats fighting in a laundry bag. On the other hand, an industry with hundreds of members and thus a low concentration ratio, may hardly compete at all. Anyone witnessing the struggles of Pepsi vs Coca Cola, IBM vs Xerox, Hertz vs Avis, or the intense rivalry of the Big Three auto manufacturers will realize the truth of this. Of far more importance than mere numbers are things such as the rate of offer improvement, innovative spirit, willingness to try new methods of sales, finance, production, etc.

Competition in the real world

It is now well documented that when classical economists spoke of competition, they meant rivalrous activities consistent with the verb "to compete." Coincident with the development of the price theory models of the neoclassical structuralist economists, however, competition lost virtually all of its behavioural meaning. Competition came to mean the "structure" of the market which, in turn, meant little more than the number of firms. "Perfect competition" became the standard by which other markets were judged, and, of course, in the perfectly competitive market in equilibrium there is no rivalry at all. For the definition of equilibrium presumes that all firms are already acting optimally. Any change at all would worsen matters.

Because of this unfortunate theoretical development, economists virtually cut themselves off from a study of competitive behaviour in a real world setting. They focused instead on price performance. While the courts could hardly ignore behaviour, they were enough influenced by neoclassical economic thought to ignore all behaviour except that explicity linked to price. As a result of these developments, the defendants in a combines case are virtually barred from telling their story of how inter-firm rivalry has resulted in offer improvements. This on the ground that such evidence would be irrelevant to the consideration of competition! It is a strange world.

The verb "to compete" is now being rediscovered, accompanied by a swing from structuralism toward behaviourism. Sooner or later the courts will have to admit a broader range of evidence, so that companies will be able to show that even a history of uniform prices does not impede or even slow down the rate of offer improvements. Indeed uniform *pro forma* prices may be accompanied by the maximum possible rate of price reductions.

If we are to have a new competition bill it must surely be based on concepts of competiton that are consistent with real world processes. Accepting a structuralist price theory model in which the ideal price is arrived at in a market in which there is, by assumption, no real world competition at all, is simply absurd.

Common sense

Were the contrast between the two schools of thought presented in such stark terms as these, and were the judges the ordinary business-person, housewife, worker, farmer, or student, using the common sense for which Canadians are so well and widely known, the debate would have been over before it was begun. We all know that in sports, love, business, the arts, the animal world, truly ferocious competition will oft-times take place between and among the few. You don't need a cast of thousands to ensure competition. This, in a nutshell, is the message which emerges from this study by Professor Armstrong.

But the debate is rarely cast in such terms. Instead generations of students have been subjected to (force-fed) structuralist theory in simplistic first-course economics textbooks. Structuralism has hidden itself from the scrutiny of the general public behind a welter of statistics, geometry, jargon, and all but incomprehensible mathematical studies. In order to understand fully the fallacies of anti-combines policy in their entirety, the concerned layperson must therefore subject himself to a not inconsiderable amount of theoretical detail, graphical analysis, and economic jargon. We are fortunate then, to have Professor Armstrong serve as our guide.

There has never been a more articulate, eloquent, and entertaining instruction book on economic principles, than this present one. In simple, easy-to-understand steps, Armstrong brings us in gentle stages from the obvious and simple, to a rather comprehensive understanding of the issues underlying anti-combines legislation. After reading this book, the reader will never again suffer the almost total incomprehension of the issues underlying anti-combines policy — the fate of most of the lay-public.

II   Behaviourism and Structuralism

In order to gain an overview of the two competing visions of competition, we contrast their elements, in summary form, as regards households, markets, firms, economic welfare, management, competition and conspiracy, and public policy implications. We list the summaries of the two positions side-by-side on the page, although because of the great differences in the two approaches, they cannot be matched point-by-point:

1. The household

Behaviourism

a) Households fill multiple roles and are vitally interested in the offers made to them as consumers, workers, savers, and investors.

b) The needs of households in all their roles are many and complex.

c) The offer made to each household with respect to each product or each job must also have many dimensions to correspond to those needs.

d) The price of a product, or the wage that goes with a job, constitutes only one of the many product or job-offer dimensions.

e) Households expect change, variety, and improvement as consumers, workers, and investors.

Structuralism

a) Households play multiple roles but their role as consumers is the main concern of competition policy.

b) Their needs are simple, confined basically to quality and price, and quality is usually given.

c) Products and offers to households are correspondingly simple.

d) Price is the main concern of the consumer.

e) Price is a single number and constitutes the pain against which is measured the pleasure derived from using the product.

f) The households' offers to sellers can be expressed as simple schedules of quantities and prices.

2. Markets

Behaviourism

a) Unconcentrated markets, the closest real world approximations of the perfectly competitive model, are not noted for their high rate of competition, or offer-improvement.

b) A firm that adds to the range of choice available by making a unique offer that households freely accept may be called a monopoly (a single seller) but its action is almost always wholly desirable.

c) Unless entry is prohibited, it cannot be assumed that "monopoly" prices (prices charged by firms making unique offers) are higher than "competitive" prices (prices that would be charged for the same product if offered by many firms).

d) Competition in a behavioural sense cannot be visualized as a steadily increasing function as the market structure ranges from monopoly to perfect competition.

Structuralism

a) The perfectly competitive model is the ideal.

b) A monopoly comprises a single firm in an industry making a unique offer.

c) The monopoly price is considered to be higher and the monopoly output lower than the competitive price and output.

d) The real-world markets are usually seen as a continuum from monopoly to perfect competition.

e) Competition is generally viewed as a function that increases as the number of firms increases.

f) Concentration measures provide a means of positioning actual industries on the continuum of competition.

g) Freedom of entry is usually seen as an additional structure variable determining the amount of competition, but barriers to entry (capital requirements, advertising, research and development, etc.) are stressed.

2. Markets (Cont'd)

e) Competition, meaning offer-improvement, improved choice, etc., is likely to reach a maximum anywhere in the area between one and a large number of firms.

f) The concentration ratio for different industries tells us nothing more than the relative importance of larger firms. It does not measure competitive behaviour, the amount of competition, or the performance of the industry.

g) Freedom of entry is a most important safeguard of competition, but it is not possible or desirable that entry be "free" in the sense of being a (costless) good.

3. The firm

Behaviourism

a) Power is widely distributed within an organization and between the organization and outside participants.

b) Contracts between the firm and its participants cannot completely specify performance.

c) The prosperity and survival of the firm rests on all individuals and groups that have power, and they include all internal and external participants.

d) The needs of customers, workers, and suppliers are multi-dimensional, and managerial responses to the needs of all participants must be equally multi-dimensional.

e) Price (wage, etc.) is at best only one dimension and is often not a single member.

f) In order to assure the prosperity and survival of the organization, managers must maintain the goodwill of all those with power; i.e., customers, workers, suppliers, etc.

Structuralism

a) Whatever power is possessed by a firm rests with the top managers.

b) If workers or suppliers have any power, it is surrendered when they make a contract with management.

c) Contracts completely describe the terms of exchange and subsequent performance.

d) Needs of participants (workers, customers, etc.) are simple and can be measured and met in monetary terms.

e) Change is relatively unimportant.

f) The number of variables under managerial control, even in a monopoly, are few and simple.

g) B.Comms. need not apply.

3. The firm (Cont'd)

g) In general, goodwill is maintained by:
   i) making better offers than those available elsewhere;
   ii) generating expectations that future offers will be even better than present ones;
   iii) convincing participants that there is a fair distribution of value among workers, investors, suppliers, and customers.

h) Security for the firm will be achieved when management can make better offers to all participants than are available elsewhere, and can hold out the prospect of being able to maintain the superiority of its offer-improvement rate over time.

i) It follows from the foregoing that the job of management is to make changes that will improve *all* offers, though, of course, all participants will not share equally in every successful change.

j) The task of management must be seen first and foremost as the creation of value for the purpose of making better offers.

4. Economic welfare

Behaviourism

a) The perfectly competitive model implies an absence of intra-industry choice and a low rate of offer-improvement. It cannot, therefore, be considered as an ideal for a world that values variety and progress.

b) Even if welfare losses occur because of an absence of perfect competition, they would in all likelihood be made up by offer-improvement in a world of competing monopolists.

c) Monopoly in the unique-offer sense does not misallocate resources.

Structuralism

a) Optimum resource allocation is achieved in a world of perfect competition.

b) Perfect competition does not now characterize all industries. All the more reason, then, for the objective of public policy to approach the ideal as closely as possible.

c) Monopoly power exists in greater or lesser degree in any market that is not perfectly competitive; it always misallocates resources.

d) Excess capacity constitutes a misallocation of resources that would be eliminated if there was adequate competition.

4. Economic welfare (Cont'd)

d) Excess capacity cannot be dismissed as a misallocation of resources. It is an important part of the offer to customers, workers, and managers. It provides a measure of security to the firm and to the economy, and over time it will probably result in lower costs.

e) The most appropriate test of performance is the rate of offer-improvement as judged by free choice.

e) A uniform level of profit across all industries, with some allowance for differences in risk, would give a practical indication of adequate competition provided there was no X-inefficiency (laziness, reduction of effort).

5. Management

Behaviourism

a) Managers are rational in the sense they prefer larger rewards to smaller ones: but rewards include much more than money and goods.

b) Managers, like other people, do *not* dislike work; as a group they work long and hard.

c) Successful managers work harder than less successful managers.

d) Managers, like virtually everyone else, put a high value on satisfying basic needs.

e) When basic needs are met (e.g., no imminent threat of bankruptcy) managers will be motivated to satisfy higher needs.

f) In general the needs that are higher up in the need-hierarchy are more consistent with independent assertive action than with collusion.

g) In that range of higher need-satisfaction there is no reason to think that managers are indifferent to whether or not they break the law.

Structuralism

a) Managers are rational in the sense that they prefer larger rewards to smaller ones.

b) Since in general monopolistic rewards are bigger than competitive rewards for shareholders and managers, managers will prefer monopoly to competition.

c) Managers are lazy and do not work hard unless forced to do so by competitive pressure.

d) Managers want security, which is presumed to come from the achievement of monopoly power.

e) Monopoly prices are higher than competitive prices and are therefore preferred.

f) Managers dislike innovation, and develop and use monopoly power to resist change.

g) Managers are not concerned about breaking the law — at least not the law concerning competition.

6. Competition and conspiracy

Behaviourism

a) Successful competition implies a rapid rate of offer-improvement by innovation and imitation,

Structuralism

a) The desire to conspire (for the sake of larger rewards) is universal; the opportunity is not.

6. Competition and conspiracy (Cont'd)

exploiting opportunities to make or to offer better choices, independent assertiveness, hard work, becoming more knowledgeable and expert, playing fair, and developing power and using it for the above purposes.

b) While adopting a common *pro forma* price may be relatively easy, agreeing to stop or slow down offer-improvements to buyers is very difficult.

c) There are always many dimensions in an offer which can be used to transfer value from sellers to buyers. Agreements are thus exceedingly difficult to draft and police.

d) Any such agreement would leave all firms more vulnerable to new entrants, inter-industry rivalry, and imports.

e) Comprehensive agreements involve too many people and, therefore, leave firms exposed to actions by either rogues or dishonest employees.

f) A comprehensive agreement to limit innovation would merely make explicit the fact that better offers could be made in the absence of such an agreement. The agreement itself would provide a blueprint for entry by breakaway executives.

b) Managers in an industry made up of small firms are unable to conspire effectively.

c) In industries with only a few firms it is easy to conspire, implicitly or explicitly; not to do so would be irrational.

d) The smaller the number of firms, the tighter can be the conspiracy; profits are, therefore, higher.

e) Entry by other firms would be a threat if it were absolutely free. But in fact entry is often made difficult by capital requirements, advertising, research and development, patents, secrets, and so on.

7. Implications

Behaviourism

a) Arrangement of an explicit or implicit conspiracy that could slow down the rate of offer improvement would be exceedingly difficult to accomplish.

b) Successful competitive strategies that produce better offers (including higher profits) could also produce higher levels of concentration. Therefore, a weak correlation between profits and concentration does not establish

Structuralism

a) According to the foregoing theory, explicit or implicit conspiracy is easy and will be common enough to create a positive relationship between concentration and profits.

b) Excessive profits are unfair and constitute a misallocation of resources.

c) The economy would be better served by increasing the number of firms in each industry where

7. Implications (Cont'd)

that concentration causes high monopoly profits.

c) High profits are not unfair. At worst they constitute only a temporary misallocation of resources in the static or unimportant sense, and are a necessary condition of progress. (They attract investment where it is most needed; as this occurs, profits tend to be reduced.)

d) Some of the greatest breakthroughs in technological progress have been managed by large, highly concentrated firms. Government nationalization has rarely worked well and has usually led to inefficiency and deficits.

possible, and by preventing further decreases in numbers (hence divestiture and anti-merger legislation).

d) If a structural solution (more firms) is not practicable, we must use a tougher combines law — one that either regulates firms, or punishes collusion more severely.

III The Nature of Competition

Once the idea of competition as a textbook, structural condition is dropped and it is recognized that competition is something that happens in the real world, then and only then can one come to grips with the meaning of competition. The elements of competitive behaviour should be quite clear to everyone who has ever competed in business, in love, or in sports. These are the main points which emerge from Professor Armstrong's study regarding actual, real-world competition:

1) The first element of competitive behaviour is the twin activity of innovation and imitation. Competitors must always be concerned with making better offers. When they begin to lose out to more attractive offers they will have no choice but to imitate their rivals in order to hold their position.

2) The second element of competition is choosing and offering choice. This element is closely allied with the first. When businesses offer a new product or a new version of an old product they are broadening the field of choice. When buyers select they are providing guidance on the direction of change that they will desire.

3) Competing managers adopt a stance of independent assertiveness. This does *not* imply that they must be stupid or undertake actions that will destroy themselves or their industry. It does *not* mean that they should ignore rivals any more than a boxer should go into a ring and shut his eyes so that he won't notice what his

opponent is up to. It does *not* mean that they behave atomistically and ignore the degree of interdependence that will be determined by the nature of the product and market. It does *not* mean that if the product or brands are quite homogeneous they should avoid the same *pro forma* price. It does *not* mean that they should always be engaged in a price war that drives price below the level that will allow them to make acceptable offers to employees and shareholders. What it does mean is that they strive to be number one, or to be better than they are, or at least to try to survive.

4) According to the structuralist, price theory model of perfect competition in equilibrium (in which it is supposed competition is at its apex) the buyers or sellers have hardly any power at all. This is indeed another illustration of how silly it is to try to learn about the real world by the use of models that do not and cannot be applied to the real world. Competition in the world as we know it only begins when someone acquires and starts to use power for the sake of making and choosing offers. The acquiring and using of power — and the countering of the power of others — are essential ingredients of the behaviour we call competition.

5) We normally observe that managers (boxers or lovers) who are competing are also working hard.

6) Successful competition also requires the acquisition of expertise.

7) Competition always involves the acceptance of fair and equitable rules. We expect competitors in courtship and sports and even in war to play by rules that the community accepts as being fair. Competitors in business are, or should be, bound by the same kind of ethical standards.

8) Finally, business competition, paradoxically, is a means through which the diverse members of a large society *co-operate* with each other. Only through competition can millions of people, personally unknown to each other, co-operate in the creation of modern complex goods and services.

IV Policy Implications

Only when it is agreed that we know what we are talking about and are all talking about the same thing, can we have much hope in agreeing on sensible legislative proposals.

Based on his study, Professor Armstrong, rejects the idea that competition can be described by, or judged by, the structural view of the firm or of markets. Competition is what competitors do. Only if we recognize this self-evident truth can we explore the rules that can logically be incorporated into the laws governing the conduct of the competitive game. Among the Armstrong policy implications are the following:

1) The first legislative principle to recognize is that real world imperfections are not a sufficient excuse for a new law. Before we can possibly justify a legislative change it must be demonstrated that the benefits will exceed the costs. For example, before we bring in a legislative change that would "screen" all important mergers and reject some of them it would have to be shown that:

   a) Canada would be better off to have more smaller firms, than fewer larger firms, and

   b) that the improvement would more than compensate for the cost of government and private bureaucracy that would be required to implement the screening proposal.

2) It is easy to cry for "change," for "rationalization," for "strengthening" of our laws. Old laws have already been interpreted. We have some idea of what they mean. They have conditioned people's behaviour. They are part of the infrastructure. This is not by any means to suggest that there should be no change — far from it. But there should certainly be no change based on slogans such as "reform" and "strenthening." Changes should be based only on careful and objective analysis and on the reasonable promise of a net benefit to society.

3) If and when the law is to be changed there are a number of additions and alterations that should be made to reflect the proper meaning of words, and to make crystal clear the intent of the legislation.

   a) The preamble to the bill should make it clear to businessmen and to the courts that the principle objective of competition is the progressive improvement of the offers that firms make to their customers and to the suppliers of services.

   b) Before courts pronounce on the competitiveness of an industry they should be required to examine total rivalistic activities and offer improvements. The reasonableness of any specific act should always be judged in the context of all competitive activity.

   c) The preamble to the act should make it clear that it is *not* an objective of the government to reduce the amount of concentration in any specific industry. The national interest is in the speed with which all offers can be improved, *not* in the number of firms.

   d) The law should not permit the prosecution to imply guilt by saying that just because four companies are the suppliers in a given industry, they therefore "control" it. Even a monopolist must share its control with unions, suppliers, governments, and especially, consumers. What power is left will be reduced by the threat of entry from other domestic or foreign firms. If four firms are competing they will have no collective control whatsoever, and the important decisions in the industry will be made in effect (or confirmed) by consumers.

e) The preamble to the bill should call particular attention to the importance of the openness of the Canadian economy, to the great need for and the fact of declining tariffs, and to the fact that so much of Canadian business is subject to ever-increasing import competition, or must compete with foreign firms in world markets.

4) If governments are genuinely concerned about monopolistic elements (i.e., positions of power that cannot be challenged even on the basis of bad performance) then they should look to the monopolies that they have themselves established, to the marketing boards that they have set up, to the single unions in essential services that they have permitted, and even strengthened. No company or group of companies in the private sector ever comes even close to attaining the unchallengeable monopoly power held by such groups. There is no reason whatsoever that a law designed to encourage competition should not apply to *all* participants in the economy.

5) With regard to mergers, a worthwhile improvement in the law would be to place the issue under civil rather than criminal jurisdiction. Whether any particular merger is good or bad is a matter of measurement and judgement. It is in no sense a criminal act.

6) The provisions of the law concerning conspiracies should be clarified. It should be made clear that what we do *not* want is agreements that would stop or slow down the rate of offer improvement or make an unfair transfer of value from one group to another.

7) It is clear in reality, and it should be clear in the law, that similarity of *pro forma* prices for reasonably homogeneous prices cannot be considered as evidence that collusion has occurred. Even similarity of real transaction prices would not in itself be proof that a price agreement had been made. It certainly would not prove that there was a conspiracy that had the effect of stopping or slowing down the rate of offer improvement.

8) In this regard it should be made quite clear that those facts of life and those facts of rivalry called "conscious parallelism" and "mutual interdependency" must never in themselves be construed as being anti-competitive.

9)   The prominence given price in the existing competition bill should be modified. Price is only one dimension of an offer and sometimes not even the most important. What is important is offer improvement and neither the business community nor the courts should ever lose sight of the fact.

The organization of the Armstrong study of competition is as follows. In Chapter 2 he introduces the *behavioural* concept of competition. Three successive approximations are made: rivalry, socially useful rivalry, and a brief overview of seven different behavioural dimensions of competition. Next is an examination of a *structural* definition of competition. This is a section that economists will want to skim over (merely making sure in passing that the models are being fairly presented). Non-economists, however, have to read it fairly carefully if they are to understand what is meant by perfect competition, monopoly, and the neoclassical view of the essential nature of the firm. This is followed by a section called "the nature of managerial work;" it lays the groundwork for a behavioural model of the firm, of households, and of markets, and provides an alternative to the usual price theory model that is the basis of most main-line economic thinking about competition.

Chapter 3 examines in more detail six of the seven behavioural dimensions of competition introduced in Chapter 2. Power, the dimension that is omitted, is more difficult and, therefore, is given a chapter to itself. This chapter (Chapter 4), besides exploring the various meanings that have been given to power in the context of the economy, relates the concept to the price-theory or structural view of the firm. Power is then considered in relation to the behavioural concept of competition. The study of power leads naturally to an examination of the relationship between power and size and finally to the issue of the appropriateness in business (as opposed to sports, for example) of trying to balance power among rivals.

A study of monopoly — the subject of Chapter 5 — follows logically from the subject of power. After considering the quite different meanings that are given to the term, the geometry of "monopolistic" and "competitive" prices or offers is dealt with. Exposed is the fallacy in the view that the more firms there are, the more competitive the industry will be.

Chapter 6 tells the behaviourists' side of the story; it seeks to determine the probable relationship between the number of firms in the industry and competition as defined by its behavioural dimensions. It will be seen that the structural and behavioural approaches to competition and the optimum number of firms give quite different answers. In Chapter 7 the topic is the concentration doctrine — the proposition that there is a link between the profitability of an industry and the fewness of firms in it. It is widely, although not universally, assumed that the explanation for the link is explicit or implicit collusion. It is in response to this issue that Armstrong compares the different theories of competition. The chapter ends with a consideration of some of the arguments for accepting one theory or the other. The final chapter (Chapter 8) applies the analysis of the study to the policy issues, raised by the proposed amendments to the *Combines Investigation Act.*

The Fraser Institute has an abiding concern for a competitive Canadian economy and is publishing this volume in the interests of encouraging more informed and wide public debate about the issues raised by the proposed amendments to the CIA. However, the author has conducted his work independently and the views he expresses may or may not conform singly or collectively with those of the members of the Fraser Institute.

December, 1981   Walter Block

About the Author

DR. DONALD EUGENE ARMSTRONG

Dr. Donald E. Armstrong has had a background that is particularly relevant to the study of competition in both theory and practice. He was raised in a small town in Alberta where the family businesses included a small farm (as close to "pure" competition as one can get in this world); a dry goods store (an oligopoly) and the town's own theatre-dance hall (the only show in town — a monopoly?).

At eighteen he joined a government-run organization — the Canadian Army — in which he experienced competition of a different sort. After being discharged with the rank of Lieutenant he went to University.

He obtained Arts and Commerce degrees *cum laude* at the University of Alberta and a Ph.D. in Economics at McGill University, with one year of post-graduate study at the University of Manchester. Major academic awards include the D.A. McGibbon Gold Medal in Economics at the University of Alberta as well as Fellowships from McGill, Manchester, and Imperial Oil.

As an administrator, Dr. Armstrong has served as President of the Montreal Economics Association, the McGill Faculty Club, the Canadian Association of Schools of Business, and has served a five year term as Director of the School of Commerce. His main administrative job at McGill has been to set up a new Graduate School of Business. (Now the Faculty of Management). After the school was established Dr. Armstrong served for four years as its first Director. For two years he also headed the Red Feather Drive at McGill.

Dr. Armstrong played a leading role in organizing the Financial Research Institute and served as its first President. One of the goals of the Institute was to provide research and management tools to companies, that were small in the North American context, in order that they might compete more successfully.

On the public side of his consulting and research activities Dr. Armstrong has prepared studies or has acted as advisor or expert witness for the Gordon Commission, the Borden Commission, the Royal Commission on the Revision of the Financial Terms of Union Between Newfoundland and Canada, the Royal Commission on Transportation, and the Royal Commission on Bilingualism and Biculturalism. It is, however, as a consultant for industry that he has done most of his work. He has served as a Project Director at the Stanford Research Institute in California, and has acted as the Manager of a Canadian firm of economic consultants. Currently Dr. Armstrong is a principal in Manecon — A Meco Company offering economic consulting services to industry.

Dr. Armstrong's experience in business has been widespread both as to the number of industries served and as to the range of problems. There has, however, been a tendency for his activities to be concentrated in the competitive aspects of industrial marketing in both national and international markets.

Recently Dr. Armstrong acted as an expert witness for the Aluminium and Sugar cases both of which were won by his clients.

The competitive triumph of Dr. Armstrong's life has been to compete successfully against a vast field of talent in winning the hand of Muriel Buchanan of Calgary; (B.A., B.Ed., cum laude, Alberta; M.A. Economics, McGill), who is now Professor of Economics at Concordia University, and formerly an Associate Dean in the Faculty of Arts. After the merger the Professors Armstrong acquired three subsidiaries aged 17 to 24.

Chapter 1

Introduction

Birds do it; so do flowers. Politicians must be good at it. Churches and armies do it on a grand scale. Many of us delight in watching it on T.V., and we like to pretend that we did it successfully against a vast array of talent and beauty when winning the favours of our beloved. Businessmen do it, of course, and if they do it in a way that is displeasing to the authorities, they may go to jail!

This little book is all about it — about that universal phenomenon called competition. More specifically, it is about the *concept* of competition, especially competition among business firms and between those firms and their customers and suppliers. Since such competition is central to the operation of the market system, this book should be relevant to many contemporary economic and political issues. Whenever we hear a politician, a journalist, or an academic say that the market system is not working, or that competition is dead, or that economic power is being concentrated in the hands of fewer and fewer large companies; whenever we hear it said that the government must intervene in the economy; we can be sure that the speaker has an explicit or implicit theory about what competition is, or should be, and that he has made a judgement about how it is working. To paraphrase a writer of a leading textbook on his advice to students: be warned, the image that you have of competition will shape your thinking on the appropriateness of different market structures and of different governmental policies.[1]

The objective of this study is to put forward a view of competition that should appeal to common sense, and that is consistent with the way most of us use the term in love or in war, in sports or in business. It will be argued that this view provides the most logical way for the term to be used in economics and law, when these disciplines are applied to business.

After reading this book the citizen, it is hoped, will be in a better position to judge the issues being raised about competition policy in Canada. He will also be better able to participate in the great debates now going on between more government regulation and less, or between such well-known economists as, say, John Kenneth Galbraith[2] and Milton Friedman.[3]

CRUCIAL IMPORTANCE OF COMPETITION

The outcomes of these debates are important, for they promise to shape not only our economic system but also our social and political systems. Indeed, the issues affect all of us so deeply that they should not be left to the experts. Furthermore, since competition is an integral part of the daily life of each of us, we shall find that if we think about the subject in a systematic way, and are willing to put forth a little effort, we can all become experts. This book is written first and foremost for the intelligent voter and opinion leader who lives in a competitive environment, and who wants to understand how the competitive market system works.

The book is also written for those who compete. It is said that we are all captives of our experience: one experience outweighs several chapters in a learned book. My experience comes from several hundred clients, colleagues, and competitors whom I, as a manager and as a consultant, have encountered over the past 25 years in several countries and in more than 20 industries. It is these mentors who made me work and think and lose sleep and, above all, who taught me about competition.*

If the book is to have an impact on public policy, economists and politicians must also be persuaded that the thrust of its arguments is sound. This multiple readership poses serious problems of presentation — so much so that it is worth spending a few moments addressing the issue of communication.

To managers it should be said that economists have had insights into some of the dark corners of competition. Many of these are not obvious on experiential grounds. At the same time it will no doubt appear to practitioners that the theoreticians have developed models or simplifications of reality that must make their theories suspect. No doubt the managers who persevere to the end of this book may feel they have been exposed to more economics than they need to know for the successful pursuit of their competitive activities. Perhaps this part of economic theory can be rationalized in the same way as is the study of Latin — it is useful in explaining the origin and meaning of words and ideas.

Managers may have no more opportunity to speak economics than Latin. But they can rest assured they will never be able to understand the arguments of some of those economists who draft and

---

*It is to this group of managers — clients, associates, and competitors — to whom this book should be dedicated. They are too numerous to mention but many will recognize themselves, their situations, and their wisdom in this book. To all of them I would like to say thank you.

propose policy unless they expose themselves to the same sort of intellectual exercise as did the economists when they learned their trade.

COMMUNICATION BETWEEN ECONOMISTS AND BUSINESSMEN

If it is hard for businessmen to give economists a fair hearing, the reverse is equally true. "It is a curious fact that there are certain areas of endeavour where those who teach do not practice and those who practice do not teach. In general, the skilful practitioners of business do not teach 'economics'. . .Likewise. . .those who teach economics. . . do not practice business."[4]

Sometimes the academic half of the two solitudes seizes upon this difference to support a claim for objectivity. But if managers are the victims of experience and self interest, economists are every bit as much victims of early training and of an intellectual vested interest in established doctrine. If it is true that seeing is believing it can be equally true that believing is seeing. It can hardly be questioned that the acceptance of theories early in our careers shapes our point of view, the questions we ask and the reassuring evidence we retain in our memory banks.

Yet, on the matter of competition, economists should still have an open mind. It was less than 15 years ago that an economist — one who specialized in the history of economic thought on the subject of competition — said, "There is probably no concept in all of economics that is at once more fundamental and pervasive, yet less satisfactorily developed, than the concept of competition."[5] It was another economist who said that the study of the Peloponnesian Wars was a better preparation for the understanding of competition among a few firms than was the study of economics — a proposition that Professor Kilgour qualified by saying that, "competition may be a fight but it is like boxing rather than war, for it is subject to rules."[6]

UNDERSTANDING COMPETITION

It is as likely that economists can improve their understanding of the nature of competition by listening to businessmen, as businessmen can improve their understanding of competition by looking at the economists' models, and both groups, economists and businessmen, can gain additional insight into the competitive process by glancing occasionally at competition in quite different fields of endeavour.

While we must be ever mindful of the dangers of a false analogy, an examination of competition in other fields poses no greater danger than using a model that leaves out an essential ingredient or that subtly builds a conclusion into an unstated assumption.

Chapter 2

Competition: What Is It?

Competition anyone? Anyone for competition? Tennis? Perhaps a friendly game of poker? Will Avis ever be number one, and will I.B.M. be broken up because it *is*? Will Johnny Carson keep his ratings? "Competition" is used to describe such a multitude of actions in so many fields that one wonders whether it is possible to provide any kind of intellectual structure for its consideration.

WHAT, ROUGHLY SPEAKING, IS COMPETITION?

First approximation

Roget's *Thesaurus* places "competition" next to "rivalry," and in many contexts the two terms are used synonymously. Webster defines competition in part as "the act or action of seeking to gain what another is seeking to gain," and this is almost the same definition as is given for rivalry. "To rival" is to "strive to gain some object in opposition to" someone or something. As a first approximation, competition can be equated to the performance of rivalrous acts.

Second approximation

It is clear, however, that rivalry is a broader term than competition. If we want to reserve the term "competition" for those actions that are socially useful, then there are acts of rivalry that we would hesitate to label as competition. Webster's definition of competition goes on to limit the activities of competition to those "under or as if under fair or equitable rules and circumstances." Rivalry, on the other hand, may include a range of rivalrous situations from love-ins and conspiracies at one extreme to hitting below the belt and murder at the other.

If, as a second approximation, we can accept the idea that rivalry can be shown along a single horizontal axis (x) running from zero (no rivalry at all) to infinite rivalry (call it murder), and if we can conceive of a second axis (y) that measures the social and economic desirability of the different levels of rivalry, then we might imagine a graph that looks something like Figure 1.

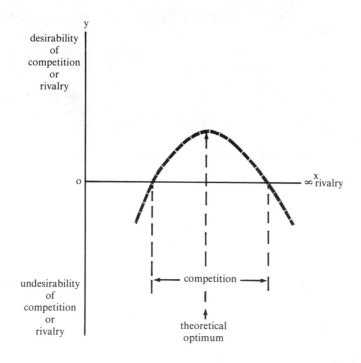

Figure 1 — Competition and Rivalry

The graph tells us that very low and very high levels of rivalry are undesirable and that there is some middle ground with more acceptable levels of rivalry. We may imagine the existence of boundaries marking the limits of legally or economically desirable rivalry, and we may label the distance between these boundaries "competition." We may assume that Mr. Hoyle, the Marquis of Queensberry, the Better Business Bureau and the Geneva Convention have all been interested in making sure that rivalry did not exceed these bounds, and it may be presumed that it is only the rivalry within such limits that our legislators and our courts want to promote under the name of competition.

Like many approximations, this diagrammatic treatment of competition as a subset of rivalry yields decreasing returns to understanding as we analyse it more carefully. To avoid making a further contribution to confusion, therefore, let us pass on to something more precise.

AND WHAT, MORE PRECISELY, IS COMPETITION — A THIRD APPROXIMATION

A clutch of the neighborhood armchair coaches has just agreed that the Saturday night game between the Leafs and the Canadiens was very competitive. What exactly did they agree to? If we went to each in turn and asked him to explain what he meant, we can be sure we would get a number of quite different answers. Here are a few possible replies:

1. "The players went all out; you could just see the sweat pouring off their faces."
2. "The playing was really professional for a change. You should have seen Savard. . ."
3. "It was a closely fought battle."
4. "The best team (ours) won."
5. "The refereeing was strict and fair."
6. "The Leafs were much improved, the extra practice sessions are beginning to pay off."
7. "The players were good sports and there was less fighting than usual."
8. "It was a good crowd: it applauded the good plays and booed loudly whenever a player stepped out of line."

These responses embrace some quite different concepts — effort, balance and good sportsmanship, for example — and they cannot possibly be measured along a single axis. This brings us to an important conclusion: competition is multidimensional.[1]

THE BEHAVIOURAL DIMENSIONS OF COMPETITION

In Chapters 3 and 4 of this study we shall examine these factors at somewhat greater length. For now they can be described briefly as follows.

The Process of Innovation and Imitation

What would we expect from two young men that would convince us that they were seriously competing for the hand of our daughter: movies, flowers (oops, hay fever), poetry, a mustache (produces giggling at the wrong time — scrap that idea), a display of physical prowess? When one of these ideas seemed to elicit a positive response, would we not then expect imitation? If name-dropping seems to impress the young lady, would we not expect the rival to start dropping names also, and perhaps to throw in a little of his genealogy? With such a display of experimentation, innovation, imitation, and counter innovation, we would feel quite comfortable in concluding that the two young men are competing vigorously for the honour and privilege of becoming our son-in-law. In business we expect the same kind of behaviour. Firms that compete are always trying to improve their offer: bigger and better, safer, less gas, faster delivery, more sex appeal, longer lasting. When one of these new attributes appears to work, rivals seize it for their own and try to improve on it. This process of innovation and imitation is the engine of progress of our economy, and is for that reason sometimes referred to as "dynamic" competition. Clearly, the twin processes of innovation-imitation are one of the key dimensions of competition.

Choice, Challengeability and the Right of Effective Protest

Economists are often divided into two schools of thought depending on whether they approach competition from a behavioural or structural point of view. The behaviourist places the emphasis on what competitors do; the structuralist stresses the structure of the market, especially the number of firms. When it comes to choice, however, both schools of thought are likely to agree that it is an important dimension of competition. A wife who has no money of her own, no training, and a couple of small children, may not feel she is enjoying the full benefits of competition. She may feel she cannot protest very effectively if her husband is always late for dinner. Should an old boyfriend appear who is attractive and rich and who has love in his heart, marriage, and two step-children on his mind, the husband may have to reconsider whether it is really wise to drop in after work for a drink with the boys.

There is a strongly entrenched idea in economics that competition and human welfare in an industry (and presumably in a hockey league or in a marriage) are a simple function of the number of rivals — the more rivals, the more competition — with the theoretically "perfect" number for the structuralist being infinity. On the other hand, a behaviourist will insist that the wife had a choice between zero and one — between marriage and no marriage. The marriage, the children, the lack of training, were, in the absence of coercion, all the result of choices. No doubt, challengeability of the *status quo* and her ability to protest will improve — i.e., cost her less — with the appearance of an additional suitor. But would she be still better off with 30 or 100? We shall have to think about that.

Independent Assertiveness

When we watch two hockey teams we expect them to display an attitude towards each other, and behaviour that we might describe variously as "battling it out" or "giving it their very best." A **degree** of independence and self-assertiveness is obviously a necessary dimension of competition. But the dimension is subtle and tricky. It would be ridiculous to expect each team to be so independent that it would go onto the ice and pretend that the rival team was not there. We would be shocked if the teams were so self-assertive that they had not come to a firm agreement on matters such as when they were going to play and what rules would guide the conduct of the game.

The same dimension of competition applies to business, and the same problems and subtleties are present. An agreement with rivals to prevent all innovation or to stop new competitors from getting into the industry would clearly not be consistent with independent assertiveness. At the same time, to charge, as has been done, that businessmen are not being competitive if they keep a close eye on their rivals is clearly ridiculous. Independent assertiveness is an important dimension of competition, but it is not an absolute: it requires the application of common sense.

Energy

If asked to describe the quantity of competition between rivals we would probably think of such phrases as the amount of effort, single-mindedness, carnage, devotion, concentration, dedication, or sweat, depending on whether the rivals are chess players, armies, suitors, cup challengers, or used-car salesmen. We shall try to capture this particular dimension of competition with the word "energy."

Expertness and Knowledge

The competitive game and some of the dimensions we have already mentioned will obviously be enhanced by the skill and knowledge of the players. In order to exercise choice intelligently, one must know the options. To be able to innovate successfully, one must have knowledge of what is wanted and what is technically and economically feasible. If the neglected wife is to benefit from competition, she must at least have some idea of what she is getting out of and what she is getting into. Night baseball is better played under the lights.

Existence of Rules and Willingness to Abide By the Rules

The idea that competition in sports, love, and even war is enhanced by playing within the rules is so well established that it would be very surprising if the same idea did not apply to the business world. Indeed, many of the adjectives appended to competition (for example, "predatory," "dog-eat-dog," "unfair") bear witness to the fact that competition is frequently judged according to the fairness with which it is conducted.

Power

Power obviously plays a key role in all of the competitive activities that come to mind, be they in love, war, sports, or business. Its appropriate role as a dimension of competition is confused, however, first because of the difficulty in defining the concept, and second, because of two false analogies, one from textbook economics and the other from sports. Because of the complexity of this dimension and the fact that academic opinion is so sharply divided we shall leave discussion of this matter until Chapter 4.

Summary: A Behavioural Definition of Competition

It may already have occurred to the reader that all of the dimensions of competition we have listed so far are words describing actions, or verbs, and that they could be presented to sportsmen, lovers, or business managers as a set of instructions to be followed in order to achieve a high level of competition. In a simplified form these instructions might be listed as:
1. strive to improve your offer by innovation or imitation;
2. choose and offer choice;
3. be independent and assertive;
4. play and work hard;
5. be skilful and knowledgeable;
6. play fair; and,
7. acquire and utilize power to accomplish the above.

The actions listed above add up to a behavioural definition of competition. They can all be associated with the verb "to compete." This behavioural approach goes back many years, and while it was not elaborated in exactly this way, it seems that when Adam Smith and his contemporaries spoke of competition, they had in mind competitive actions broadly consistent with the foregoing.

A STRUCTURAL DEFINITION OF COMPETITION

Unfortunately for our clarity of thought, many economists began increasingly to associate competition with a market structure.[2] This line of development culminated in a concept unhappily called "perfect" competition,[3] which was defined in such a way as to be devoid of any of the activities that we have described as competitive.

To qualify as perfect competition, the market has to offer a product every unit of which is exactly like every other (the condition of homogeneity) and it has to be made up of a large number of small buyers and sellers acting independently, with perfect knowledge, and with freedom to enter or leave the market. If all of these conditions are met, price would be set by the interaction of total market supply and demand, and all individuals would be virtually powerless "offer-takers." Buyers and sellers alike would have to accept the product and its price as given.

At the opposite extreme from this vision of "perfection" was monopoly. This was a market occupied by a single seller, who sold a product for which there was no close substitute. This seller, the mono-polist, was presumed to have power and since there were, by definition, no competitors, the power was unconstrained — at least by competition.

An understanding of the standard price-theory models of these two markets — perfect competition and monopoly — is absolutely essential if non-economists are to understand the structuralist concept of competition. We shall try, therefore, in the simplest possible way to explain by words and by geometry how firms and households are presumed to operate in these two market structures.

Let us begin with perfect competition.

Perfect Competition

It must be borne in mind that the condition of perfect competition demands that every unit of the product be absolutely the same as every other regardless of who produces or sells it, so that consumers have no reason to prefer the output of one seller to that of any other. This condition effectively rules out product differentiation; one seller cannot vie with another by offering a better product on more attractive terms.

Depending on their incomes and their tastes, households will place a lower and lower value on each additional unit of virtually any product consumed within a given period of time. This is the law of diminishing marginal utility, and Figure 2 presents a picture of this famous law.

This diagram tells us that if the household consumes only six units in January, the sixth unit, Q_6, will add to its total satisfaction MU_6. If, instead, the same household in the same period decided to consume 12 units, the last unit, Q_{12}, would add to utility an amount equal to MU_{12}.

The demand side

If we make the not-unreasonable assumption that buyers are able to measure their utility for products in terms of money, then we can assume that the price-consumption relationship (i.e., the demand curve) for an individual householder for, say, pounds of butter, will look like *dd* in Figure 3.

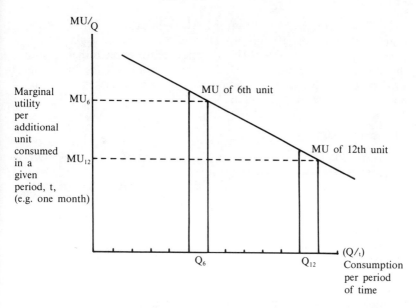

Figure 2 — Diminishing Marginal Utility

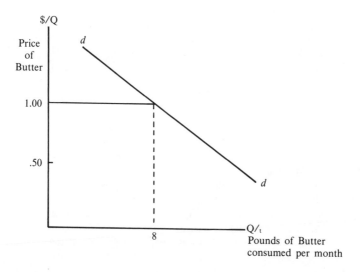

Figure 3 — The Demand Curve

If the price given to the buyer is $1.00, this demand curve tells us that the householder should buy all of the units up to eight in each period because their value (MU in money terms) exceeds their cost to the household of $1.00. If we added horizontally all the individual demand curves for all the householders in a given market, we would have the total market demand.

The supply side

The firms operating in this "perfect" market have a number of short-run cost curves that show the relationship between average and incremental costs and the amount produced in a given period. The meaning of a marginal cost curve can be seen by imagining a simple manufacturing plant with a fixed quantity of plant and equipment. The only variable input and therefore the only variable cost is labour. Graph A in Figure 4 shows the physical relationship between additional quantities of man-days (measured on the vertical axis) and additional units of output per week (on the horizontal axis). From the figures on the chart it can be seen that if the plant is to produce only one unit of output per week, 14 man-days of labour will be required. If two units are to be purchased each week an *additional* 12 man-days will be needed making a total of 26 man-days per week. An output of three units requires 36 man-days so that the addition to the labour input required to go from two to three units of production per week is 10 man-days.

If labour costs $30 per man-day then the schedule of incremental output and labour input can be translated directly into a marginal cost curve by multiplying the numbers in Graph A of Figure 4 by 30. The result appears in Graph B. The marginal cost of the fourth unit, that is, the addition to total cost of increasing production from four to five units of output per week is $240. The marginal cost of the first unit can be seen to be $420 and so on.

The average total cost and the marginal cost are normally considered to be "U" shaped, as shown in Figure 5.

It is a necessary assumption of perfect competition that both the average and the marginal cost functions rise after the firm has attained a relatively small amount of production per period of time (3,000 pounds is a quantity that must represent an insignificant proportion of the total market demand, just as the amount purchased by an individual buyer — eight pounds in Figure 3 — must be insignificant in terms of the total market). If average and marginal costs continue to decline as more is produced, then larger firms can produce larger outputs more cheaply than can small firms.

In the presence of these "economies of large scale," the industry would soon be made up of only a few large firms, for they could

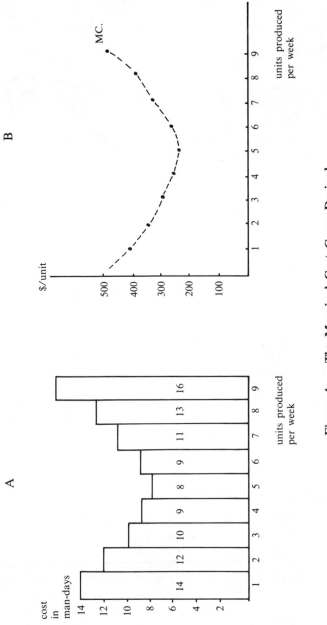

Figure 4 — The Marginal Cost Curve Derived

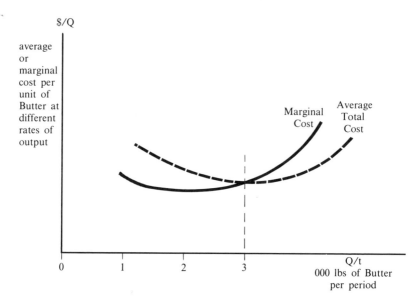

Figure 5 — "U" Shaped Cost Curves

produce at a lower cost per unit than would be possible for a large number of small firms. In such industries, with only a few large firms, society would benefit from lower costs, but there would not be perfect competition.

Earlier, we added the individual demand curves horizontally to produce an industry demand curve. In the same way we can add horizontally part of the rising portion of each marginal cost curve to produce an industry marginal cost curve; it is usually called the industry supply curve.

Supply and demand

Figure 6 shows the total supply and demand curves, together with two examples of the very large number of households and firms that comprise the "perfect" market. We may in this way illustrate how the market reconciles the individual actions of all households and firms. The total supply and demand schedules intersect at a price of $1.00 and an output of 24,000,000 pounds of butter per month: in other words, $1.00 is the price that "clears the market," and 24 million pounds is the amount bought and sold. The quantities bought at the market price by

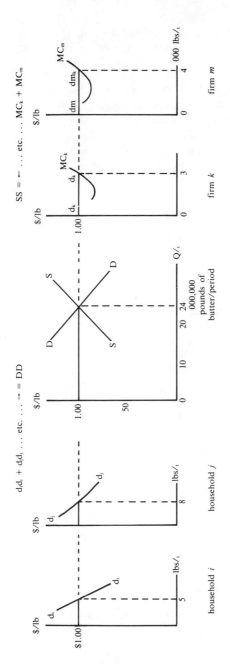

Figure 6 — Supply and Demand

households *i* and *j* are five and eight pounds a month, respectively (*j* is taken from Figure 3). These, together with the quantities bought at that price by the millions of other households in the market, add up to total purchases of 24,000,000 pounds a month, which is one point on the market demand curve. This, in turn, is the quantity that all of the thousands of butter producers are willing to sell at that price. Two such producers are also illustrated in Figure 6: firm *k* (taken from Figure 5) produces 3,000 pounds a month, and firm *m*, 4,000.

Each household and each firm is assumed to maximize its profits or net benefits. Firm *k* sells 3,000 pounds because at that output the marginal cost of producing the last unit is just equal to the marginal (and average) revenue from the last unit. Profits or contributions to overhead are received for all units to the left of the 3,000th unit, and losses would be incurred on all units produced per period in excess of that amount. Householder *j* consumes eight pounds a month for the same "profit maximizing" reason. All units from one to seven consumed per period provide an excess of value over cost. All units after the eighth would incur a loss, because the cost of each additional unit would still be $1.00, while the extra benefit, or marginal utility, would be less than that.

The only point that remains to be made is that the firms consider the demand curve for their products to be $d_k d_k$ and $d_m d_m$ equal to $1.00 a pound for any amount the firm chooses to produce. Even though the firm's managers know that there is a downward sloping demand curve for the industry, they also realize that their share of that curve is so small that nothing they can do will have any appreciable effect on price. Therefore, they accept the flat *dd* curves as being both their average-revenue and marginal-revenue curves and assume they can increase or decrease their output without affecting the price. They are "price takers," not "price makers."

Monopoly

The geometry for the monopolist is much simpler. By definition, the monopolist — let us assume it is a bakery — is the only firm in the industry and therefore the only supplier of bread. The individual demand curves for all the buyers added horizontally, as before, produce an industry demand curve that must be the demand curve for the product of the monopolist. Because the demand curve slopes downward to the right, the manager of the monopolistic firm knows that more sales can be made only at lower prices. It can be shown that so long as the demand curve, which is also the average revenue curve, is falling to the right, marginal revenue — the *net* addition to total

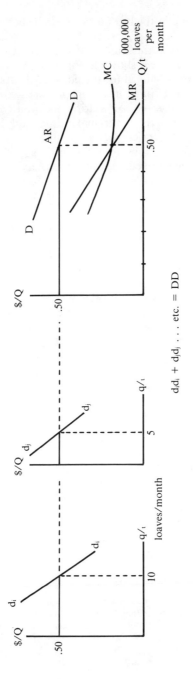

Figure 7 — The Monopolist

revenue from the sale of the last unit — must be below it and must also be falling.[4]

The geometry for the monopolist and two of the households that make up this market is shown in Figure 7. As we can see from the diagram, nothing has changed for the households. As before, they take the price as given. This time, however, price is set by the monopolist rather than by the market. As before, the households adjust their purchase rates to equate their marginal utilities and their own marginal cost (50¢) which is the price they must pay.

For the firm, conditions are rather different. The managers must first of all find the demand curve, which they may do through a process of experimentation or trial and error. Having found it,* they must do a bit of arithmetic to find the corresponding marginal revenue curve. What is important to understand from this process is that the monopolist, unlike the perfectly competitive firm, cannot sell all he wants at the going price and that an additional rate of sales per period can be accomplished only by charging a slightly lower price. Therefore the marginal revenue — the addition to total revenue received from the sale of one additional unit per period — is the new lower price less the revenue that was lost on all previously sold units because of the lower price. This proposition is illustrated in Figure 8.

Assume that 20 units can be sold at $5.00 in January giving a total revenue of $100. To sell 21 units in February the price for all units would have to be dropped to $4.90. The revenue in February is $102.90 (21 × $4.90) so that the additional revenue for the monopolist from the sale of the 21st unit is not $4.90, the price, but $2.90, the marginal revenue.

MC = MR

In order to maximize profits the monopolist follows the same rule as the perfectly competitive firm and equates marginal cost and marginal revenue. The price which the monopolist sets is given by the point on the demand or average revenue curve that lies directly above the intersection of marginal cost and marginal revenue. This is shown as 50¢ in Figure 7.

The foregoing explanation of perfect competition and monopoly has been made as brief and as simple as possible. Nevertheless, it is essentially the picture of monopoly and perfect competition as it is painted in most economic textbooks.[5]

---

*Actually, the demand curve is continually hopping all over the place as tastes, incomes, and the prices and quality of substitute and complementary household items change. Thus monopolists can only "find" demand curves in the world of ivory tower scholastic exercises.

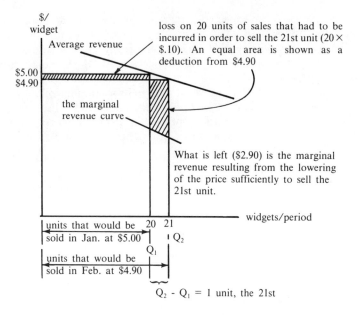

Figure 8 — Average and Marginal Revenue for Widgets

Competition — A Function of Numbers

In at least partial defence of economists who lean to a structural definition of competition, we hasten to point out that no one, even in a "perfect" ivory tower, is likely to imagine that the world is composed of markets that are either perfectly competitive or purely monopolistic. Instead, these particular markets are more likely to be taken to provide the extreme reference points for a scale on which real markets can be positioned according to whether they come closer to the models of perfect competition or monopoly. Since, by definition, there was zero competition at the monopoly end of the scale and perfect (infinite?) competition at the other, the positioning of each market on the scale will describe the amount of competition.

If we look back at the characteristics of perfect competition we can see that a large number of buyers and sellers is not the only condition mentioned. There is also freedom of entry. This, however, is closely associated with numbers for the common-sense reason that if there are many firms already in an industry it must have been, and probably still is, fairly easy to get in. If only a few "made it," entry or survival must be more difficult. Independence is also mentioned.

Independence is to be expected if there are many firms because it will be next to impossible to reach a single opinion for the entire industry, whereas a monopolist reaches one automatically. So it would appear that numbers explain, or at least reflect, most of the competitive conditions that matter.

Diagramatically the presumed competition-number relationship can be captured in Figure 9. The positively sloped line tells us that as the number of firms increases from one in a monopoly to many in perfect competition, the amount of competition increases.

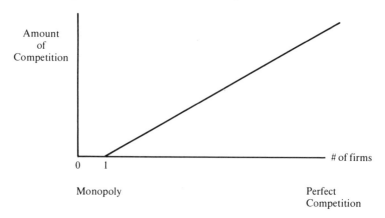

Figure 9 — Competition and the Number of Competitors

BEHAVIOURAL COMPETITION AND NUMBERS: A QUICK LOOK

Even though we have not yet explored the behavioural dimensions of competition at any length, the worldly-wise reader will already be aware that the relationship between competition and numbers presents a very different picture if a behavioural test is used. For example, it is easy to think of some few-firm industries that are famous for their high rate of innovation; it is difficult to find comparable examples in multi-firm industries. Many of the few-firm industries give us a wide range of choice; producers of butter and eggs give us very little choice.

At least some of the behavioural dimensions are likely to indicate that high levels of competition exist quite close to the "monopoly" end of the number-of-firms scale.

A first approximation of a competition-number relationship as measured by *behavioural* tests is more likely to be some version of Figure 10.

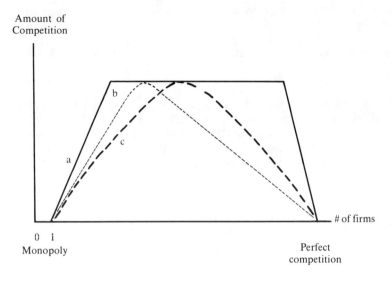

**Figure 10 — Competition and the Number of Competitors —
Another View**

THE NATURE OF MANAGERIAL WORK

Introduction

There is virtually nothing managers or entrepreneurs do that is not in some way or other related to rivalry in either product or factor markets. For this reason, what we are prepared to believe about competition must rest in very large measure on how we perceive the managerial function. The theme of managerial work is one that will appear and reappear throughout this book, for it is the thesis of this study that an understanding of competition can only be based on an understanding of managerial or entrepreneurial work.

To begin with, therefore, we shall sketch, in the briefest of outlines, the picture that is presented to economics undergraduates of the nature of the managerial problem and of the household, the firm, and the market.[6] Having done so, we shall then explore, in considerably greater detail, an alternative description of these institutions. For the sake of convenience, this alternative will be called the "behavioural model" of management, but that is only to maintain the structural-behaviour dichotomy. A more accurate characterization of our model is "descriptive," for its claim to acceptance must be that it is simply a more accurate description of what managers and entrepreneurs actually do.

The Simple Structural, or Price-Theory, Model of Management

The buyers

In the structural or price-theory model, buyers, whether households or firms, need products which, if not unidimensional, are at least simple enough to be described by a single designation like "bread," "pig iron," and the like. The interest of the buyer in the product is twofold: quality, which we assume to be given (or at least outside the scope of the model), and price.

The firms

The managers confront product and factor markets where goods are sold and resources purchased. Production functions (input-output relationships) and cost functions (cost-output relationships) are provided by plant engineers or accountants. In a perfectly competitive market the demand or average (and marginal) revenue curves are given. In a monopolistic market (one with a downward sloping average revenue curve) the curve has to be estimated or guestimated and a corresponding marginal revenue curve must be calculated. In both cases (perfect competition and monopoly) the output is set where marginal revenue equals marginal cost and the corresponding price is determined for sellers and buyers by the corresponding point on the price-sales curve. Factor services are hired or fired according to the same sort of analysis. Investments or disinvestments are governed, to oversimplify slightly, by whether profits are above or below average.

The markets

The perfectly competitive and the monopolistic markets are fairly simple and deterministic — that is, the market price follows from reasonably objective relationships, and any two reasonably intelligent managers would make the same price and output decisions. Markets in between the two extremes are more difficult and not so deterministic.

Management

According to the foregoing, there is very little scope for discretionary action on the part of managers. The "givens" really leave them with the relatively simple problem of making a "Robbinsian" type of resource allocation. The term "Robbinsian" gets its name from Sir Lionel Robbins whose famous essay on *The Nature and Significance of*

Economic Science defined economics as the allocation of scarce, versatile means among competing ends.[7] Robbins, it might be noted, was describing economics, not management. In what followed, however, it was as though economists having discovered the profession of resource allocation, created managers in their own image to work on smaller allocative problems, while they concentrated on the big ones. Macroeconomists advised governments that they had to choose between more guns or less butter or vice versa, managers were supposed to advise boards of directors that they had to choose between a little more labour and a little less material or vice versa. This designation of managers as junior economists obviated the necessity for anyone to write a book entitled *The Nature and Significance of Managerial Science.*

The Behavioural, or Descriptive, Model of Management

The buyers' multidimensional needs

The competitive struggle, be it in wrestling, love, or commerce, is always undertaken to achieve some goals or to satisfy some needs, and these goals and needs are never single or simple. A wrestling match is never just a wrestling match. It may be pathos, slapstick, choreography, drama, an aphrodisiac, or the eternal struggle between the forces of hair-pulling, eye-gouging evil and the underdog-but-eventually-triumphant forces of justice and fair play. It may even include a contest of strength and skill.

The goals of courtship are much too complex even to be mentioned in a book aspiring to brevity. Commerce is only slightly less complicated. Household and business needs for a product — even a simple product with no moving parts — are wondrously involved.[8] A baker does not want flour: he wants a certain quantity of flour to meet particular specifications including such things as a limited moisture content, no moving parts, and a carefully specified range of tolerable impurities (non-wheat solids, if you are squeamish). He wants the flour delivered in containers that are compatible with his own materials-handling equipment, and delivery schedules that shift as much as possible the cost of inventories from himself to the flour miller. Undoubtedly he would like flexibility in determining pricing dates; he might even like to influence the price he pays by being able to average quoted prices over a certain period. He wants payment dates to follow, not precede, his own sales, and if there are to be financing charges, he wants them heavily subsidized.

Of course, there is also the price of the flour, which may include discounts for prompt payment, large volume, and long contracts, as well as for his success in giving the impression that someone else has offered him a better deal on freight charges.

Of course, life is much too short to maintain a complete and up-to-date analysis of the dimensions of our needs, and on the spur of the moment few of us could list more than a few of the things we expect (or do not expect) when we buy a bag of flour. The reason is that we have found that we can safely take for granted most of the dimensions of the products we buy and sell. When changes are made in a product, they do not usually involve more than one or two dimensions at the same time. We can experiment briefly by comparing the new with the old, accept or reject the change, and forget about it. We have better things to do with our time than to be psychoanalysed every time we want to buy a pair of slacks, and few of us would have much patience with those who would seek the "deeper" meaning of a tin of mushrooms. Like theoreticians, we all use simplified models of the real world. As consumers, this does no great harm; as citizens, however, we may be led to accept assertions about products, markets, and the market system that are *too* simplistic.

The firms' multidimensional offers

In view of all of these wants and needs of the consumer, we should not be surprised to find a similar set of "dimensions" attached to the product by the seller. Flour, sugar, salt, iron ore, sulphur, steel plate, and newsprint are simple products, but without too much difficulty anyone with any sales experience can find at least 20 dimensions for each product.* Any one of these dimensions can shift value from seller to buyer and win or lose a sale. From this it must be concluded that the dimensions of simple products have to be measured by the tens or scores, while the dimensions of complex products have to be measured by the hundreds.

It is important to emphasize the multidimensional nature of both business and household needs and the multidimensional nature of the products and services offered to satisfy those needs. This must be done in order to counteract the simplistic models of theoretical economics, which usually picture a single dimension — price — as the only dimension, or the only dimension that matters.† This leads to an excessive emphasis on price and on price competition and, as we shall see, it can completely distort our view of the competitive process in a number of important ways.

One of the reasons economists sometimes fail to appreciate fully the multidimensional nature of products, or their improvement over

---

*The task could no doubt be accomplished even without experience. We have just finished listing about 15 dimensions of flour without even mentioning colour, the type of grain, or nutritional values.

†This is implicit in the usual price-model diagram as for example in Figure 3.

time, is that an added or altered dimension can be very quickly taken for granted and forgotten. We would probably be quite indignant if we discovered, after we got home, that the box of breakfast cereal we had just purchased did not have a recloseable top, or that our salt did not pour, or that our brown sugar was not moist, or that our facial tissues did not pop up, or that a new watch that failed to work was not returnable. If it could be arranged that every now and then all customers were sent — by mistake of course — a 1911 automobile, a 1925 vacuum cleaner, a 1946 record player, we would soon learn not to take for granted the number and quality of the dimensions of current offers.

The firm — multiple participants

For almost any competitive activity there are several interested participants, each of whom plays one or more roles. An individual hockey player as a member of a team will compete against other teams. For some purposes — obtaining the most points, being named most valuable player, receiving a larger share of the available salary fund — he will compete against players on his own team. In acting and reacting in a game, he will have to give some thought to the club owners, the box office, the referees, the fans, the tax collectors, and the manufacturers of the products he has endorsed. One could think of everything he is and does as a hockey player and call it his "total offer." Clearly this offer is going to have to be fashioned in the light of the sometimes conflicting interests and claims of the different groups and individuals involved in the sport. Indeed it may be more useful to think of his total offer as being composed of different, though closely related, offers to each of the participants.

The same kind of considerations apply in business. Sometimes competition is rather narrowly defined as the rivalry that occurs among sellers of the same product competing for the favour of a given group of customers, but the concept is much broader. It is, of course, a fact that two or more sellers may be competing for the same buyer, but the terms of the victory are as important as the victory itself. Indeed, if the terms are not favourable, making the sale may be only a Pyrrhic victory. A seller does not compete for sales: he competes for *profitable* sales.*

Obviously, the competitive struggle must involve not only the rivalry among sellers for profitable business; it must also include the struggle between buyer and seller for the most advantage (perhaps the

---

*"Viable" is actually to be preferred to "profitable" because the former reminds us that sales must be made on terms acceptable to the buyers and *all* the firm's suppliers — not just the shareholders.

most profit or the most value) that can be obtained from each transaction.[9]

Buy, buy, sell, sell

All of the dimensions of competition we have enumerated apply in differing ways and degrees to the seller-seller and the buyer-buyer rivalry as well as to the buyer-seller rivalry. Hence, the rules of good conduct that preclude one seller from telling lies about another would at the same time require him to honour an agreement with a buyer.

But seller-seller, buyer-buyer, and seller-buyer rivalries are by no means the end of it. The manager of a selling firm who is trying to frame an offer better than that of another seller, which will attract his rival's customers, must necessarily involve the services of workers and shareholders in that offer. These participants must also be satisfied with their role and their share of the action. The seller may win friends among his customers by speeding up delivery and lowering the price, but he will lose friends back in the shop if his generosity means unpaid overtime and/or lower dividends.

A person unfamiliar with business may be surprised to learn that some of the greatest competitive struggles that occur on behalf of the various participants occur *within* a single firm.[10] Salesmen who spend most of their time with buyers tend to become the captives of their clients. They will often campaign vigorously on their behalf for a better deal. Of course the salesman may be doing no more than obeying his self interest. A better deal will make him more popular, increase his sales and his commissions, and teach those degenerates who work for a rival company a good lesson. While customers and competitors may give him a bad time now and then, his worst enemy may well be the vice-president, finance in his own company who, on behalf of the workers and shareholders in the company, keeps vetoing the "sweetheart" deals with his clients.

Intra-firm rivalry

One is likely to find the same sort of conflict between the vice-president of personnel and his colleagues on the executive committee. The "friend in court" of the workers, the vice-president, personnel, wants happy, productive, and loyal workers just as badly and for many of the same reasons as the vice-president, marketing wants happy, buying, and loyal customers. And it should not be at all surprising to find that the vice-president, purchasing brings the suppliers' points of view to the executive committee meetings.

On reflection, it is self evident that all of the offers made by a firm to all of the participants must be mutually consistent (the offer to the customer to deliver next week can only be made if there is an offer to workers providing for overtime), and in the long run all of the offers to all of the participants must be mutually satisfactory. Therefore it is logical to expect that within the firm there will be individuals representing the point of view of each of the participants.

In a completely different context Adolf A. Berle in discussing the Black-Douglas doctrine of the corporation suggests that while the corporation is not a natural person, it certainly is a *composite* of natural persons. He says "the corporation would have standing to represent and defend the aggregate of individual rights held by or entrusted to the corporation." What is of special interest is that Berle goes beyond the shareholders to include "perhaps also the contract or other rights created through bargains reached collectively with employees; possibly even rights under agency and other arrangements reached in agreements with, let us say, salesmen and dealers."[11]

Social responsibility — or common sense?

Those who have been writing on the social responsibility of corporations have stressed the need of corporations to consider the welfare of all participants. According to one study, "five out of six executives surveyed agreed that it is unethical for corporation executives to act in the interest of stockholders alone and not also in the interest of employees and consumers."[12]

One can see the concern of managers for all participants as something required by ethical standards, as an evolving legal requirement, as an obvious need if conflicting interests are to be reconciled, as a promoter of long-run profit maximization or, as we shall argue later, as a simple recognition on the part of management that all participating groups, including employees and customers, have sufficient power to threaten the security and well-being of the organization unless their interests are considered and their co-operation secured. Whatever the starting point, one arrives at the same conclusion: any model of the firm that does not specifically acknowledge that managers must be concerned about the offers made to *all* participants is going to be misleading.

Market Classifications

It is necessary in any discussion of competition to recognize that markets differ from one another. The result is that competitive behaviour appropriate to one would be quite inappropriate, and perhaps even impossible, in another. What follows is a brief discussion of some of the key differences that separate one market from another.

Bargaining versus trade-at-set terms

Of the many different possible ways of classifying markets, one of the most important and perhaps the least understood is the classification that divides markets into bargaining, trade-at-set terms, and combinations of the two.

The terms of a settlement reached after a competitive struggle, or the rules under which a competitive battle is fought, may be the result of explicit bargaining or negotiation. Or they may be set (or appear to be set) unilaterally, on a take-it-or-leave-it basis by one of the participants. The difference between these two situations may be more apparent than real and certainly cannot be taken as an indication of power or the balance of power.

The seller with a better mousetrap may be able to demand and receive a premium because of the superiority of his product. The young maiden with a superior set of dimensions may be able to attach rather stiff conditions to the granting of an interview in a parked car; if the dimensions are only so-so, there may have to be more give and less take.

The ability to make what is, in some respects, a superior offer enables a seller to obtain advantages in regard to other dimensions of the offer. For example, the seller with a superior product can give his customers the advantage of the better product and retain the advantage of a higher price. The point is, however, that he will be able to do so whether he bargains individually with each buyer or whether, in effect, he bargains collectively, making what is at any time a take-it-or-leave-it offer.

The economics of information

What determines whether a given market is likely to be governed by trade-at-set-terms or bargaining is less likely to be the superiority or strength of a buyer or seller than the recognition of the high cost of individual bargaining.[13] ("If you are going to argue about it, forget it.") When we buy a new or used car, we are aware that there is usually some room for negotiation. If we take the time and effort to negotiate with several different garages, we usually discover that the first offers will be modified. On the other hand, when we go to a department store to buy a spool of thread, we expect to be confronted with a take-it-or-leave-it offer; it would not occur to us to try to bargain. In any event, for small items, who could be bothered?

While we have come to expect take-it-or-leave-it markets for many of the things we buy at the retail level, we should remember that this type of market is of fairly recent origin; it was the necessary mass-marketing, mass-consumption, companion of the mass production that marked the industrial revolution. In Adam Smith's day consumer markets were places of higgling and haggling. It became clear, however, that haggling was a very expensive market process for both buyer and seller. With no posted prices a buyer had to make a survey of the merchants to find out not only what the initial asking price was but how far the various tradespeople could be beaten down: to buy the material for a gentleman's shirt was a major undertaking. It was largely in response to the high cost of bargaining that retail markets adopted take-it-or-leave-it marketing techniques.*

Price setting does not equal price determination

It should not be imagined that in a take-it-or-leave-it market all the decisions are made by one party, or that the person who determines most of the conditions of a take-it-or-leave-it offer has all, or even most, of the power. Let us look briefly at the bargaining processes and make a few comparisons between these markets and markets in which there is trade-at-set-terms.

In a bargaining-type market it is useful to distinguish among what might be called *pro forma* offers, real offers, and final offers. An illustration will make these distinctions clear. It is customary for most businesses to publish a *pro forma* offer — perhaps in a catalogue with a description of each item and a price list. It might be regarded as a starting offer, which normally will be as attractive as similar offers of rival firms. Potential buyers usually expect to be able to take advantage of a *pro forma* offer without negotiation. They may expect to improve the terms through bargaining, but they do not expect bargaining to make the terms worse. This usually means that a seller's *pro forma* offer should be high enough to cover the cost of doing business with the buyer whom it is most costly to serve.

There are offers — and offers

The *pro forma* offer may be the actual offer on some transactions. In that case, for those who must, or who do, accept it, the market is essentially of the take-it-or-leave-it variety. For others, it may be only the starting point. Behind the *pro forma* offer there may be a real offer, and this real offer may still be subject to bargaining and negotiation. The final offer is the one that is embedded in the contract, or would have been if an agreement had been struck.

---

*It was no accident that Timothy Eaton, who was one of the pioneers in North America of one price for all, ("A Child Can Safely Shop in This Store"), was one of the first to be able to expand on the basis of large volumes.[14]

Competition is all-embracing

A consideration of this process demonstrates why competition must be considered to embrace both seller-seller and seller-buyer rivalry. Discussions between buyers and sellers will be influenced not only by the *pro forma* offers of other sellers, but also by the sort of deals that a buyer forecasts he can make with other sellers. Thus the limits placed on the terms of a particular negotiation will be set by the participants' conclusions or forecasts about other seller-buyer contracts that may be available. As a practical matter, it would be quite impossible to separate out the extent to which a particular contract has been determined by (a) competing *pro forma* offers (seller-seller *pro forma* competition); (b) forecasts or estimates of the contents of competing, available contracts (which would, in themselves, be an amalgam of seller-versus-seller concessions and buyer-versus-other-seller negotiations, whether actual or hypothetical); and (c) the pure seller-buyer negotiations that put the finishing touches on the contract.

At first glance, this bargaining process may seem to be very different from the take-it-or-leave-it process; and, to a certain extent it is. The difference, however, is as much form as substance, and the results may be the same.

Consumer sovereignty

Because the expense or impracticability of individual bargaining forces sellers into a take-it-or-leave-it form of making offers, this does not mean that buyers have lost their voice, their right of protest, or their bargaining power. The buyer-seller interaction in trade-at-set-terms, while a different sort, will be just as important as it is in a bargaining situation. A large number of buyers, each taking, or not taking, relatively small quantities of a product on set terms, will provide sellers with a constant flow of information. Some of this is oral: customers complain, "it's cheaper next door," or they may say "your salesman is attractive." This information will usually be augmented by commercial intelligence supplied by comparison shoppers or surveys. By far the most important source of information, however, is the ebb and flow of purchases as buyers "bargain and negotiate with their feet." Large stocks of unsold and unwanted inventory can quickly change "take-it-or-leave-it" to "bargain-sale" days.

Many markets, especially those in which there are both large and small firms, will have a mixture of bargaining versus trade-at-set-terms. The same *pro forma* offer may be a take-it-or-leave-it offer to a small customer who is expensive to serve, but only (serve as) the basis for negotiations with a larger customer with lower per-unit servicing costs and more bargaining power.

Homogeneity of offers and mutual interdependency

It is useful, indeed it is necessary in studying competition, to differentiate between industries in which mutual interdependency and consciously parallel actions are inevitable, and those in which mutual interdependence does not exist. In the latter category we have three types of industries. The first is a pure monopolist, who has no close rivals and obviously does not need to be concerned about what actual rivals are doing, although the possible actions of potential competitors must always be considered. The second is the perfectly competitive industry: although in equilibrium it is expected to move in lock step; it is not assumed this happens in response to mutual interdependency. Third, there are those "industries" that are in fact a collection of industries in which each firm offers a product that is sufficiently unlike any other product that there is no need to maintain identical prices or identity in any other dimension of the offer. In such an "industry," each firm is a monopolist in its own niche and is protected to a certain extent by the uniqueness of its offers. Industries in this category include those that produce furniture, computers, trucks, mining equipment, and so on.

It is only the former category of industries (i.e.: interdependency is inevitable), that faces the difficult competitive problems of mutual interdependence. While no two offers in such an industry are ever identical, the products may be so similar that the firms are obliged to maintain the same *pro forma* prices and perhaps the same *pro forma* offers. Given certain conditions of knowledge and expertise, it may even be necessary to maintain the same *actual* offers, including virtually identical prices.

Most of the combines cases involve this particular category of industries. The problem faced by such industries will be considered at length in Chapter 6. For the moment, suffice it to note that there are certain product and market conditions that compel the firms in those industries to act in mutual awareness of each others' actions and to be consciously parallel over time in the offers they make to customers and/or suppliers. To behave otherwise would be stupid.

Vulnerability to atomistic price wars

It is difficult to think of any business, unless of course it is protected by the government, that is not vulnerable to the changing wishes and demands of a free market. Any firm, no matter how gigantic, can fall victim to a change in tastes, or a technological innovation, or it may simply become unable to keep up with its competitive Joneses. If changes occur quickly enough, the firms that lose out may think of themselves as victims of a price war — although a "superior-offer war" would be more descriptive. So long as the superior offers (including the prices) made by the victors allow them to continue to make superior or satisfactory offers to consumers, shareholders, workers, and other suppliers, the victims have no cause to complain about anything except their ability to maintain the competitive pace.

The potential for change, scale and learning

The last basis for classifying industries is their potential for change. At one extreme of this scale could be corner-store retailing, in which both the product offered and the technology for making the offer are relatively simple and static. The offer made has relatively few dimensions, and they are not very difficult to understand.

At the other extreme could be an industry such as the one that produces hand-held calculators. The product has a considerable number of dimensions, some of which are difficult to comprehend. The process by which the product is made is complex, and it seems to be subject to change without notice.

There is of course a great deal more to potential for change than just complexity. History, however, suggests that at any given time there exist industries that are relatively mature, static, and frequently characterized by a small-firm technology. They continue to live along side other industries that are adding dimensions, attracting resources, and making progressively better offers to customers, workers, and shareholders. It would be surprising if the appropriate competitive behaviour at the static end of the scale was not different from competitive behaviour at the dynamic end.

Appendix A

Optimum Resource Allocation

The economic questions that must be answered by any economic system are what to produce? How much? For whom? By whom? And when? There are basically only three different ways of answering these questions. The first is by an economic system of tradition. Tribal societies tend to evolve static economies in which people do today what they did yesterday. The son of a hunter becomes a hunter. He catches the animals and divides the meat in the same way as did his father and grandfather before him.

Tradition-based societies are generally presumed by those in them to allocate resources optimally — if such thoughts are entertained at all — because this is the traditional allocation. The chief and the high priest receive more of the meat because this has always been so. For those who would question the status quo, there is generally a theology that explains the rightness of how things are.

Because of the obvious inability of a tradition-based society to deal with volcanoes, the coming of the white man, or original sin, such societies tend to evolve into societies of command. The kingly and/or the priestly class become interpreters of the theology or ideology and assume the right to decide (usually in the name of a deity such as the Sun, the Moon, or Chairman Mao) what should be produced, for whom, by whom, and when. The allocation of resources under the command system is also presumed to be optimum, especially by those who do the commanding or believe the ad campaign run by the commanders.

The market system

The third method of determining the answers to the basic economic questions is the market system. Entrepreneurs must judge or guess what people would like to buy. The reasonableness of these plans and forecasts enables them to persuade resource owners (workers and savers) to help them produce their products. The existence of such entrepreneurs provides, simultaneously, a range of products, investments, and job opportunities. By investing and working, households acquire income and their dollars are then used to "vote" for the various products.

Obviously, the key to success for the entrepreneurs is to offer attractive enough returns to labour and capital to obtain and hold their co-operation, and at the very same time to win enough of the dollar votes of households to pay the factor owners.

When one compares the resource allocation of the market system with the way resources are allocated by either tradition or command, the most striking difference is the amount of freedom involved in each. In tradition-based societies, people are duty-bound to obey the rules of the past as interpreted by the leaders. In command societies, people are bound to follow the rules of the commanders. In a market system, however, individual householders are free to try to fill the role of entrepreneurs; they can seek employment in different regions or industries; they can spend or save, and if they save, they can invest with different entrepreneurs. What they spend can be allocated in any way they want, and their collective dollar voting determines what is produced. The allocation of resources in a market system is very much under the control of households. An entrepreneur may guess that women would like silk stockings, and for a while he may be right. But if another entrepreneur guesses that women might prefer nylons, and if the second entrepreneur is right, there is very little that the first entrepreneur can do about it. It must also be remembered the dollar votes in a free market can be allocated to churches, Shakespeare, ballet, education, political parties, or pot.

Market systems for democrats?

On the basis of what has been said, one might conclude that democrats, at least, would prefer to see resources allocated by a market system than by tradition or command. Economists are not content to leave the argument between the market and command systems to be settled by a shouting match and the Berlin Wall. Instead, they have developed a model in which it can be shown that with a given distribution of income, technology, tastes, etc., perfect competition will allocate resources to each industry in such a way that it will be impossible for a dictator to command the movement of a worker from one industry to another and thereby improve welfare. In other words, the answers provided by the system to the questions of what should be produced, how much, for whom, by whom, and when cannot be improved upon.

Not only does such a model appear to kill (overkill perhaps) the socialist or command economy alternatives; it is an elegant and intellectually satisfying model as well. In any event, good or bad, relevant or irrelevant, it is hardly possible to make sense of the subsequent discussion about competition without understanding the optimum allocation of resources as promised in this perfectly competitive nirvana.

Let us begin the exposition with a perfectly competitive bacon industry. The diagram in Figure 11A represents the demand of a representative household for bacon. The sloped marginal utility (MU) curve indicates the marginal private benefit (MPB) the household receives from the consumption of each additional pound of bacon in a given period of time — a month, let us say. The price to the household is assumed to be $2.00 per pound. This is shown by the horizontal line (MPC), the marginal private cost of each pound of bacon consumed per month. The diagram indicates that this typical household will buy ten pounds of bacon per month. This is because the tenth pound produces just a bit more benefit to the household than the value of the $2.00 which must be sacrificed to obtain it. The thin clear rectangle represents the marginal private benefit (MPB) of the last unit of bacon purchased.

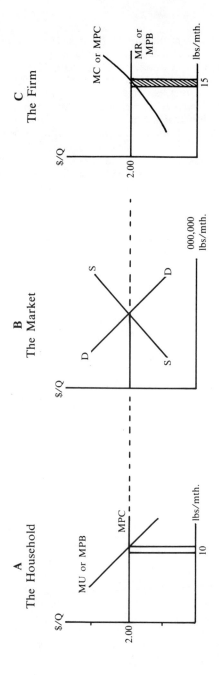

Figure 11 — Household, Market, and Firm: Bacon and Eggs

Hog prices

Figure 11C provides the relevant functions for a typical hog producer. This producer has a rising marginal cost (MC) or marginal private cost (MPC) function, indicating that, for this producer, additional increments of output cost more and more. The price received by the farmer is also $2.00. (The farmer must obviously produce, slaughter, package, and sell the bacon in the market.) This farmer will find it best to produce 15 pounds of bacon per month, because at larger outputs, each additional pound will cost more than the $2.00 he receives for it. At lower levels of output, the additional revenue would exceed the additional cost.

Figure 11B shows how the $2.00 price is derived. The DD curve is, roughly, the horizontal summation of the individual MU curves, and the SS curve is approximately the horizontal summation of the marginal cost curves.

The trick in this analysis is to be able to understand that the clear rectangle under the MU curve in 11A represents the extra benefit received by the household, while the shaded rectangle under the marginal cost curve represents the cost to the firm (hours of work, materials consumed, etc.). They are both equal to $2.00. The marginal private benefit to the household (MPB_H) equals the marginal private cost to the firm (MPC_F). That is, ($MPB_H = MPC_F$).

If all social costs or social benefits are recorded in the marginal private benefit (MPB_H) and marginal private cost (MPC_F) curves, we can assume that private benefit equals social benefit. If the benefit happens to an individual, it happens to society as well. The private cost is also a social cost: if an hour of labour is used up by a firm, it is lost to society. In this perfectly competitive industry, therefore, the marginal social cost of incremental production is equal to the marginal social benefits of an equivalent amount of incremental consumption. Thus, there are no "externalities."

We can now see how much effort (cost) is likely to be expended in any one direction. People stop working when the extra effort and backache of producing an additional unit of product just equals the satisfaction that can be derived from it.

Bacon and eggs

Now let us assume a two-industry, perfectly competitive economy that produces only bacon and eggs. We assume that the intersection of supply and demand produces a price of $2.00 per pound of bacon, and a price of $1.00 per dozen for eggs.

Figure 12 shows the previous bacon consumer and producer, and in addition, a typical egg consumer and producer. Just as we found that the extra cost to society of producing the last pound of bacon was balanced by the extra benefit to society from consuming this last pound ($MSC_F^{Bacon} = MSB_H^{Bacon}$), so too it can be shown that the equilibrium, market-clearing price of eggs will find a level that will produce the same joyous state: $MSC_F^{Eggs} = MSB_H^{Eggs}$. At the margin, people would work twice as long to produce a unit of raspberries as they would to produce the last unit of

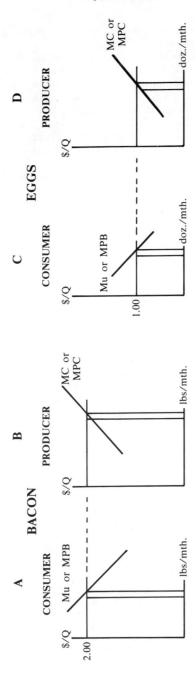

Figure 12 — Consumer and Producer: Bacon and Eggs

strawberries if (again at the margin) the last unit of raspberries gave twice the satisfaction of the last unit of strawberries.

Let us suppose, however, that the government decides to test the theory that resources have been well allocated by the market. It directs that some resources be shifted from one industry to another. Suppose that the decision is made to produce one less pound of bacon, which will free up two dollars' worth of resources, and to direct these resources into the egg industry. Figure 13 shows what will happen. There is obviously no change in the total amount of resources being used.* What, however, will happen to satisfaction? Not very much, obviously, but as we shall see, there will be a small change, and for the worse.

Because the marginal cost of eggs is rising, two dollars' worth of resources will not produce quite two dozen eggs. Furthermore, because the marginal utility of eggs is falling, two dozen more eggs will produce a shade less than two dollars' worth of satisfaction. Conclusion: the forced transfer of resources from one perfectly competitive industry to another has reduced welfare. Therefore, resources should have been left where the market had determined they should be. The perfectly competitive market produces an optimum allocation of resources that cannot be improved upon by command.

Monopoly strikes again

Now for the bad news. Assume a world made up of a perfectly competitive bread industry, and a single-firm-monopoly beer industry. Figure 14 shows a typical bread consumer and a bread producer; it also shows a typical beer consumer, and the one and only beer producer. The perfectly competitive bread market (not shown, but see Figure 11 for the derivation) determines a price for bread of $1.00 a loaf. As convenience would have it, by the time the beer producer estimates his (the industry's) demand curve, calculates marginal cost and marginal revenue, it turns out that the profit maximizing price is also $1.00. The marginal cost (the marginal private cost and also the marginal social cost) is fifty cents. It is important to realize that, under present assumptions, the bread producer is a price *taker* (bread prices are determined by the entire market), while the beer producer is a price *maker* (given the demand curve he faces, the beer producer determines for himself the most profitable price-quantity configuration.

Is there an optimum allocation of resources in this world of both perfect competition and monopoly? Can human welfare be increased by a shift in resources? The answers to the two questions, are respectively, "no" and "yes." Figure 15 shows what would happen if the government gave the order that one less loaf of bread should be produced (which frees up one dollar's worth of resources) and that the resources should be used by the beer industry. Again, we assume that the government can do this costlessly.

Resource use remains constant, but one additional dollar applied to the production of beer will produce about two units of beer. The value placed by

---

*We assume, not altogether correctly, that there is no bureaucratic cost entailed by this shift of resources.

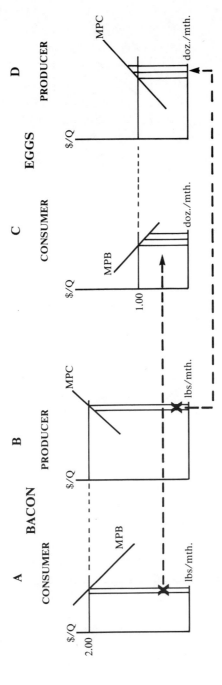

Figure 13 — Optimal Allocation: Bacon and Eggs

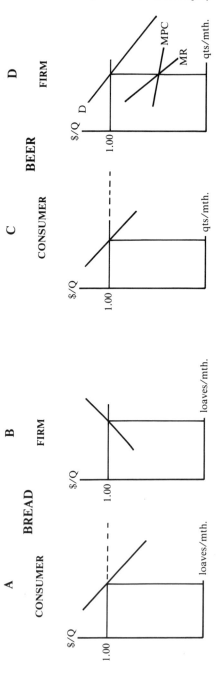

Figure 14 — Competitive Bread, Monopoly Beer

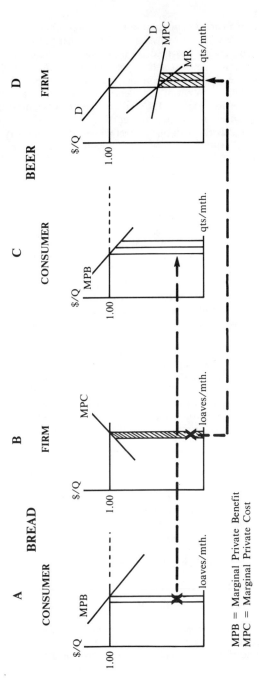

MPB = Marginal Private Benefit
MPC = Marginal Private Cost

Figure 15 — The Beer-Bread Allocation

a typical consumer on an additional quart of beer is almost (but not quite) $1.00, and two quarts of beer will be worth almost $2.00. Clearly, welfare has been increased. Total resource use was held constant: the thin shaded rectangle in 15B is equal in area to the two shorter rectangles in 15D. Benefits have increased, however: the clear rectangle under the MPB curve in 15A measures approximately one dollar's worth of satisfaction, but the two clear rectangles under the MPB curve for beer in 15C indicate an increase of satisfaction amounting to almost (but not quite) two dollars.

Conclusion: in a world with one perfectly competitive industry and one monopoly, resource allocation is *not* optimal. Welfare can be increased by the forced shift of resources from the more competitive to the less competitive industries.

There is more

The story is usually left at this point, even though there is another world to explore, a world with a uniform degree of monopoly. To illustrate, let us assume a two-industry economy of wine and cheese. Figure 16 shows again a typical consumer for both products facing a given price determined by the monopolists. As fate would have it, the wine producer finds that the optimum price for wine is four dollars per litre. The cheese producer finds the optimum price for cheese is two dollars per pound. In both cases the marginal cost happens to be exactly one half the price. This is indeed what we mean by a uniform degree of monopoly — a uniform value for the ratio of price and marginal cost.

What happens in this world if an order is given to shift resources from one industry to another? Is welfare increased? The answer is "no." We can see easily enough in Figure 17A and B that an order to produce one less litre of wine will reduce satisfaction by $4.00 and will free up $2.00 worth of resources. When these resources are put to work in the cheese industry they will produce about two pounds of cheese worth a little less than $4.00 in total ($2.00 each). The "little less" occurs because the marginal utility curves slope downwards and to the right.

Conclusion: In a world in which there is a uniform degree of monopoly ($P/MC = k$), (price over marginal cost is constant), in each industry, no increase in welfare can be obtained by shifting resources among industries.

The world of a uniform degree of monopoly is called second best (perfect competition is supposed to be best) because it can be shown (with quite a bit more effort) that the world of a uniform degree of monopoly overvalues leisure and undervalues work. An individual would still allocate working time properly among various jobs but would spend less time at the office and more time with the spouse and kids going on Sunday-school picnics and walking in the woods.

Personal values

How many demerit points one debits the world of the second best is a matter of the values attached to work versus leisure. However, the weighing of the two standards of resource allocation cannot end here. Our world of bacon and eggs

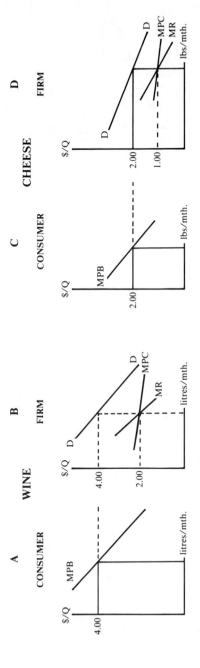

Figure 16 — A Wine and Cheese Party

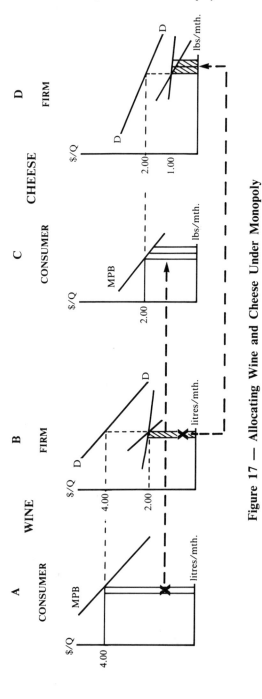

Figure 17 — Allocating Wine and Cheese Under Monopoly

was one of army-issue, one-size-fits-all products. Change is virtually ruled out because innovation destroys the conditions of perfect competition. Visitors to this world of bacon and eggs would see no rivalry. Bacon producers would not be vying with each other to produce more sizzle, or less fat, or that old-time home-cured, smoky flavour. Indeed our visitors could be forgiven if they came to the conclusion that they missed the sign posts somewhere along the way and were visiting a society of tradition instead.

By contrast, our world of wine and cheese would drive our visitors into a tizzy of excitement. The first thing they would note is that no one sells wine. Instead they sell Bordeaux, Chablis, Mosels, Dom Pérignons, and Baby Ducks (Baby Ducks?). The world is one of innovation and change. Our visitors would have no trouble at all seeing why a wine and cheese party in a world of competing monopolists would be much more fun than a bacon and egg party in a world of perfect competition.

Assumptions of perfect competition that produce the conditions of a static optimum allocation of resources must inevitably raise questions about the relevance of such a standard. For the vast majority of products at any time and for all products some of the time (perhaps most of the time), the conditions of perfect competition cannot be satisfied. It seems rather pointless, therefore, to undertake what, in any event, can only be idle speculation about how these products would be produced, how they would be priced, etc., under other unattainable and even undesirable conditions. As Hayek said,

> In conditions where we can never have many people offering the same homogeneous product or service, because of the ever changing character of our needs and our knowledge, or of the infinite variety of human skills and capacities, the ideal state cannot be one requiring an identical character of large numbers of such products and services. The economic problem is a problem of making the best use of what resources we have, and not one of what we should do if the situation were different from what it actually is.[1]

The relevance of the perfectly competitive exercise is that the custom has evolved among economists of comparing our real market economy not with the economies of command and tradition, which are the real alternatives, but with the optimum resource allocation of perfect competition. This is not a valid comparison at all. One cannot have the static allocation of perfect competition without the static world that goes with it.

Chapter 3

The Dimensions of Competition: A Closer Look

In the last chapter we enumerated seven dimensions of competition. In this chapter, we shall turn our attention to a more thorough examination of the first six. The seventh, power, being somewhat more involved will have a chapter to itself.

INNOVATION AND IMITATION

Introduction

Athletes, companies, or lovers who are really competing will always be looking for ways to improve their performance, and they will be forced to react quickly to improvements made by others. If, for the moment, we can agree to call each improvement an innovation and each reaction to a rival's improvement an imitation, it seems almost self evident that this innovation-imitation process is an essential element of competition.

While it is possible to trace the link between competition and "new divisions of labour and new improvements of art" back to Adam Smith,[1] it cannot be said that it was an important idea to either Smith or his followers. Indeed, neoclassical thought with its emphasis on static, optimum resource allocation and two-dimensional price theory, was, at best, indifferent to the process of change. At worst, it was hostile. This is perhaps because change (often dismissed as product differentiation) posed a threat to the relevance of the whole intellectual exercise. As a result, it was not really until 1942 with the first edition of Joseph Schumpeter's book *Capitalism, Socialism and Democracy* that economists were told in ringing terms that they were on the wrong track.

> But in capitalist reality as distinguished from its textbook picture it is not that [traditional] kind of competition which counts but the competition from the new commodity, the new technology, the new source of supply, the new type of organization. . .This kind of competition is. . .so much more important that it becomes a matter of comparative indifference whether competition in the ordinary sense functions, more or less promptly. . .[2]

Reminders of the Schumpeterian position have been frequent. Some examples are given below.

Clare Griffen, 1955:

> I think we should recognize that the pattern of many small concerns in an industry may have the effect of keeping price close to cost and at any moment of time the resulting narrow profit margin may yield an advantage to the consumer. But in a longer view, more is to be gained by reducing cost or improving the product.[3]

In a section called, "Dynamic and Static Interpretations of Competition," the authors take the MacQuarrie report to task for the statement, "Effective competitive control requires the existence of large numbers of sellers and buyers so that no one exerts any observable influence on the market but is in fact controlled by it." They argue that, "this is not a picture of the kind of competition that is necessary for, or even compatible with, the dynamic economy, and is not the kind of competition that the legislators had in mind when enacting this statute."[4]

George Stigler, 1957:

> The way in which the competitive concept loses precision when historically changing conditions are taken into account is apparent. It is also easily explained: the competitive concept can be no better than the economic theory with which it is used, and until we have a much better theory of economic development we shall not have a much better theory of competition under conditions of non-repetitive change.[5]

The argument of this section is that a key element needed to achieve that better theory of economic development is the innovative-imitative process. Unless it is explicitly taken into account, the resulting competitive concept is simply misleading.

Edwin Mansfield, 1968:

> Technological change is a key element in a competitive struggle among firms.[6]

Economic Council of Canada, 1969:

> In using economic analysis for purposes of competition policy, it is important to view competition and efficiency in dynamic rather than purely static terms. That is, they must be seen in a context of economic change over time, with new products, industries and methods of distribution constantly coming forward and old ones dying off.[7]

Lawrence A. Skeoch, 1972:

> . . . the central focus of policy relating to industrial organization [in context, — competition policy] should be to promote dynamic change. . .Such a policy must emphasize not the efficient allocation of existing resources among alternative uses in terms of keeping down costs and profits, [the usual concern of structural perfect competition] but the encouragement of new methods of production and distribution, the development of new institutions for liberating and expanding the growth opportunities in the economy.[8]

Despite these frequent reminders and the simple common sense of the Schumpeterian observations, static, innovationless price theory has remained the stock in trade of most economists. As Robert Solow has complained:

> The multifaceted dynamics of technological advance and industrial transformation — the underpinnings of increased productivity — are almost wholly excluded from the purview of Establishment economics. The notion that a competitive price-directed market is the underlying economic reality lingers on, a fixation even of those who proclaim the organizational revolution.[9]

In 1981 it should be respectable to bring innovation to the fore in any discussion of competition; what about imitation? In a somewhat different context the linkage of the two processes can be found in the innovators and imitators in Schumpeter's works. It also appears in J.M. Clark's discussion of the attempt "to excel" and "to equal":

> The attempt to excel may be called aggressive competition, in effect if not in intent; it may or may not be aimed at a particular rival's business. The attempt to equal a competitor's offer or minimize a rival's advantage is clearly defensive. Under competition the one implies the other, and it takes both kinds to make an effectively competitive situation.[10]

What Qualifies as Innovation and Imitation

There is a tradition in economics, which admirers of Schumpeter are loath to upset, that reserves the word "innovation" for important changes in products or technology. For our purposes, however, it will cause less confusion to apply the term to any change in an offer, that is not clearly an imitation.[11] Using the term in this way means that it will be unnecessary to try to make the distinction between what is and what is not important. Importance, after all, can only be in the eye of the beholder. A change important enough to persuade one person to stop buying an old familiar product and try a new one may, and undoubtedly will, leave over 99.9 per cent of the world's population unmoved.

Furthermore, the difference between what is a big innovation and what is a little one depends very largely on the number of small changes one is willing to include within the category of a single innovation. Schumpeter in his work on the business cycle talked about the automobile and the locomotives as being innovations. Certainly, when we look back 70 years we can see that the development of the automobile industry has had a significant impact on the economy. The car, however, is by no means a single innovation. We did not progress immediately from a 1910 horse and buggy to a 1981 automobile. What happened was that in 1911, in response to a few almost imperceptible changes, and some more persuasion, a few more brave souls switched from a reasonably predictable, but polluting, horse and buggy to a bone-rattling horseless carriage that was unsafe even when standing still.* If we try to determine the reason for a relatively simple decision on the part of a manufacturer to switch over from, say a copper to a nylon component, we normally find that this decision was preceded by years of development, or rather by years of different rates of development, of copper and nylon. *Natura non facit saltum*, and even inventors and especially developers must usually take many small steps to get where they are going. There is nothing wrong with many small steps; if enough of them go in the same direction we shall, after the fact, pronounce the movement to have been a grand innovation in the Schumpeterian tradition. This means, however, that an observer cannot gage the importance of a single innovation by the subsequent purchases by new customers, for the customers may be reacting to a whole sequence of changes. For all of these reasons, we have little choice but to categorize all changes as innovations whether they are grand, headed for grandure, or just a minor adjustment by one seller, in one market, prompted by his attempt to obtain a marginally-interested customer.

A "bad" innovation?

Two questions may arise from our insistence that any change in an offer, apart from an obvious imitation, must be treated as an innovation: what about innovations that are obviously not improvements? And what about changes in that part of the offer involving price? Let us deal first with changes that are not improvements. It seems logical to suggest that we should welcome any test that would warn managers away from changes that they would regret. However, since success can only be judged by the choice people make, any test must be based on an after-the-fact assessment of changes that worked and

---

*For the information of younger readers, the starting crank was a reliable source of sprained, bruised or broken thumbs, wrists, forearms, and jawbones.

changes that did not work. Therefore, there does not seem to be any particular advantage to be gained from reserving the term "innovation," which is a process, for only those changes that "worked."

There is, however, a more practical consideration. No doubt there are some changes that almost everyone recognizes as a failure at some point of time; but most changes get a mixed verdict that varies over time. Any change worth talking about will affect more than one group of individuals and more than one individual in each group. It is doubtful whether all those affected will be unanimous in their verdict. Music while you shop? Pleasant for those who like that kind of music, but unpleasant for those who do not.

Changes are also likely to affect more than one dimension. Suppose there is a change that introduces better, longer-lasting material, but at a higher cost and price. Almost all consumers will like the new material, and almost all consumers will not like the higher price, but the good and the bad must be taken together. On balance, some will prefer the new offer; others will not. Among those who do not, the dislike may be a first reaction to the new price, but that reaction may change when they discover that the product really does last twice as long.

Undesirable differentiation?

There is another kind of change that some economists might like to disqualify as an innovation because it is felt to be an undesirable kind of differentiation. On this subject, the Economic Council of Canada had this to say in its *Interim Report on Competition Policy*:

> Still other concepts and principles are useful for assessing product differentiation and the many types of nonprice competition that are encountered in imperfectly competitive markets — for example, competition in respect of product features and after-sales services. A basic principle here is that competition is to be valued according to the real net benefit it yields to the ultimate consumer. Some types and degrees of nonprice competition may pass this test while some may not. For example, the net benefit to the consumer of trading stamps and some other promotional devices has frequently been called into question. Despite such criticisms, it is still too widely assumed that *any* form of vigorous business rivalry amounts to healthy competition and is therefore good for the economy.[12]

This study by the Economic Council was undertaken at the request of the federal government, which was looking for guidelines for a new competition policy. The suggestion that trading stamps may not meet the test of providing adequate real net benefit to the consumer, therefore, could be interpreted as an invitation to the government to ban them. But what justification is there for declaring trading stamps illegal? If consumers do not like trading stamps they do not have to accept them or patronize businesses that offer them. There is no more reason for outlawing trading stamps than there is for declaring that offering customers a choice of colours in cars or telephones is undesirable because obviously costs are thereby increased, and the *net* benefit to consumers can be questioned. The path to dictatorship is paved by the good intentions of those who would like to substitute their judgement for the judgements of others.

Innovation and market structure

Yet another basis for differentiating between changes in offers has been suggested by Milton Friedman. In explaining why so much emphasis was placed on monopoly, he cited the "over-estimation of the importance of those technological changes that promote monopoly by comparison with those that extend competition."[13] In the former category he includes mass production with its attendant increasing concentration in certain industries. In the latter, he suggests developments such as trucking that offers additional competition to the railways.

   This, however, raises the question of the legitimacy of trying to distinguish between innovations that increase the number of firms that compete in a particular market and those that do not. Suppose there were many small lumber mills cutting up logs in a manner that used much labour and very little capital. An innovator — or, more likely, several innovators — devises capital-intensive methods for mass production that lower costs considerably. Prices decline (in real or relative terms). The old labour-intensive companies go bankrupt or sell their holdings or merge, and the number of lumber-producing companies falls from several thousand to 20, half of which are, relatively speaking, giants. Are the series of changes that produced these results monopolistic or competitive either in the process or in the outcome?

Process vs outcome

Presumably each of the individual changes was undertaken on the expectation that the lumber producers would be able to make a better offer to one or more participants. If consumers, in general, did not benefit from the developments, they could have continued to support companies using the old technology and changing the old prices. Surely the *process* is competition. But what of the outcome? It is anticompetitive only according to a structural definition of competition — one that sees more firms as necessarily more competitive, and fewer firms as less. The case against adopting such a definition is very strong, if we want to retain the term competition to describe a process that is economically desirable. More to the point, we should note that the innovative-imitative process could very well reduce the number of firms in each of the lumber, aluminum, gypsum, plastics, glass, steel and cement industries, and at the very same time increase the number of end uses for which these industries compete with each other. Of one thing we can be sure; Milton Friedman would be the last person to suggest that the government try to differentiate between innovations that would, and innovations that would not, increase competition.

The preceding discussion also suggests that there is no basis for excluding price from the list of changes that belong to the innovative-imitative process. Even if consideration is limited to an examination of one dimension at a time, of one offer made by a single firm, there can be no hard line drawn between price and non price dimensions. A change in *pro forma* price may not change the real price at all. A credit concession may be translated quite precisely into a price equivalent. A change in the material used in the product may also be expressed in terms of a certain price equivalent for one customer, but it may be different for other customers and/or involve considerable uncertainty. Furthermore, an innovation seldom if ever involves only one dimension. It would be unusual if it did not affect the offers made to at least two different groups. Within the firm, innovations will produce a mixture of changes in price and non-price dimensions for different groups.

Orthodox price theory

As far as a household is concerned the orthodox price theory model encourages us to think of the product as the pleasure and the price as the pain. But this is a caricature of the real world. Painful dimensions for certain products may include interest costs, the burden of transportation, the inconvenience of storage, the risk that they will be stolen and the danger that they will not suit our particular style of beauty. Price is by no means the only entry on the debit side of an offer and the physical product is seldom an unmixed blessing.

For practical reasons if for no other, the innovation process must be taken to embrace all offer changes whether great or small, whether they seem to reduce the number of firms in an industry or not and whether they involve price changes or not.

Finally we must take a brief look at what constitutes imitation. At its simplest, an imitation is an exact copy of an offer made by a competitor. In the real world, however, competing offers are seldom identical. A change in the spirit of imitation may include enough that is different to make it indistinguishable from an innovation. The late

Charles Revson, who was President of Revlon, is reported to have said, "if you copy something. . .you copy it so well and so differently that nobody recognizes the fact you copied it. That's creative copy."[14]

The opportunity to improve on what has gone before is an advantage. One may also gain from preparing an imitative offer that purposefully differs from that of the rival so that it comes closer to meeting the needs of a specific subset of the market (differentiation). It may, therefore, be very difficult in practice to distinguish between an innovation and an imitation. In any case, dynamic competition does not consist of one change, innovation or imitation; it consists of a continuous but bumpy process of action and reaction. We now turn our attention to this process.

The Process[15] of Innovation-Imitation

The process of innovation and imitation will be different in form if not in substance, depending on whether the market is one of bargaining, trade-at-set-terms, or some combination of the two. Let us begin with bargaining.

The whole bargaining process can be cast in terms of innovation and imitation. Suppose an industry sells a fairly simple product that is technically quite homogeneous. All firms in such an industry will probably have very similar *pro forma* offers. When bargaining takes place, it necessarily means that one supplier, on his own initiative or at the request of a buyer, is willing to change one or more aspects of his offer and make it different from that of his competitors. At this point, we can say that the offers are now heterogeneous: one of the sellers has introduced an innovation which, if it is to succeed, must be considered an improvement by at least some buyers. If this innovation is successful, it procures profitable sales. There will very likely be some imitation, as other sellers react in order to protect their shares of the market. By so doing, they will act in the direction of restoring homogeneity.

If the innovation involves an improved process, other sellers may not be able to copy immediately. In the short run, they may fight back by changing another dimension (granting higher volume discounts, for example). This would increase the amount of heterogenization — in the short run at least — although the effect of the additional change may be to bring back into equality the value of the two different offers. In time, however, the reacting firms may find it better to adopt the new process and stop granting the volume discounts. This will restore or at least increase homogeneity.

Set-term markets

In a market in which there is trade-at-set-terms, one seller may introduce a change in one of the dimensions of his offer. This will make the offers of the industry somewhat less homogeneous. If the change appears successful — if sales and profits increase — then other sellers will be encouraged to imitate or to make improvements in their offers. This will allow them to hold on to their market shares and their profits. If the reaction is imitative, homogeneity will tend to be restored. If some other dimension is changed, heterogenization will result. In either case, all offers must be improved. In the actual market process, there may thus be relatively little difference between bargaining and trade-at-set-terms from the point of view of this innovation-imitation process.

The offer-improvement process arising from this progressive leapfrogging of innovation and imitation can be visualized as a series of perpendicular and parallel movements. To take the simplest kind of example: consider the introduction of plastic bags for brown sugar. At time A, in Figure 18, two competitors X and Y were making roughly

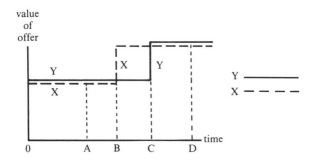

Figure 18 — Offer Improvement: Plastic Bags for Brown Sugar

equal offers that involved packages made of kraft paper. At time B, company X introduced a plastic bag which kept the brown sugar moist and easy to handle. This was such an obvious improvement and consumer acceptance was so unmistakable that the reaction time between B and C was no more than the time required by company Y to order plastic bags and adapt its packaging machinery. At point D, the offers were once again similar, and in only a short time customers had forgotten what a nuisance it had been to try to keep brown sugar moist and workable.

Some complications

Let us consider a slightly more involved case: at time A, in Figure 19, companies X and Y were making similar offers of granular sugar to

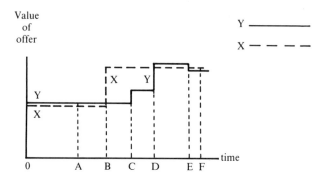

Figure 19 — Offer Improvement: Granular to Liquid Sugar

industrial users. At B, company X introduced liquid sugar in bulk. This was a very important innovation, especially to some large users. Y could not immediately respond by offering liquid, but when it realized that it was losing customers, it offered a price concession at C. This was not sufficient and so a second price concession was offered at D, in part to try to recapture some business. During this period it became obvious that the price concessions were costing more than it would to offer liquid sugar. Thus at time E, company Y introduced liquid sugar, dropped its discounts, and returned to an offer more similar to that of company X. As a result of this process one more improvement had been made in the offer. Even though sugar has no moving parts and has been around for a long time, one can quite easily identify many such perpendicular and parallel cost-reducing and offer-improving innovations and imitations, in the course of a single year.

The great advantage of treating the innovating-imitating process as a series of parallel and perpendicular movements is that we can conceptualize the benefit of this dimension of competition as being the slope of the path of offer-improvement over time.* In the case illustrated in Figure 20, for example, we can say that the two firms in

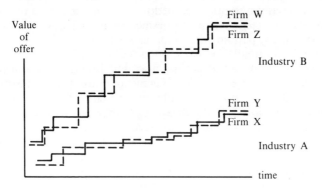

Figure 20 — Offer Improvement: Inter-Industry Comparisons

Industry B are performing better than those in Industry A. We must be careful, however, how we interpret inter-industry comparisons of performance since there will be numerous factors that determine the potential slopes of offer-improvement paths for different industries. We can hardly expect a mature industry producing a simple product that has been around for a long time to be as dynamic as an industry that is just beginning on a base of new technology.

Multidimensional Needs and Offers and Multiple Participants Revisited

We have considered the conceptual link between the innovation-imitation process and competition. We have defined innovation as a change and have described the process in both bargaining, and in trade-at-set-terms, markets. We must now remind ourselves of the multidimensional needs of buyers, the matching multidimensional offers of sellers and the multiple offers that must be made to the different participants in a firm and in a market. Four propositions emerge from this broadening of our perspective. The first is that the innovative-imitative process must involve *all* price and non-price dimensions, without distinction.

---

*It must be stressed that the diagram is for illustrative purposes only. Since the vertical axis can have no clearly defined units, the depicted curves cannot, of course, be measured.

It is an unfortunate tradition in economics (arising one suspects, from the intellectual investment that would-be economists are forced to make in price theory) that views price competition as the only thing that matters and non-price competition as being made up of one part singing commercials, one part salesmen (who arrive when you are in the shower), one part an addition to products of baubles, bubbles, and bagatelles, and finally, perhaps, one small part of quality.[16] The last part may be dismissed or heavily discounted by those who believe in the myth of the golden past. This dismissal of non-price competition is not acceptable. We do not usually buy the cheapest car available, or the cheapest vacation, or the cheapest of anything. We cannot possibly assess an offer without taking into account each and every dimension of it[17] — though, of course, for repeated purchases, most of a product's dimensions will be taken for granted.

The second proposition is that every change will not necessarily be an improvement for every participant. A price increase *per se* will not be welcomed by a buyer, though the sum of a price increase and a quality improvement may, on balance, be considered a better offer by some.

The third and closely related proposition is that management must balance all of the offers it makes. It is therefore not sufficient to do as we have done in Figure 20, and look only at an offer-improvement path from the point of view of buyers. Workers, shareholders, managers and suppliers also want, expect and even demand offer-improvements over time. Consumers might, in fact, prefer a price increase unmatched by any improvement in quality to the alternative of a withdrawal of union services so that they have no product at all.

The fourth and final proposition is that in the absence of stupidity, accident, miscalculation, or sheer perversity every change purposely made by management must have as its objective the improvement in the offer made to at least one of the participants.

Reaction Time

Is there anything that can usefully be said about the appropriate timing of the response? A number of authors[18] and the patent provisions of our law[19] take this into account by allowing and even protecting uniqueness of offers for some limited time. If the research and development of one firm can be copied immediately by a rival, what sense is there in investing in progress? In matters of public policy we must take care that in trying to increase the rate of offer-improvement through imitation we do not take measures (subsidizing entry, abolishing patents, compulsory sharing of know-how) that bring the innovating process to an abrupt halt. The Canadian government has been pursuing a policy of compulsory licencing of pharmaceutical innovations. No doubt some price reductions will result in the short run. The more interesting issue, however, is whether Canada will have a research capability in this industry in 10 years time.

A Prelude to Power

Power is the subject of the next chapter. It is worth noting here, however, that the innovative-imitative process requires that firms possess power. Each dimension of a product opens up the possibility of varying the offer, but only for the manager who has the power to choose between different options or to create new ones.

Limited as price theory models are with respect to the dimensions that can be administered by managers, there is generally some scope for choice. Even in the exacting model of perfect competition, Arrow[20] has reminded us that only in a state of equilibrium is the market at rest. But since the market is in disequilibrium, most, if not all of the time, some managers will have to ask a different price and a buyer will have to agree or disagree. Other buyers and sellers will have to decide whether or not to follow. These decisions all imply the existence and exercise of power. If this is true of perfect competition, where change is minimal, we must conclude that a more complex market with many more dimensions will require the existence of even more power.

Competition Within the One

Structuralists have mistakenly confined their discussions of competition to industries in which the number of firms ranges from one (monopoly) to many (perfect competition). But rivalrous behaviour does not begin with the arrival of the second firm: it begins with the arrival of the first.*

The first street railway, the first electrical generating plant, the first automobile, the first home delivery of milk had to compete — sometimes none too successfully — with the previous state of affairs in which there was no street railway, no electricity, and a horse and a cow in the backyard. The early automobile advertisements[22] often contained detailed financial accounts showing the superiority of the automobile over its rival — the horse-drawn vehicle.[23]

When the innovator introduces a new product, not everyone buys it; indeed there may be only a disappointingly few who try it. This automatically means that for many, or even for most potential buyers, the monopolists must continue the struggle against the alternative of

---

*Joseph Schumpeter recognized this point many years ago when he wrote, "the business-man feels himself to be in a competitive situation even if he is alone in his field. . . ."[21]

zero. Furthermore, even those who are venturesome and decide to try the new product may buy only one unit. For those buyers, the monopolist will have won the battle between zero and one, but the struggle will continue to the second unit, and the third, and so on. The idea that a monopolist has captive buyers who must do just as he says and buy the quantities he dictates at the price he determines is not one that fits the real world outside of government "service," the delivery and terms of which are backed by police powers.

Monopoly — a realistic assessment

Because the monopolist must in fact compete against zero sales and against a sales volume that is lower than desired, he must innovate. To put this issue in concrete terms, the innovating, cost-reducing, product-improving record of Bell Canada is much better[24] than that of the corner-grocery-store industry, and there are several reasons why this should be so. In a large firm there is likely to be a good deal of intra-firm or inter-division rivalry. Within the Bell system this kind of rivalry was encouraged by the exchange of operating statistics by similar units. When a division fell behind, it was very likely to imitate the process that put another division ahead of it.

Competition within the one may be a new idea to economists who were taught in their introductory course that monopoly means no competition. If managers or behavioural psychologists were being asked to comment on the matter, however, the idea that one person or one social unit would compete with the record of yesterday would be "old hat."[25] They would know either from experience or the laboratory that "feedback" is one of the most important motivators available. Most people want to grow, and if given an opportunity to see their own scoreboard, they will try to better their past records. Individuals and departments will compete with their own pasts. One M.B.A. graduate climbed several rungs of the hierarchical ladder in a week because of the miracle in productivity he performed by doing nothing more than posting and updating a graph on the daily output of his production unit.[26]

Doing better

From after church on Sunday until the first temptation arrives on Monday, we may feel that we are winning in the competition between the person we wish we were and the person we are. The new husband will feel compelled to outperform the dear departed. Louis XIV, a monopolist with clout, still had to outshine Louis XIII. A new broom must sweep cleaner, and it would be an unwise manager who did not seek to outdo his or her predecessor.

Finally, a very important source of innovation and imitation is the inter-company peer rivalry that occurs in all functional areas. Managers who perform financial, marketing, information, computer, personnel, planning and other functions meet regularly with their counterparts in other companies. It is very much in their professional interest to see to it that their own division performs well in relation to similar functional groups in other companies. Good performance will increase their self-esteem, their value to their company and — not incidentally — their mobility. An objective analysis of Bell's growth and performance reveals an impressive record. Intra-firm rivalry, inter-temporal personal and divisional rivalry, buyer-seller rivalry, and inter-firm rivalry at the functional level appear to have had a great deal to do with the record of progress that Bell has achieved. It should be added parenthetically that this progress has been made not because of regulation, but in spite of it. Regulation, *per se*, pays virtually no attention to innovation or imitation and, in fact, discourages the whole process.*

A dramatic contrast

In Chapter 2 we tried to capture diagrammatically the distinction between the structural and behaviourist school with respect to the way in which they were likely to view the relationship between competition and the number of firms. Figure 21 illustrates that distinction. In both cases the curve showing the relationship begins at one firm.

Our present discussion suggests that the diagrams need to be altered. With regard to the innovative-imitative dimension of competition, both curves should be shifted so that they begin at zero firms as shown in Figure 22. The present one must compete with past ones, potential ones, other ones, one's past, one's dreams and with zero; and one's innovation and imitation may be substantial and, conceivably, close to optimum.

---

*Obviously, if the rate of return to shareholders is fixed it matters very little, to them at least, whether the firm innovates or not. Indeed, if as is usually the case, an innovation involves some risk and increases the likelihood that the allowed rate of return is not earned, the shareholders would be wise to resist innovations.

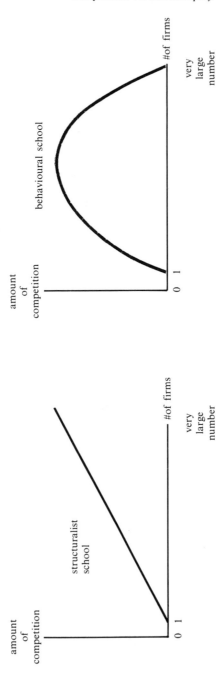

Figure 21 — The Number of Firms and Competition: Structuralists *vs* Behaviourists

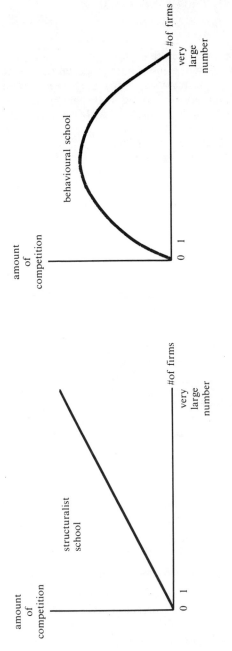

Figure 22 — Structuralists and Behaviourists Revised

CHOOSING AND OFFERING CHOICE

Introduction

It is easy to accept the idea that choice is an important dimension of competition. The user of a monopolistic postal service, the voter who can vote for only one party, a young lady with only one man who seems interested, all have one thing in common: they must accept the "product" being offered or make do with what may be a very poor substitute, or nothing at all.

Choice has been seen by different economists different ways, but in virtually all cases it plays a central role in the concept of competition. Frank Knight gave choice pride of place when he said, "what competition actually means is simply the freedom of the individual to 'deal' with any and all other individuals and to select the best terms as judged by himself, among those offered."[27]

Since monopoly is a unique offer, choice can be seen as the element that destroys monopoly and promotes competition. For example, Professor Kilgour states "The essence of full monopoly power resides in being the sole source of a product; so that the buyer must meet the seller's terms or go without. The essence of competition is to free the buyer from the power by access to alternative sources of the product."[28]

Since structuralists generally see a close relationship between the number of firms and competition, it might be assumed that they would also see that same close relationship between choice and competition. As we shall see, however, in a world of perfect competition there is no meaningful intra-industry choice, and, as we have already noted, even product differentiation is suspect.

In most of the structuralist economic literature that deals with choice, attention is focused on the number of firms. We must, therefore, examine the nature of choice and of choosing, which means breaking these complex activities into their different components. Next, we shall consider the role of choice in the economy. This involves a brief look at choice in the classical economic literature and how choice and choosing came to be treated in the static, neoclassical world of perfect competition. We shall then contrast this static world with the dynamic world of change. Passing references will be made to the striking similarity of the roles played by choice in economics and politics.

The second task will be to deal with the "amount" of choice, which, at the conceptual level, involves concepts like range, relevance and density. Of particular interest is choice at a point of time as compared with choice over time. The latter must take change and the addition and subtraction of offers into account.

Third, we shall make explicit the proposition that the number of offers is not at all the same as the number of firms, and finally we shall add yet another brief observation on power.

The Nature of Choice and of Choosing

There is more to making a choice or to offering a choice than first meets the eye. The process begins with an assessment of needs or wants. This is followed very quickly by a recognition of constraints. There is no point in wanting the moon if one's ladder is too short. The third step is a search in which the buyers determine the offers being made by other buyers and sellers, and the terms on which final deals have been and are being settled.

Step four includes some explicit or implicit calculation of the pleasure and pain of the different options. The calculation may be a very simple seat-of-the-pants judgement, or it may involve hours of work in a testing lab. Quick and simple judgements may be used to narrow a large field down to a few candidates, which then become the objects of more intensive study. Depending on the type of market, the choice may be a matter of take-it-or-leave-it, or it may involve bargaining on some or all dimensions of the offer. All four steps involve the use of existing, and perhaps the development of new, knowledge and expertise.

Finally, the choice can be essentially static and repetitive, or it can be innovative as in the case of the discovery by the buyer of a new way of satisfying an old want, or the putting together of a new purchase offer that is more attractive to both buyer and seller, or the use of suggestions or threats to inspire a supplier to make a better offer.

These elements can also be considered from the point of view of a seller. Like the buyer, suppliers can be expected to assess their own needs and constraints: to search, to calculate, to frame initial offers for bargaining, and final offers for the trade-at-set-terms. If, as often happens, the suppliers are larger, more specialized, or more expert than the buyers, the entrepreneurial element will be more important. An innovation may be nothing more elaborate than a retailer trying out a new line of convenience foods; it could be as complicated as a chemical company undertaking a multi-million-dollar feasibility study designed to create and offer a new process for refining a complex metallic ore.

In Chapter 2 we mentioned choice as being only one dimension of competition. But as we have just seen, choosing and offering choice are themselves complex, multi-faceted activities.

The Role of Choice in the Economy

It is difficult for us to understand the role of choice in the real world unless we make quite explicit the role of choice in the text-book world, for this view has conditioned the thoughts of economists and laymen alike.

Classical economists wrote about competition against a background of mercantalism — a system in which governmental constraints attempted to throttle individual initiative and preserve monopolistic positions. The lack of freedom of outsiders to enter closed guilds, industries, territories or professions was one of the major issues of the day and, as good anti-mercantilists, the classical economists spoke glowingly of the advantages that would follow if people were freely allowed to enter any field of their own choosing. Hence, Adam Smith wrote

> The quantity of grocery goods, for example, which can be sold in a particular town, is limited by the demand of that town and its neighborhood. The capital, therefore, which can be employed in the grocery trade cannot exceed what is sufficient to purchase that quantity. If this capital is divided between two different grocers, their competition will tend to make both of them sell cheaper, than if it were in the hands of one only; and if it were divided among twenty, their competition would be just so much the greater, and the chance of their combining together, in order to raise the price, just so much the less. Their competition might perhaps ruin some of themselves; but to take care of this is the business of the parties concerned, and it may safely be trusted to their discretion. It can never hurt either the consumer, or the producer; on the contrary, it must tend to make the retailers both sell cheaper and buy dearer, than if the whole trade was monopolized by one or two persons.[29]

In a similar vein, John Stuart Mill said that "competition is not so active among a limited as among an unlimited number."[30]

Simplistic extrapolation

In the light of such remarks it seemed to be nothing more than a simple extrapolation for neoclassical economists to evolve the perfectly competitive model. This seems to do no more than extend the argument from "two is good; but 20 is better," to "infinity must be perfect." But the classical economists had no more experience with 20 sellers in a single market than we have today, let alone experience with markets composed of an infinite number of buyers and sellers. The classical economists did not prescribe government intervention to increase the number of competitors; instead they advocated freedom: governments should leave it to the parties themselves to decide whether to enter or leave an industry. As we have just read, "Their competition might perhaps ruin some of themselves [that is, *reduce the number of competitors*]; but to take care of this is the business of the parties concerned. . ."

Regardless of the intent of the classical and neoclassical econo-mists, let us accept the perfectly competitive model as part of our intellectual inheritance and inquire what choices would be available to buyers and sellers in such a system. We shall look first at buyers.

If buyers lived in a perfectly competitive world, each of them would be free to choose the products of all the different industries according to their tastes and pocket books. But there would be no intra-industry choice. Because of the assumption that the offers within an industry are homogeneous, a buyer would have no reason to prefer the output of one firm over that of any other.

Little choice anywhere

Not only do the assumptions of perfect competition rule out intra-industry competition, but they do not suggest a wide range of inter-industry choice either.

Suppose that the "very large number" for firms required to achieve perfect competition in Canada is only 1,000, and that the condition "relatively small firms" can be satisfied by decreeing that firms on average have ten employees. Our labour force of about 10 million in Canada[31] could, therefore, be organized into about 1,000 perfectly competitive industries making 1,000 different products.

What impact would this have on total choice? The catalogue of one department store in Canada has over 900 pages.[32] On many of those pages ten or more different products are offered. Yet this cata-logue does not usually carry more than two brands of each product; it covers no services, groceries, housing, transportation, investment or financial services. It does not sell government products or services, and it has almost no components, parts, "intermediate" or investment goods, which are many times more numerous than consumer goods.[33] It can hardly be claimed that perfect competition will maximize choice. Our 1,000 firms in 1,000 perfectly competitive industries would pro-vide us with more choice if they all differentiated their products, and offered us, instead, 1,000,000 products produced by 1,000,000 competing monopolists.

Even though choice may be limited in a perfectly competitive world its existence, in combination with all the other conditions of perfect competition, would produce a static consumer sovereignty and an "optimum allocation of resources."[34] This means that consumer choices (with given incomes) determine how much of each product should be produced. As a result, an all-knowing, all-powerful economic dictator cannot increase human welfare by ordering the transfer of resources from one industry to another. In a static and unchanging world, therefore, free choice and perfect competition would ensure that we had precisely the right number of headboards, scrub boards, and buck boards, given every household's tastes and income. We would be unlikely, however, to have Xeroxes, computers or most of our present-day pharmaceuticals.

At a microeconomic level it is free choice that permits each household to select the best mix and quantities of products, given its income. At a macroeconomic level, choice and the other assumptions of perfect competition produce an optimum but static allocation of resources.

Choice and change

Choice plays an even more important part in a changing, dynamic world. At the micro level, free choice still enables the individual household to allocate available income among all products. In so doing it attempts to optimize its satisfaction. The two main differences between the static world of pure competition and the real, dynamic world in this regard is that, first, the buyer (whether householder or firm) can generally exercise intra-industry, as well as inter-industry, choice; and second, the buyer will usually be able to choose between new and old offers. This ability to indicate preference for this brand over that, or for this offer over that, is very important. It provides customers with a steering wheel with which they can control the path of change.

Whenever a firm makes available a new offer, whether evolutionary or revolutionary, households and companies are usually presented with an opportunity to experiment with, and express an opinion on, the new and the old. Sometimes the new is so obviously superior that the old very quickly disappears. Nylon stockings very quickly replaced silk stockings.

Sometimes the old survives the competition of the new and both continue to exist in an enriched repertoire of offers. Cassettes did not replace records; both continue to be sold side by side. Sometimes, of course, the new products, or the new version of the old products, or the new and promising techniques lose out in competing with the old, and the trial proves to be an error.[35]

Back to reality

In the real world the seller is in quite a different position than his counterpart in the textbook. The perfectly competitive firms could read the price in the newspaper. He merely has to choose the most profitable output. In most real markets a supplier can take very little as given, and will find more questions than answers in the newspaper. Management must face scores and perhaps hundreds of "explanatory variables" in all its product and factor markets. By guess or by measurement it must choose the best packaging material, store hours, credit terms and so on. Then it must estimate as best it can what sales and what output will result from these choices. It must determine what simultaneous choices can be made in its factor markets for labour and suppliers. And these are only the short-run, day-to-day choices!

In the longer run, almost everything becomes variable, from basic technology to plant location. The range of possibilities within which management is called on to make choices increases as does its vulnerability to the choices made by others.

In either a perfectly competitive world or in the real world, choice is the instrument by which each individual seeks to maximize his or her own welfare. In the perfectly competitive world, choice plus some other conditions produces a technically optimum distribution of resources. But imposing this artificial system on the market place will encourage neither a high standard of living nor much in the way of progress. In the real world, free choice (plus some other conditions) gives householders control over the direction of change.

Economics and politics

The similarity between this dynamic role of choice in the real world of economics and the real world of politics is too close to escape our attention. If we are prepared to accept Schumpeter's analysis that democracy is primarily concerned with competition for leadership,[36] then it becomes clear that while a two-party system may appear to offer only a limited choice at a point of time, it nevertheless offers a wider range of choice over time.

The reason for this is clear. So long as citizens preserve the right to change parties (and leaders), competition for power will force both parties to move in line with public opinion.[37] If proof of this simple proposition is needed, one need only look at the political platform of the radical parties of 100 or 50 years ago and compare them with the platforms of the "conservative" parties of today. With only a few exceptions, the Communist Manifesto looks conservative compared with the current platforms of our major political parties in North America today.

Quality improvement

It would be almost as much a mistake to look at the similar political platforms of two political parties at a single point of time and conclude that voters had no real choice as it would be to look at the offers being made by two manufacturers at the same time and conclude that the similarity of the brands leaves consumers with no real choice. The significant fact is that both of the main parties in either the United

States or Canada have changed their platforms so much over time that they bear little resemblance to the platforms of the same parties 50 years ago. The same observation can be made about products. It may very well be that the goods or services offered by two airlines or two sugar companies today are not very different from each other. The point is, however, that they are very different from the offers made by those same companies 50 years ago. And not only are they different, they are undeniably better.[38] As Stigler put it, "the main trend of quality change has been toward improvement, and it has been a strong and continuous trend."[39]

The analogy can be pursued further. The reference to political choice helps us to understand that the existence of choice and the existence of freedom go hand in hand. The difference between having only one party and having the choice between two is the difference between dictatorship and Schumpeterian democracy — the right of effective protest.

The existence of choice in either politics or in the market gives us not only freedom, but responsibility as well. Indeed, morality has little meaning unless there is choice, and this simple fact should be borne in mind by those who would limit our economic choice. If it is not a Palagian heresy to argue that moral man must be confronted with the choice of good and evil and that we must rely on his moral sense to choose good, then it may not be too outrageous to argue that man must have the opportunity to choose good and bad products, and that we must rely on his good sense to choose well.[40]

The Amount of Choice

If it is logical to accept choice as a dimension of competition, can we take the next step and say the more choice there is, the more competition we are likely to have? Before we can hope to answer such a question, we need to have a clear idea of how choice might be measured or at least how we might recognize whether choice has been increased or not.

In order to facilitate the task of conceptualizing the problem, let us imagine the simplest of all products with only two dimensions: thickness and price. In addition, let us impose the condition that everyone in the market believes that within some range, more thickness is always better than less. Finally, let us assume that thickness incurs costs and that costs and prices increase with thickness.

With such a simple product we can identify three elements that taken together describe the amount of choice. The first and most obvious is "range." We can presumably say that the greater the distance from the cheapest and thinnest brand to the thickest and most expensive brand, the greater is the range of choice.

The second element we shall call "relevance." It is specified that more thickness is better "within some range." The qualification is necessary because at one extreme, the product may be so thin that it cannot be handled, and at the other, so thick that it cannot be moved. Beyond these points, offering additional choice is obviously irrelevant on technical grounds. But range will not be settled solely on technical grounds, for in our two-dimensional example, price and cost must also be considered. Well before the products become technically impossible, they will become economically inappropriate; and they can be inappropriate from the point of view of either the seller or the buyer or both.

So long as extra thickness means extra cost, the buyer will at some point avoid technically better (thicker) brands because the extra value is not worth the extra cost. For his part, the seller will recognize that it would be easier to sell a brand of a given thickness for a lower price, but he also is bound by what is economically possible. Cutting the price in half might be within the acceptable range of offers for customers, but the resulting offers to workers and shareholders might be quite unacceptable.

Relevant offers

Obviously no offers can be counted as relevant unless they are acceptable to at least some buyers and some sellers. Because different buyers and sellers value products (thickness, labour, etc.) differently, and because they value their money differently, relevant boundaries cannot be predetermined on an objective basis. The pragmatic test, however, is simple: if someone is willing to make an offer and someone else is willing to accept it, the offer falls within the relevant range of the possible and the desirable.

The third element that can be identified is what might be called the "density" of the choices. "Density" is taken to be a function of the distances between offers. Even if the utility of thickness is the same for all customers, so long as their incomes or the utilities for other products are different, not all of them will want the same thickness-price mix, and we may assume that the more offers there are and the better (more evenly?) distributed they are within the relevant range, the more choice there will be. The more heterogeneous are the needs or wishes of buyers with regard to thickness (whether they are different buyers, or the same buyer with different uses) the more important it is to have different thickness-price offers.

There is, of course, no product in the real world that has only two dimensions, so "range", "relevence", and "density" must be translated accordingly.[41] Despite obvious and insurmountable measurement difficulties this conceptual framework can still be used to throw light on certain issues such as the relationship between choice, perfect competition and monopoly. It is readily apparent that additional identical offers will do very little to enhance the amount of choice. Whether the number of firms making *exactly* the same offer is one or 1,000 will not matter to choice-seeking buyers. The superiority, if any, of having more rather than fewer identical offers, must rest on grounds other than choice. It is one of the many anomalies of the neoclassical position that perfectly competitive and perfectly monopolistic industry can offer buyers the same range of choice: one or zero!

When a firm in a perfectly competitive industry makes a unique offer, either it will be accepted, or it will not. If it is accepted (on a large enough scale to make the offer viable) then we can say that choice has been increased. But since any firm making a unique offer is by definition a monopolist, then monopolization by definition is the *only* way to enlarge choice.

Statics and dynamics

There are two time frames in which the amount of choice can be judged: at a single point of time, and over time. The offers existing at a point of time provide the repertoire from which products and services can be selected in order to optimize the use of current income and/or wealth. Presumably the more (different) offers there are at that point of time, the easier it will be for people with different tastes and incomes to maximize their satisfaction. If the economy is static, there will be little interest in looking at choice over time; but if products or offers are changing, intertemporal comparisons will be important.

Let us look back at our simple price-thickness product to see what impact innovation might have on this industry. Suppose that initially the offers range from a 1-inch variety costing $1 to a 20-inch one at $20. Suppose further that market experiment with price-thickness combinations beyond this range have failed. Assume that brands are available at each 1-inch interval and that each brand is produced by a different company, so that the choices are made available by 20 companies, selling 20 different products.

Now let us suppose that an innovator discovers lamination and is able to produce a 1-inch product that can sell for $0.90. If the new product is obviously superior to all existing varieties, regardless of thickness, what will happen to the amount of choice?

Evil monopoly

Clearly, the new company and the new product will replace 20 companies and 20 products. Has choice been reduced? If choice is to be measured at a point of time, in terms of numbers of products or number of companies, one would be bound to agree that it had. On the other hand, if choice must always be considered over time, then buyers have had an increase in the amount of choice from 20 companies and 20 products to 21 companies and 21 products! Even after 20 bankruptcies have occurred, the new manufacturer must continue to compete with the old, because the former products can be reintroduced at any time if the new product does not continue to be more attractive.

No sensible person is likely to dispute the proposition that the innovation increased choice over time. The problem is to consider how this increase can be characterized and, if possible, how it can be contrasted with choice at a given point in time.

In order to illustrate, imagine that all offers can be represented as points on a flat surface. In Figure 23, the ellipse A encompasses all offers made in 1950. Similarly, the circle B describes all offers made in 1980. The shaded areas of the ellipse outside the circle (C) represent discontinued offers. The cross hatched areas of the circle outside the ellipse (D) are new offers that were not available in 1959.

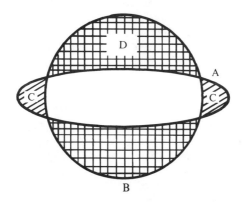

Figure 23

The 20 old products of our thickness-price example would be found in the shaded area of the ellipse (C); the superior offer of laminated material would be found in the new-product, cross-hatched area of the circle (D). While the circle and the ellipse represent choices at a point in time, the thickened, outside perimeter around both the ellipse and the circle describes the dynamic or intertemporal choice.

Total intertemporal choice

By selecting the outer boundaries of intertemporal choice as the relevant criterion for the measurement of total choice, we simply make explicit the obvious fact that the invention of a laminated product did increase choice. There should be no difficulty in continuing to include the old products in total intertemporal choice; not only because they did exist, but, more important, because they could exist again if the superiority of the new offer is not maintained.

It is almost universally accepted that the freedom of entry — the possibility of new offers by new companies — is an important competitive element. Since old offers have proven both their acceptability to consumers and their technical feasibility, freedom of entry (really the freedom to make similar offers) should not only include the possibility of making totally new offers, but also the possibility of reintroducing old ones.

It must be admitted, of course, that the probability of reinstating old offers will in most cases be remote indeed, especially if they involved lower wages and lower consumer satisfaction. One hundred years ago a fur coat with a hand-embroidered lining could be purchased for under $100. Such an offer would still be attractive to consumers. But the offers that would have to be made to workers, trappers, and investors in order to make such an offer to consumers would be completely unacceptable.

The Number of Offers and the Number of Firms

So far each firm has been assumed to make a single offer. There is no reason why this should be so; in fact most firms make multiple offers. One automobile dealer may offer a series of products that range from an old, second-hand car sold "as is" for $50, to a top-of-the-line, all-the-accessories vehicle for $20,000. Stigler and Kindahl[42] have pointed out that a steel company could make 135 million product offers in just the narrow category of hot-rolled carbon-steel shafts. This is without getting into credit terms, delivery schedules and the like. Even a very simple product like sugar boasts a price list that includes 17 different kinds of sugar that come in 50 different packages, and that does not include special blends at negotiable prices or the different types of bulk handling equipment or the permutations and combinations that can be obtained when roughly 1000 product-package categories are multiplied by all of the different delivery, credit, volume and other terms that can be specified.

There are a number of reasons why it is economically efficient to have one firm make multiple offers. Economies of scale and of learning will often apply to the total volume sold in different product categories, if they have parts, raw materials, technology, sales, delivery or manufacturing facilities in common. Then too, it may be important to the buyer for different products to be compatible: anyone who has tried to do any electrical work in England knows how much easier life would be if parts and components were all manufactured by fewer and more co-operative companies. This latter consideration, plus time and money spent in searching, ordering, delivering and financing, suggests that multiple offers by the same company often produce economies of scale for buyers as well as for sellers. The advantages of having a single company make multiple offers are quite obvious.

THE CONCEPT OF INDEPENDENT ASSERTIVENESS

My amateur (and amateurish) activities in the ring many years ago once involved sharing a dressing room with two professional wrestlers. They put on a good show, and we disillusioned amateurs were the only ones who knew that what went on in the ring had been choreographed a half hour earlier in the dressing room. What the spectators were watching was "show-biz," not competition; the dimension that was missing was independent, assertive behaviour.

Independence and self-assertion of spirit and behaviour are important elements of competition. Making the relationship precise, however, is not so easy. Considerable confusion arises however, because there has been an attempt to infer competitive behaviour from the price-theory models of perfect competition, monopoly and oligopoly. Let us try to make explicit what inference can be drawn from price-theory models.

If we have an industry made up of 1,000 small farms producing a homogeneous product sold to a large number of small buyers, we can make some reasonable assumptions about what an individual farmer would know and how he would behave *vis-à-vis* his rivals. If the farmer has taken even an introductory course in economics, he will have been told, correctly, that if all farmers produce more, other things equal, the price will decline. However, he will also know, with or without a course in economics, that if only *he* produces more, the price decline will be imperceptible and the cost of the decline will be spread very thinly over so many other farmers that they will not be too concerned about what he does.

Marketing boards

Suppose that our farmer is producing as much as it is profitable to produce at the going price but that he feels that the going price is too low. He could, of course, try to persuade all his fellow farmers to produce less, but this would be too expensive for him to undertake personally, and in any event would be unlikely to succeed. He might instead organize a co-operative or a political action group to force the government to establish a marketing board and thereby raise the price.[43]

His first-year economics course, however, would have told him that this higher-than-the-market price will increase production (always *ceteris paribus*) and reduce sales, creating a surplus the government will have to buy and store. Since the accumulation of stocks cannot go on for very long, the government will eventually have to order a reduction in the amount produced. When this happens, the joy of the higher price will be partly or completely offset by reduced sales.

What the farmer probably had in mind, however, was higher price and *more* production. This being so, our farmer will have an incentive to cheat and produce above his quota if he can. Even if one of his neighbours finds out about it, the farmer can argue that his cheating is costing the neighbour very little, so perhaps they should both cheat. If cheating becomes general, quotas will have to be cut further or policemen will have to be hired to stop the cheating.

It is also quite possible that the "activists" who campaigned for the collectivist marketing board solution will be able to apply pressure on cheaters or noncomformists. The conditions of perfect competition suggest self-centered, individualistic behaviour (a view that we shall qualify later) but results that are perceived to be unsatisfactory could easily lead to collectivist (and non-perfectly competitive) behaviour.

Few sellers

Next, let us look at the other end of the competitive scale and consider a perfect monopolist (a single supplier of a product for which there is no very close substitute). The monopolist of course recognizes that his behaviour and that of his customers would be interdependent. He would no doubt give thought every now and then to the closest substitutes for his product and to the possibility of the appearance of an even closer substitute. Generally speaking, however, apart from the truism that no monopolist is an island, he should enjoy a relatively high degree of independence, however defined. He could thus assert his own self-interest.

Finally, let us consider an oligopolist (a firm in an industry that includes only two, three, four or a "few" other sellers). To make the independent assertiveness comparison as sharp as possible, let us assume that our oligopolist is one of three firms selling a completely homogeneous product and that the offers are potentially different in only one respect: price. In such a case, the same market relationships will apply as in the case of the perfectly competitive industry: more production will mean a lower price, other things being equal. In this case, however, the possibility of one firm's lowering the price without being detected, is very small. An individual oligopolist may have the same incentive to cheat as an individual farmer, but the chance of doing so without being discovered is remote indeed.

No competitor is an island

There are two closely related behavioural assumptions we might reasonably make about perfectly competitive firms. The first is that an individual farmer, say, will pay very little attention to the output plan (which, it must be remembered, is the only variable) of any other *individual* farmer. He will, of course, be vitally interested in the collective output behaviour of all his rivals, because that is one of the determinants of price; indeed, he may be prepared to devote considerable energy, time and money to changing the collective actions of his competitors, but such efforts, if successful, will, of course, destroy the conditions of perfect competition. Co-operatives and marketing boards apart, the behaviour of the farmer can be described as ignoring his individual competitors, but not ignoring their collectivity.

The second behavioural assumption, which follows from the first, is that the farmer would not assume or act on the assumption that there was any mutual interdependency with any of his *individual* rivals. That is, he would not expect his output decision to have an appreciable effect on any one of his rivals. He would not, therefore, expect it to elicit any appreciable retaliation or reaction.

The proposition that ignoring competitors is good (i.e. perfectly competitive) and watching them is bad (i.e. monopolistic or oligopolistic) can be found in most combines trials in which the issue is conspiracy. The prosecutor will usually try to produce evidence in court that firm A knew what B, C and D were up to. That such action is judged to be anticompetitive is implicit in the collection and presentation of the evidence, and it was made explicit in the judgement on the important metal-culvert case in which it is stated: "It would seem unlikely that any of the accused producers would have made inquiries to prospective buyers concerning competitors' bids and the results of the bidding if there was not a common interest in determining whether the open price policy was being followed."[44] In other words, in the absence of collusive intent, one businessman can have no interest in watching his rivals.

Turning the other cheek

This is hardly a conclusion that could be based on the study of competition in love, war, sports or any other field of human endeavour. Any boxer who climbed into the ring intent on being so perfectly competitive that he ignored his rival would have that particular idea knocked out of his head soon enough. I count myself lucky that I did my boxing before I did my economics. Fortunately, it never crossed my mind that I would be more competitive in the ring if I just minded my own business; otherwise I might have qualified for the "Perfectly Competitive Boxing Citation" (usually awarded posthumously).

The ignoring-of-rivals interpretation of independent assertiveness cannot (or perhaps we have to say, *should* not) "stand up in court." If we look a little more carefully at the perfectly competitive model, we discover that even the farmer is not quite as independent as he may at first appear. We were careful to point out earlier that he "would pay very little attention to the output plan (which, it must be remembered, is the only variable) of any other *individual* farmer." But even in perfect competition a product has many dimensions in addition to quantity. The farmer must not be different from other farmers with respect to any of them, otherwise he will be guilty of product differentiation, and would thereby destroy the conditions of perfect competition. *The perfectly competitive firm can hardly ignore its rivals since it has to be exactly like them.* Such a condition can hardly give a farmer much room for independence or self-assertion. Only the monopolist would be happy with the judgement that being independently assertive meant ignoring rivals.

Mutual interdependency

A more serious but equally unacceptable interpretation of the independent-assertiveness element of competition is that it means absence of mutual interdependency. If we approach the issue of mutual interdependency through game theory, we can find an apparently precise distinction between dependency and interdependency. Player A's choice of strategy may not depend on the choices made by B (for any of a number of reasons: lack of information; costs of analysis or of gathering information that exceed possible gains; no discernible relationship between B's strategies and A's payoffs). If so, A makes choices of strategies independent of B. In the context of game strategy, however, it would also be clear that A and B are not really players in the same game: they are not really direct competitors. A could be selling holidays in Bermuda and B could be selling machines that make button holes. Alternatively, A and B could both be wheat farmers! When the choice that A makes does affect B, and vice versa, Nicholson calls it "a decision under conflict".[45] But he could as easily have called it mutual interdependency.

According to the traditional view, a manager's independence and the state of competition in the market are severely compromised as soon as the manager recognizes he will have to take into account his competitors' reactions to his own actions. In the orthodox interpretation of independent assertiveness, in other words, the higher the degree of mutual interdependency, the less competition there is.

If this is so, the oligopolist is condemned to being anti-competitive by definition. But even the farmer (the definitive example of perfect competition) does not get an unequivocal "not guilty." For the farmer who is a good businessman will make his plans in the light of what he thinks all his competitors will do. While there is a big difference between being one of 1,000 and one of three, it is clear if rather paradoxical that the only way to escape any suspicion at all on the charge of mutual interdependency is to be a monopolist.

Back to reality, once again

Should we conclude from all of this that watching rivals or recognizing mutual interdependency reduces, and perhaps reduces to zero, the dimension of competition called independent assertiveness? Let us back away from price theory once again and consider the issue from the point of view of other disciplines or activities.

We do not ask boxers, gladiators or bullfighters to behave as though they were alone in the ring: it would be foolish to imagine that they could or should be unaware of their rivals. It would not occur to us to charge a chess player with being anti-competitive just because he is aware that every move he makes will have an impact on his competitor and will no doubt elicit a response. We accept that football teams are trying to be "competitive" when they spend time and money scouting the opposition and setting up defences against all possible attacks.

When describing the process of innovation and imitation illustrated in Figures 18 and 19, we mentioned the successive leapfrogging of two business rivals as they innovated and initiated. This example was inspired by the examination of the month-by-month marketing plans of three sugar companies. There was no doubt whatsoever that each company watched its rivals as carefully as do boxers in a ring. There was no doubt, either, that they did everything they could to better their opponents. In view of the fact that sugar has been used for many centuries it is astonishing that there could still have been so many cost, quality, packaging and transportation innovations. It goes without saying that each of the innovations introduced by the sugar manufacturers was of benefit to one or more of the buyers, and the companies knew very well that each advantage was temporary because, if successful, most of them could and would be imitated by their rivals.

Price-theory concepts

There is no doubt that if we were innocent of price theory and approached competition through a study of love, war, sports, or business, there would be little chance of being led to the conclusion that watching rivals or recognizing mutual interdependency is anti-competitive. Indeed we would be more likely to conclude the exact opposite: that competition does not even *begin* until two parties recognize they are rivals. But this is just another way of saying that they recognize their mutual interdependency.

We have spent considerable time describing what independent assertiveness is *not*: it is not the ignoring of rivals, and it is not a denial of mutual interdependency. It is now time to try to clarify what it is and why we have chosen the rather awkward term independent assertiveness.

One of the themes that has appeared in the economic literature from time to time, and one of the propositions flowing from the observation of competition in other fields, is that a competitive organization seeks first and foremost its own self-interest. This concept lies behind the *laissez faire* doctrine espoused by Adam Smith in his famous statement that the individual who "intends only his own gain, . . . is . . . led by an invisible hand to promote an end which was no part of his intention. . . . By pursuing his own interest he frequently promotes that of the society. . ."[46]

Independence in economics

Henry L. Moore writing about competition in 1906 said, "Every economic factor seeks a maximum net income. This is the essential meaning of the term." He goes on to show that this meaning of competition was adopted by Edgeworth, Malthus and Cournot, and in a footnote quotes Quesnay as saying "To obtain the greatest possible increase of enjoyment with the greatest decrease of expense is the perfection of economics."[47] Frank Knight said much the same thing: "What competition actually means is simply the freedom of the individual to 'deal' with any and all other individuals and to select the best terms as judged by himself, among those offered."[48] Kilgour also stressed self interest.[49]

While it may not always be spelled out, it seems clear that when such quotations are taken in context there is a presumption that people seek their self-interest through individual rather than collective action. This is essentially why we have selected the term "independent assertiveness." The "assertiveness" suggests the advancing of one's own cause: the independence suggests that it is done by independent or individual, as opposed to collective, means.

The theme of independence plays a much larger role in the literature than does self-interest, either as a positive statement linking competition with independence or as a negative statement linking collusive, nonindependent action with monopoly. For example, Richard E. Low, states "One conduct test [of competition] is the independence of rival firms."[50] J.M. Clark, in the tradition of price theory, said "For the competition to be effective, the crucial thing seems to be that prices be independently made. . ."[51] And Frank Knight linked the meaning of competition to a state in which "competing units are numerous and act independently."[53]

Economic aggression

The third theme, which is very closely related to self-interest and independence, is aggressiveness. It is not quite enough for competitors to be independent or to be primarily interested in their own welfare: a clutch of hermits might meet those two tests. Competitors should also be reasonably aggressive in the way they approach the competitive game. Kilgour suggests that they should recognize that "Competition is not a tea party."[54] Whatever they do, they should give Stigler no further reason for believing that they "treat each other with the utmost kindness."[55]

Ideally, independent assertiveness might be described as behaviour consistent with the objective of being better than one's rivals. Anti-competitive behaviour that fails the independence test involves making an agreement that halts or seriously retards the struggle for superiority.

The foregoing paragraph is prefaced with "ideally " because while it is to be hoped that all participants in every race will aim to be number one, it must be recognized that some will be striving to improve their relative position while others will consider it a triumph simply to stay in the race. More broadly and realistically, therefore, independent assertiveness may be described as behaviour consistent with the struggle to be relatively better, whether better than everyone else, better than some others, better than one's own past performance, or better than those who fail. Anti-competitive behaviour that fails the independence test, then, includes making an agreement that halts or seriously retards the progress inherent in the competitive struggle.

Collusion and competition

Does this definition imply that all agreements among rivals are anti-competitive? Not at all. Relationships among groups are seldom wholly rivalrous or wholly co-operative. At one point of time two parties may be predominantly rivalrous, and yet at another, predominantly co-operative.* Even at a time when rivalry predominates, there may be some matters on which co-operation is socially useful, inevitable, and even required by law.

This co-existence of rivalry and co-operation should come as no surprise, for it is a feature of competitive situations in all fields. For example, we expect our football players to be unco-operative with other teams when it comes to revealing game signals or game strategies, but we would be indignant if they carried this lack of co-operation so far that they refused to tell their opponents (or the fans) when they were going to show up for a game.

Similarly we might want to see considerable independence among sellers in the introduction of product improvements. Yet we encourage our companies to collude on research products and we are prepared to command them to co-operate on the use of a common set of rules and standards to describe the quantity and quality of their products.[56]

Once a year a manufacturer and his agents may fight vigorously over contract renewals and cost sharing, but most of the time they will co-operate closely to make sure householders buy the brand in which they have a common interest. Consider an actual problem that confronted one of my clients.[57] The Canadian industry of which the firm was a member imported a relatively homogeneous raw material. My client was long on inventory and, moreover, had a shipment that it did not really need arriving in one week. The president of the firm was approached by a competitor who was desperately short of inventory and did not have a shipment arriving for a month. The competitor proposed swapping shipments. Should my client agree? What were the competitive implications? Should my client try to take advantage of its rival's misfortune or bad planning to win away some of his customers.

In this case it was decided to co-operate by swapping shipments. Management could see no lasting advantage to adopting a policy that would appear to buyers as showing a dog-in-the-manger attitude. Furthermore, it was judged that this particular swap, and indeed a policy of swapping, would result in lower costs for all Canadian manu-

---

*In a fundamental sense, the whole competitive economic system may be looked upon as a vast cooperative effort. The marketplace underlies and supports specialization, comparative advantage, the division of labour and trade. Without these, human life would be truly "nasty, brutish, and short."[55]

facturers in the industry. Indeed that particular swap obviously saved one month's carrying costs on a boat load of raw material.

In his book *The Antitrust Paradox*, Walter Bork rejects the idea of equating the competition that is the requirement of the law with rivalry because "the event that triggers the application of law is often the elimination of rivalry. . ." This "invites the further, wholly erroneous conclusion that the elimination of rivalry must always be illegal." He goes on to say, "Our society is founded upon the elimination of rivalry, since that is necessary to every integration or coordination of productive economic efforts and to the specialization of effort."[58][59]

Peaceful co-existence

The idea that we should be prepared to accept the co-existence of competition and co-operation is also supported by the fact that acts of rivalry occur over time, sometimes quite long periods. A rivalrous strategy may comprise a long sequence of events involving a number of quite different activities and, of course, different players. The different activities may include the haggling over the rules ("what will the neighbors think"), the struggle ("what sort of boy do you think I am"), the settlement of terms ("my father thinks doweries are old fashioned"), and the subsequent co-habitation ("I never promised you a rose garden"). When we consider the wondrous variety of actions and reactions that are possible in any commercial or non-commercial strategy, we should not be surprised to find a mixture of rivalry and co-operation in almost any sequence of events or over any considerable passage of time.

This discussion of independent assertiveness enables us to show how a simplistic price-theory model of the firm can build a conclusion into the assumptions of the model. A good deal of the work in simulation and game theory is designed to find out whether oligopolists adopt a co-operative or an aggressive attitude. But why should it be either/or? Perhaps it is because the experimenter thinks of the company as a person whose actions or attitudes can be measured along a single, unidimensional scale. Not surprisingly, given the grip of price theory, that one dimension will normally be price (though some times it may be market share). Thus Shepherd writes, "cooperation results in stable prices and [and/or?] market shares among the participants. Even where the cooperative devices are not known, such stability can show that cooperation is present."[60] And again, "price is the sharpest competitive weapon. . .price is *the* device to be controlled."[61]

Price, however, is only one of a number of dimensions of an offer. An investigator should, therefore, be duty bound to withhold judgement about the degree of co-operation or independence until a reasonable sample of dimensions has been studied. *Pro forma* price should not receive much attention unless it is also actual price. The behaviour of price should not be considered without reference to the range of possible price differences, and the scope for variations in average prices over time.

United we stand — competitively

There is no obvious reason why the firms in an industry should not end up with the same *pro forma* prices, adopt the same package sizes, co-operate to discourage unions from using a whipsaw, form a united front against a foreign, monopolistic supplier of a raw material, and support a common advertising campaign to promote the generic product against those of other industries; and at the same time be aggressive in cost reduction, offer improvement and price cutting (within the limit of what is possible). Such a mixture of co-operation and independence might well be the combination that maximizes the rate of offer-improvement. To look at only one of these factors and on that basis make a judgement about the state of competition in the industry tells us more about the assumptions made by the investigator than it does about the industry.

ENERGY

No enumeration of the elements of competition would be complete without mentioning the dimension that is often the most obvious — the grunts, groans, curses, decibels, sweat and blood of competition. In Chapter 2, we chose the decorous label of "energy" for all of these sounds and furies.

When we pay our money to watch a competitive sport, we expect to see the expenditure of a lot of energy or effort. When we pay our money to read about a businessman of fact or fiction, we expect again a story of energy and devotion to duty — plus, perhaps, some other characteristics. The biographer (unauthorized) describes the president of Revlon as follows:

> Whatever else he was — nasty, crude, lovely, virile, brilliant, inarticulate, insecure, generous, honest, ruthless, complicated — Charles Revson was a man of single-minded persistence and drive, entirely dedicated to his business.[62]

The boss in *The Man in the Grey Flannel Suit* says:

> "*Somebody has to do the big jobs!* . . . This world was built by men like me! To really do a job, you have to live it, body and soul! You people who just give half your mind to your work are riding on our backs!"[63]

A survey by Don Rothwell[64] of 700 managers, from foremen to senior executives, found not only that executives put in long hours, but also that time and effort spent on the job correlated closely with achievement as measured by position and salary.

Yet, strangely enough, there is a counter-myth that is illustrated in a statement by Judge Wyzanski, "Some truth lurks in the cynical remark that not high profits, but a quiet life is the chief reward of monopoly power."[65] Cynical or not, seeking the quiet life is an oft-repeated charge levelled against businessmen, especially by academic economists.

More general in its language, though in context clearly aimed at business, is Harvey Leibenstein's concept of X-efficiency: "for a variety of reasons people and organizations normally work neither as hard nor as effectively as they could."[66]

Whether managers are workaholics, or X-inefficient quiet-loving folk, there appears to be general agreement that their energy level is a facet of competition.

FAIR AND EQUITABLE RULES

That competition needs rules that constrain rather than encourage rivalry is an old idea. One of the first to describe the consequences of unchecked rivalry was Thomas Hobbes who wrote in 1651,

> . . . if any two men desire the same thing, which nevertheless they cannot both enjoy, they become enemies. . .So that in the nature of man, we find three principal causes of quarrel. First, competition; secondly, diffidence; thirdly, glory.[67]

It was of course these quarrels that pitted "every man against every man" and made necessary the *Leviathan* to set rules and enforce them.

In a more modern idiom, we have suggested that competition should be likened to boxing rather than war because boxing "is subject to rules."[68] Perhaps because rules are sometimes of more interest to the smaller of the two competitors, the Government of Canada declared over 150 years ago

> prompt and signal vengeance will be taken for every fresh departure by the Enemy, from that system of warfare, which ought alone to subsist between enlightened and civilized nations.[69]

Thus did we hope to encourage the Americans to honour the fair and equitable rules of warfare in 1812.

In sports we are no less imbued with a desire for fair play. To that end, we employ a host of referees, umpires, judges, time-keepers, score-keepers and officials who do everything from calculating handicaps to administering blood tests. The course of fair and equitable love is smoothed by chaperones, policemen, duennas, priests, lawyers, eunuchs, Ann Landers (for difficult cases) and a host of interested parties who do everything from locking (and unlocking) chastity belts to, again, administering blood tests.

Clearly all is *not* fair in love and war — or sports. Fair rules and the willingness to abide by the rules are so obviously an important dimension of competition in other fields that it would be surprising indeed if competition in business did not also require fairness and equity. In business, the boundaries of good competitive conduct are prescribed by the law, by our values, and by our ideas of fairness. Presumably we can say that the fairer the rules and the more scrupulously they are observed, the more competition is enhanced, although as we shall see in Chapter 6, this proposition has been challenged.

Chapter 4

Power and Competition

INTRODUCTION

This chapter will explore the relationship between competition and power, an important subject. According to Adolfe A. Berle:

> More ink has been spilled — and more blood shed — in the twentieth century over economic power than for any other single concept. . .Theory rather than human well-being lies at the stated root of these struggles.[1]

In the views of a number of economists, power is really *the* issue that lies behind most of the discussion about competition. In his introduction to *Industrial Concentration, The New Learning*, Donald J. Dewey had this to say:

> If the country does not really fear the economic consequences of industrial concentration, then what is antitrust all about? The answer that I would give. . .it is about discretionary authority in the private sector of the economy.[2]

Hartle suggested that something might be achieved "by looking at competition policy as an attack on the existing power structure."[3]

If power is so important both in itself and for its role in competition, one would think that economists would be agreed on at least the meaning of terms. As we have already seen, however, economists are not agreed on the meaning of competition; and there is even more disagreement on what power is. Seneca and Haight had these discouraging words to say:

> Unfortunately, the concept of power has. . .proven to be perhaps the most inscrutable in the whole of political science, resisting both clear conceptualization and convenient measurement.[4]

To the differences of opinion on the meaning of competition, add the inscrutability of power, multiply through by the subtety of the relationship between the two, and it should not be difficult to imagine the possibility of a 180-degree difference of opinion about the role of power in competition.

The view of the majority of economists is that economic power is the result of a lack of competition. If there is adequate competition there is no power.[5]

This essay argues almost the exact opposite: without power there can be no competition. Competition can only begin when participants in the match, be it economic, political or sportive, have, or acquire, power. Competition is a process in which power is possessed, used, fought over, lost, retained or increased. Instead of associating power with monopoly as is usually done, it will be argued here that apart from the power backed by government sanctions, and/or physical force, power, in general, is more accurately associated with recent competitive achievements than with monopoly. It cannot be hoped that such diametrically opposed views can even be understood, let alone reconciled, unless we have prior agreement on the meanings of power.

Understanding power

This chapter will present eleven different, although related and overlapping, definitions of power. We shall then proceed to infer what power one should expect firms to have in the usual price-theory models of perfect competition and monopoly. We shall argue that this exercise provides us with an explanation of the prevailing view of the relationship between competition and power. This done, we shall re-examine price theory from a slightly different point of view — to show that a quite different conclusion can be drawn.

In the first section of this chapter, our primary concern is with competition and power within static, price-theory models. The next step will be to consider power in the context of the behavioural dimensions of competition. This approach will allow us to discuss the role of power in each of the dimensions of competition that we considered in Chapter 3. Using this analysis, we can take a fresh look at two perennial problems: what is the relationship between power and the size of an individual firm, and should we be concerned about the balance of power in the market among sellers or between sellers and buyers?

THE MEANINGS OF ECONOMIC POWER

Freedom to Choose

One of the broadest and, because it was written by Kenneth Boulding, one of the most lucid treatments of power, is to be found in *Principles of Economic Policy*. In the chapter on economic freedom we read:

For the individual, freedom is simply an aspect of his power, and his power is measured by the area within which choice is possible. . . .Power, in other words, is measured by all the things you *could* do if you desired.[6]

Boulding then goes on to introduce the useful idea of "possibility boundaries," which are the financial, physical, legal and moral limits that constrain our choice, our freedom, and therefore our power.

Morgenthau and Dahl: Conditioning the Behaviour of Others

Seneca and Haight provide a definition of power which they attribute to Morgenthau and Dahl and which, they say, "represents the established treatment of the subject."

At the most general level, power terms in modern social science refer to *subsets of relations among social units such that the behaviors of one or more units* (the responsive units, R) *depend in some circumstances on the behavior of other units* (the controlling units, C). . .If power terms include *all* relations of the kind just defined, then they spread very widely over the whole domain of human relations.[7]

According to the Morgenthau and Dahl definition, every person who is capable of performing any economic act whatsoever has power. The person who buys a loaf of bread or sells an hour of work will have some impact on the behaviour of many other people.

Berle reinforces this concept of power:

In economic life, every decision made affects, in some way, every life in the modern world. This is the peculiar quality of economics. The impact of economic-power decisions may be imperceptible or great, but it is always there.[8]

Since everyone obviously makes economic decisions, power must be widely diffused. If this position is accepted, it is of critical economic, social and political significance. Power is suspect; power is feared. If it is generally believed that all power resides in just a few hands, then the social and political consequences are likely to be quite different than if it is felt that power is widely, though not necessarily uniformly, distributed.

Lasswell and Kaplan: "The Ability to Impose Severe Sanctions"

According to the definitions of Boulding and Morgenthau and Dahl, we are all participants as actors or "actees" in many different power structures. Since it is not usual to cast everyman as Hero, it is perhaps natural to look at subsets of power that are more likely to be reported by newspapers on the front page. "One such subset consists. . .of relations in which 'severe sanctions. . .are expected to be used or are, in fact, applied to sustain a policy against opposition' — a subset that Lasswell and Kaplan call power."[9]

The "severe sanctions" immediately call to mind the dictator, the mafia, the motorcycle gang, perhaps also in some circumstances, the mistress, the gossip and the priest. As we shall see when we move more explicitly into the economic field, we encounter the difficulty of drawing the subset boundaries. When does economic power in the Morgenthau-Dahl sense become power in the Lasswell-Kaplan sense?

Market Power I: Control of Supply or Demand

If a sophomore class was asked to list all of the people or institutions that could be said to jointly determine or control the market variables such as price, volume of sales, quality, growth, etc., for any specific market, we would surely expect quite a long list. If, for example, we want to itemize the groups that have power in a market for, say, fertilizers would we not expect to find:

— government agricultural departments that undertake to demonstrate to farmers the optimum amount of fertilizer per acre?
— private and public research departments that are continually modifying the products?
— government agricultural income-supplement or price-support agencies?
— the institutions and factors that determine the price of raw materials?
— all of the buyers and all of the competing sellers of grain in world markets?
— the unions?
— feed-lot operators who sell "natural" fertilizers?

Obviously one could go on for some time.

When the Crown Prosecutor addressed this problem of control of the fertilizer market in Cominco Ltd. *et al.* combines case, he produced a very short list. The *Particulars of Indictment* had this to say:

> The Defendants, as virtually the only manufacturers of fertilizer sold in that area described in the indictment, hereinafter called "Western Canada," during the period of the indictment, *substantially controlled the business of fertilizer* in Western Canada during the period.[10]

What theory of power leads to the conclusion that suppliers, even all the suppliers, have total control over a market? Even if one confined one's attention to pure price-theory analysis, one still has to recognize the presence and power of buyers. Furthermore, even price theory directs attention to costs and to factor markets and to the existence of alternatives.

Despite its lack of visible support in real markets, this theory of market power seems to be firmly embedded in Canadian jurisprudence. In the judgement of *R v Canadian Coat and Apron Supply Ltd. et al.* we read: "The 'market power' referred to means the ability of one or a group of businessmen in a particular market at a particular time to control it."[11]

Market Power II: The Ability to Set Price and/or Withhold Quantity

There may not be many economists who would insist that the suppliers exercise 100 per cent of the power in a market. But an amazing number of them have ended up saying almost the same thing by associating power with the ability to set price and withhold supplies. This idea goes back a long way. Adam Smith stated:

> monopolists, by keeping the market constantly understocked. . . sell their commodities much above the natural price, and raise their emoluments, whether they consist in wages or profit, greatly above their natural rate.[12]

and again:

> the monopoly of the colonial trade. . .by the expulsion of all foreign capitals. . .by lessening the competition of capitals. . . necessarily raised the rate of profit.[13]

Walter Block indicates that one of the two views of monopoly held "within what might be called the broad Austrian camp" can be found in this version of market power.

> According to the Mises-Kirzner view, monopoly price can exist on the free market, and a necessary part of its definition is a *purposeful* withholding of resources on the part of the mono-polist.[14]

Scherer also associates market power with price setting. "All three types of firms [pure monopolists, oligopolists and monopolistic competitors, that is, all firms except those in a perfectly competitive industry] possess some degree of power over price, and so we say that they possess *market power* or *monopoly power*.[15] The logic of Scherer's position is, of course, that for all firms except those in perfect competition the price-sales curve is downward sloping as illustrated in Figure 24. The firm could, presumably, pick the price of $1.10 instead of $1.00; this is the same as saying that it could supply 600 units or it could withhold 200 units and sell only 400.

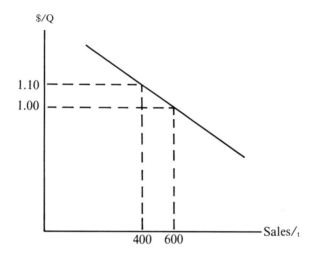

Figure 24 — The Demand Curve

We are all monopolists, now

As we shall see, however, the perfectly competitive firm that is supra-marginal or above average in profitability (a condition that should apply to about half of the firms) can also produce more or less (withhold supplies). It can even afford to sell its output below the market price, should it wish to do so. With the unimportant exception of perfectly competitive firms, Scherer seems to be in agreement with the position of Joan Robinson who suggested that we call all firms monopolists, and agree that we live in a world of competing monopolists.[16] If virtually all firms are monopolies, we should now be able to drop the redundant and pejorative term, and say that we live in a world of competing firms.

The Reuber-Wilson treatment of power is similar. It can be found in their statement of "basic assumptions" that underlie their "entire discussion" of the recent merger-policy proposals.

> (a) there are or likely will be major departures from competitive markets in the sense that either sellers or buyers have power, individually or collectively, to control supply or demand.
> (b) this market power has significant detrimental effects upon market performance in the sense of raising prices and/or costs above and reducing output below competitive levels.[17]

Point (a) by itself seems to agree with the position taken by the Crown Prosecutor in the fertilizer case that market power is simply the control of supply or demand. Taken with (b), however, it suggests instead that raising price and reducing output are what constitutes the harmful exercise of market power. Berle takes the same position when he writes, "The first great power of corporate management is its capacity to determine the price for the products or services sold by it."[18]

Economic folklore

Perhaps the reason for the popularity of this version of market power is that it seems to follow from one of the most oft-repeated bits of folklore in economics. It is widely and sometimes uncritically accepted that the monopoly price is above the competitive price.

The way one might arrive at this conclusion is to imagine that "once upon a time" we lived in a world of perfect competition. Then one day a big bad monopolist bought up all the small firms producing product X and obtained authority to prevent any new firms from entering the industry. Having established a monopoly, the villain found that the industry demand curve was the same as his own, and since it was sloped, he could calculate marginal revenue and set price where this marginal revenue equalled his marginal cost.[19] It must also be assumed in this scenario that there is no change in technology and no change in demand.

In these circumstances, and in these circumstances alone, it can be shown that the monopolist's price is above that of the individual firm in perfect competition. The monopolist in this case would undoubtedly cause some of the submarginal firms to shut down and in a real sense would "withhold" or reduce supplies from the previous, perfectly-competitive level. The diagrams (which are produced in the next chapter) and the words that accompany such a story are called comparative statics. The great merger movement at the turn of the century gave some semblance of respectability to the foregoing scenario, although mergers did not generally succeed in capturing 100 per cent of the market, or in preventing entry, or, it would seem, even in raising profits.[20]

The "good" monopolist

Let us now try a different and more dynamic scenario. Let us imagine, as before, a world of perfect competition made up of five perfectly competitive industries, A, B, C, D, and E. Now suppose that one of the firms in industry A innovates and produces a new product and a new industry, F, which, for the moment at least, would be a monopoly. Of course, if no one likes product F, the economy will revert to its former five-industry status. But suppose that product F is a success in the sense that enough consumers like the offer to make the firm viable. Given its success, the total offer made by the monopolist had to be more appealing to some customers than the offers being made by the perfectly competitive firms. It can hardly be said, therefore, that for value received the price of product F is in any sense higher than the price of other products.

It might be argued that if a large number of firms desert industries A to E and enter F, thereby establishing perfectly competitive conditions in that industry, the price of product F would fall. In other words, the price of F produced under monopolistic conditions would be higher than it would be if produced under competitive conditions. Whether it would or not, however, depends completely on the nature of the cost curve. If it turns out that very small firms can produce the product more cheaply than large firms then, presumably, industry F will become perfectly competitive and small firms will predominate. If, on the other hand, long run costs curves fall and larger firms prosper, then the perfectly competitive solution will not be appropriate *for the very reason that the perfectly competitive price,* i.e., the price that would prevail under perfectly competitive conditions, *is too high.*

Moreover it should be recognized that even if the industry remains a monopoly it cannot charge more than the perfectly competitive price. If it did, small firms using small-firm resources and small-firm technology (which is what perfect competition is all about) would start entering the industry.[21]

Market Power III: The Ability to Make Above-Average Profits

As every businessman and every economics sophomore knows, it is quite possible for a firm to be a monopolist (in the sense that it makes a unique offer, has a downward sloping price-sales function, and selects the price) and still not make a profit. Perhaps for this reason a number of authors state, and quite a few more imply, that market power exists when a firm can make above average profits.

Richard Caves clearly implies such a meaning in his discussion of "Economic Structure and Market Power." Consider, for example, his statement that:

> the first round of statistical studies of market power in Canada seemed to find a role for the concentration of domestic sellers in creating market power. . .Our own findings support the role of trade as a curb on market power by showing that concentrated sellers can earn excess profits where they face little import competition, but are unable to grasp them when some import competition is present. . . ,[22]

and again,

> Studies. . .agree that profit rates (and presumably monopoly power) are lower. . .[23]

Clearly, regardless of market shares or sloped demand curves, the firms that do not earn excess [above average] profits have no market power. Those that do better than average would seem by definition to have market power.

Finally, the effort that has been put into concentration studies is based in large part on the premise that fewness begets market power, and market power begets profits. It follows, therefore, that market power (usually designated as monopoly power) and profits go hand in hand. It should be noted, however, that if a monopolistic firm or its shares are sold at a price that accurately reflects future profits (whether these profits are monopolistic or not) the new owners will make no excess or monopolistic profits. This is why the creation of monopoly in the past does not suggest that the monopoly profits can or should be recaptured from those who own and operate the monopoly today.

Market Power IV: The Existence of the Monopolistic Power of Severe Economic Sanctions

The first three versions of market power hardly seem very menacing. Even a monopolist who appears to have complete control of industry supply must share the total market power in that industry with buyers (whose control of demand is just as complete), managers, suppliers, unions, and with other competing monopolists. To say that market power derives from the ability or the requirement to set price as well as all other dimensions of the offer is simply to say that all firms not in perfect competition in equilibrium have market power. Even to say that firms or industries with above-average profits have market power is not very frightening. One does not have to be much of a statistician to know that the Canadian population can be broken down by age and sex with the result that half, (*exactly one-half*) is above average.

In short, the first three versions of market power are rather like the Morgenthau-Dahl concept; power is very widely diffused and therefore not very interesting. This has led some economists to be rather more narrow in their specification of market power and to reserve the term for situations in which power is being, or could be, used by its holder to impose severe sanctions on customers. This is the economic equivalent of the Losswell-Kaplan concept of power.

Adolfe Berle writes:

> Zenith [in power] is reached when an economic institution attains monopoly in its field, particularly when the goods or

services it monopolizes are important, if not essential, to the life
of the community or customers it serves. Then, responsive to its
own self-interest, the organization — in practice, the men vested
with its power — can provide the goods or services within its
control *at any price or on any terms it chooses to dictate*. . .[24]

This quotation sounds like the preface for a Western in which the
villain seizes control of the only water hole in Arizona. In fact, however, Berle goes on to discuss limitations on the power of the
monopolist.

Kaysen and Turner in their *Antitrust Policy* 1959 write,

> market power shall mean the persistent ability of a person, or a
> group. . .to restrict output or determine prices [presumably higher
> prices] without losing a substantial share of the market, or without
> losing substantial profits.[25]

Inelasticity

It is probably safe to assume from this quotation that market power is
much more than the ability to set price. In economic jargon Kaysen
and Turner seem to be saying that in order for the firm to have market
power, it must have an inelastic demand for its product: substitutes for
its products must be so inferior, and the product so essential, that
consumers will take almost the same quantity even if the price is raised.

This idea is developed more explicitly by Green who writes,

> The steepness of the slope [of the demand curve] . . . indicates the
> degree to which the seller can raise prices without losing all of
> his customers. This ability reflects the seller's market power — i.e.,
> his ability to raise price above MC, and profit (rather than lose)
> thereby. Thus product differentiation is not only a facet of market
> structure, it is also a reflection of the potential exercise of some
> degree of market power.[26]

The ability to raise price to average cost plus normal profit is
hardly enough to put a firm into a position to impose a severe sanction.
If a firm cannot do at least that well, the *investors* will be the victims of
severe sanctions. To be able to impose a severe sanction on its customers (and thereby bestow a benefit of equal proportions to one or
more of the other participants) it must, as Professor Green suggests,
face a steep or inelastic price-sales relationship at prices above the
level that would provide normal profits. We should remind ourselves
that without the support of physical or government harassment, the
only way a firm can collect its severe-sanction tribute (in the form of a
higher price, presumably) is to make other aspects of the offer so
attractive that the purchases are made voluntarily.

When one tries to find examples in the real market of these severe economic sanctions, the illustrations that come to mind are liquor stores, income-tax services, post offices and unions that can operate without fear of a competing entry regardless of how angry or dissatisfied customers may become. In such cases, the power of the organization or institution with which consumers are unhappy can usually be traced to the police power of the state.

Market Plus External Power

It is not easy to see how monopolistic power capable of inflicting severe sanctions could exist, or could persist for any length of time, in a free market. This difficulty has led many economists to the conclusion that *a*, and sometimes *the*, factor that must lie behind significant market power is the actual or potential use of physical force. This force must be external to the market,[27] and must be capable of being applied on behalf of the monopolist. The most obvious examples of such power are to be found in banditry or protection rackets, or in any economic activity supported by physical harassment, or the threat of such harassment. This kind of physical-plus-market power is to be found in such chronicles as The Godfather, or the "B" westerns in which the owner of the only tavern in town is the commander-in-chief of the local enforcement officers, one of whom happens to be the town's Marshal.[28]

B-movies apart, if there is any source of non-market power that can be characterized as omnipresent, omnipotent, and omnivorous, it is government. This is the second "Austrian" view of monopoly to which Block referred. His earlier quotation continues, "Rothbard, however, defines monopoly as an exclusive government grant of trading privileges, and, as such, finds it incompatible with market freedom."[29]

Juridically Correctable Monopoly Power

In order to understand this next concept of power, it is useful to know that its protagonist, Robert H. Bork, is a former Solicitor General of the United States and is now a Professor of Law. From the vantage point of his extensive experience with American antitrust legislation and enforcement, Professor Bork set out to define competition and monopoly rather than power, so that his concept of the latter must be inferred.

To begin with, Bork states that "The law has not arrived at one satisfactory definition of 'competition'," and proceeds to supply his own candidate:

> 'Competition' may be read as a shorthand expression, a term of
> art, designating any state of affairs in which consumer welfare
> cannot be increased by moving to an alternate state of affairs
> through judicial decree. Conversely, 'monopoly' and 'restraint of
> trade' would be terms of art for situations in which consumer
> welfare could be so improved, and to 'monopolize' and engage in
> 'unfair competition' would be to use practices inimical to
> consumer welfare.[30]

This definition is in the same practical vein as "workable
competition," which in effect argues that since text-book perfect
competition is unattainable and of questionable desirability in the
real world, society should settle for something that is both desirable
and attainable. Professor Bork's definition simply reminds us that
attainability has to be defined by the limitations of the judicial process.

From this it follows that the monopoly power targeted by antitrust actions can be defined by a number of characteristics. First, the
existence of power *per se* presumably would not be objectionable: it
would be only the use of that power to act against consumer welfare
that would trigger anti-combines actions. Second, monopoly power
and monopolistic actions would not be causes for state intervention
unless they could be corrected by the judicial process. This last point
implies that action by the state would not be initiated through a textbook exercise that indicated, let us say, the possibility of resource
misallocation. The injury, to be remediable, would presumably have
to be fairly obvious and significant. Monopoly or monopoly power
should not be the subject of prosecution unless it could be demonstrated that there exists another state of affairs that is superior and
attainable by judicial decree.

The Power to Direct Production

One of the reasons for considering market power at the level of the
firm or industry is that such analysis should serve to support or deny
the existence of consumer sovereignty, which is the main economic
rationale for the market system.[31] Consumer sovereignty is the
collective power of all consumers to direct production — to decide
what is to be produced, for whom, by whom, when and how. Appendix A shows that in a world of perfect competition this power rests
first and foremost with individual consumers, though one must allow
an important role for the entrepreneurs who decide to get out of bed
in the morning to make the products that are to be offered, and to the
workers who decide how much and how hard they will work.

Appendix A also shows that almost the same results can be
obtained in a world in which there is a uniform degree of monopoly.
This is a particularly important conclusion. For even when every firm

is a monopolist — when every firm makes a unique offer, "controls" its own supply, "determines" and "sets" its own price — direction of the economy is still very much in the hands of the ultimate consumers.

Silk versus nylon

Let us illustrate the relative strength of the totality of unorganized consumers *vis-à-vis* a highly competitive or a highly monopolistic set of suppliers. As an example, consider the case of silk versus nylon stockings. We know, after the fact, that nylon won the competitive struggle. The interesting question is whether it would have made much difference to the outcome if the silk-stocking industry had consisted of a large number of small firms or just a few very large firms.

The answer depends in part on one's concept of the firm and of how it operates. Had the few large firms operated as monopolists or quasi-monopolists are supposed to operate in a price-theory context, namely, by raising price and restricting output, one would have expected the silk-stocking industry to decline just that much more quickly. On the other hand, if one assumes that firms are likely to be engaged in innovative activities in many different dimensions, a few large companies might have been able to respond to the nylon threat by trying to improve their product and their offer. If successful or partly successful, the silk-stocking industry might have lasted somewhat longer. This much seems clear: the fate of the silk-stocking industry was undeniably in the hands of the consumers.

The matter would probably be left at this point were it not for Galbraith's rediscovery of the myth of the all-powerful economic establishment. He suggested that producer sovereignty had replaced consumer sovereignty with the aid of the planning departments in the large-company, non-market sector of the economy.

> So far from being controlled by the market, the firm, to the best of its ability, has made the market subordinate to the goals of its planning. Prices, costs, production and resulting revenues are established not by the market but, within broad limits later to be examined, by the planning decisions of the firm.[32]

All companies, big or small, have planning functions: management consists of little else. Big companies tend to have larger planning departments and more specialists. But all plans are based on forecasts of what others — consumers, workers, and suppliers — will do. The plans are always tentative, and apply to the policies of the company. Anyone who thinks that a planning department can dictate to consumers what they should do demonstrates (to businessmen and planners at least) a lack of knowledge about business.

Market Versus Discretionary Power*

A distinction is sometimes made between decisions made "in the market" between or among institutions, and decisions made within an institution by a command, democratic or other non-market process. Since any decisions must involve choice, and since choice presupposes power, both kinds of decision obviously involve power. The first kind of power is sometimes called "market" or "external" power; the second is "discretionary" or "internal" power.

The distinction between market and discretionary power is of particular interest in the analysis of large-firm power. There is a very strong presumption that big is powerful, and yet when it comes to market power, it is clear that some very large firms can hardly be said to have their way with unions, customers, or suppliers. On this issue Dewey had this to say:

> Discretionary authority is essentially power to make decisions that affect the lives of other people; it is, of course, more closely associated with the size of an organization than with its power to affect price by varying output. The sophomore who, in a basic economics course, has trouble seeing the difference between a firm which is merely large and a large firm which has a large market share may not be quite so obtuse as his instructor believes. It is probable that "economic power" to the sophomore signifies power over people, which is exercised by the higher management of A&P just as surely as by the higher management of General Motors.[33]

Top-down control

If Dewey's sophomore is an economics major, and even if he is a business major, he will probably have some novel ideas about decision-making in a large firm. Economic models tend to spend very little time with the processes of management, just as they have little to say about the behavioural aspects of competition or power.[34] In the absence of accurate descriptive models, the logical error of personification is an easy one to make. "The management" becomes "the chief executive officer;" his power becomes a function of size, and size can very easily come to be interpreted as the number of people who must do his bidding.

Reality is somewhat different. Even in an army, which is organized with a hierarchical structure specifically designed to maximize the chances that when the general says "right turn" only the indolent, the shiftless, the indifferent and the victims of a bureaucratic

---

*This section owes much to discussions with Dr. Danny Miller of the Faculty of Management, at McGill University and to his submission to the Bryce Commission, "Some Comments of the Distribution of Power in Complex Organizations."

failure to communicate turn left, a smart private very quickly learns that generals are not his main problem. It is his own lance corporal to whom he should be particularly polite.

An analysis of just how well mannered the private should be will quickly bring one to realize that the amount of "discretionary" power held by his superiors is very much a matter of market considerations. If the soldier is a mercenary, worth at least as much as he is being paid, if there is a shortage of suitable candidates for his job, and if it is known that the soldier has an equally good job that he can go to at any time, then his officers can hold relatively little power over him — even in an organization that must put great stress on obedience. If, by contrast, our soldier is a conscript, and if the penalty for a lack of co-operation is three weeks of peeling onions, the corporal will be accorded much respect, his slightest wish will be seriously considered, and his jokes will provoke much merriment.

Who is in charge here?

The idea that a corporate officer holds sway over all those who rank below him in the corporate bureaucracy is just so much nonsense. Consider a chief executive officer (CEO) with an excellent second-in-command (2IC) who is so respected in his own organization and in the industry that he regularly receives job-offers from other firms at or above his present salary. In other words the salary of the 2IC is no greater than his "opportunity cost." How much discretionary power does the CEO have over the 2IC? The answer is obviously, none at all.

This point has been made in a little different way by Martin and Simms:

> . . .the real source of power is not the superior but the subordinate. Men can only exercise that power which they are allowed by other men. . .The ultimate source of power is the group.[35]

Much the same argument is advanced by Herbert Simon: ". . .the arbitrary element in authority is limited to the 'area of acceptance' of the subordinate."[36]

Which way is up?

It is an important part of John Kenneth Galbraith's thesis that "Power passes down into the organization".[37] While Galbraith seems to contradict Martin and Simms and Simon, who say in effect that power passes upward, the result is the same: power is distributed throughout the organization and does not reside exclusively at the top. Stogdill reinforces this proposition with an argument reminiscent of counter-vailing power when he states: "For every source of power. . .counter-measures can be utilized by followers to reduce the extent to which they are subject to influence."[38] And in the same vein Kotter states, "One of the distinguishing characteristics of a typical manager is how dependent he is on the activities of a variety of people to perform his job efficiently."[39]

All of these propositions add up to an interesting idea. If we agree with Dewey's sophomore that a large company has much discretionary power are we not also guilty of the logical error of personification? The bits and pieces of discretionary power that are found throughout the organization are important to the people involved, but the aggregation of these powers means very little because they are not in fact aggregated. They do not come into the hands of any one person or even into the hands of any small group of people.

What must matter to an individual is the discretionary power which he or she possesses or is subject to. The critical question is whether this is likely to be greater or less if the individual is in a small or large company. This can best be answered by looking at the sort of situation in which one is subject to someone else's discretionary power.

Discretionary power and economic rent

Consider a 60-year old vice-president who is being paid $100,000 but who has a drinking problem and is holding on to his job only because of the kindness of his peers and union executives who "cover" for him. If he lost his job he would be lucky to obtain another at $40,000. He therefore collects an economic rent of $60,000. If the facts as stated are generally recognized, and if the president or the executive committee has the discretionary power to fire the vice-president, then those who voluntarily pay the economic rent must be said to have discretionary power — in the amount of about $60,000 per year. The real or imagined receipt of economic rent may condition the behaviour of the recipient. It would not be surprising if our vice-president was a reliable lighter of the president's cigars.*

Naughty novels are peopled by would-be actresses, whose next-best jobs are as waitresses, and villainous casting directors; by penniless playboys and rich widows; by illegal immigrants and sweatshop employers. In all cases discretionary power disappears with the disappearance of economic rent: when the actress becomes successful and receives offers from other studios; when the playboy is able to attract

---

*As a "one pip wonder" I once got myself into a considerable amount of "onion peeling" in an officers' mess I had just joined by calling an utterly incompetent adjutant "Captain Ronson." It was a few days and several duty rosters later that I discovered that the designation was not his name but his behind-the-back nickname earned from the incredible speed with which he could draw his Ronson lighter whenever the commanding officer took out a cigarette.

bids from competing rich widows; when the illegal immigrant becomes legal and can participate freely in the labour market. With these kinds of problems before us, the question we should ask is this: will there be any more or any less discretionary power available *per person* whether people are organized into big firms or little ones, Crown corporations or private companies, big families or small ones? The answer is, to say the least, not obvious. So long as we keep our options open and never accept a salary that is more than we are worth in the market, it makes very little difference whether we are in a small organization or a large one.*

This consideration of discretionary power allows us to see a little more clearly the role of the market in limiting the power that can be exercised within firms. There is a tendency to think of the firm as a miniature command system. This is a useful idea, so long as one does not take the next step and equate life in the command system of a corporation to life inside a command economy. The two are very different. Individuals in a market-system firm retain their right to move to other jobs. Bargains among individuals in the firm are thus governed by market considerations just as surely as the bargaining that goes on in the market between two separate firms or households. When workers or managers stay in a company and complain about how the company is treating them, it is a sure sign that they are being treated better than they are likely to be treated elsewhere in any other job.

POWER AND PRICE THEORY

Our purpose in this study is not to consider power *per se*, but rather the relationship between power and competition. Since price theory has conditioned so much of what is believed about business competition, we must begin our analysis with a review of how power is treated implicitly or explicitly in conventional price theory. We start by considering what sort of power buyers and sellers would have under conditions of perfect competition and monopoly.

Perfect Competition

Since the ideas and the geometry of perfect competition have already been outlined in Chapter 2, we can summarize the powers of the buyers

---

*But suppose that it did make a difference. Suppose *all* workers and managers preferred to work in small companies. Large companies would simply have to make their offers to their employees more attractive in other ways. If large companies did not enjoy productivity advantages that enabled them to make competitive offers they would be replaced by smaller firms with lower costs.

and the sellers quite simply. Buyers have the power, income permitting, to purchase as much or as little of each product as they want at the going market prices. Offering less than that price would result in zero purchases. In equilibrium conditions, offering more would be possible but unnecessary. Under disequilibrium conditions,[40] if buyers feel supplies are likely to be inadequate they can offer more and in that way be assured of a greater quantity for themselves.

The individual buyer, whether firm or household, has power over its own actions. But it is unlikely to feel it has any significant power over the market's terms. Collectively, the buyers' power over the market is great, but that fact may not be perceived.

For their part, sellers can decide how much of the product to unload at the going price. Under conditions of equilibrium, asking a higher price would result in zero sales and asking a lower price would be unnecessary. Under conditions of disequilibrium, any individual seller can take the initiative and raise or lower the price. He can, in this way, take advantage of a shortage or gain protection against an unwanted inventory. Income or access to wealth and to capital markets permitting, sellers and potential sellers have the power to expand or contract the scale of their operations and to leave or enter any perfectly competitive industry.

Monopoly

The usual model of monopoly pictures one large seller, the only supplier in the industry, facing a large number of individual buyers. In such an industry, where does the power lie?

First of all we can see that very little has changed as far as the buyers are concerned. Individually they have no more power than they had in the perfectly competitive market, and *collectively they have no less*. If the sum of their individual decisions is such that they buy less, the monopolistic seller will perceive, quite accurately, that his customers collectively have the power to inflict what may appear to him as a severe sanction.

On the sellers' side, matters are quite different. Whereas the perfectly competitive firm in equilibrium had the price determined for it, the single seller has to estimate the industry's (and its own) price-sales relationship. It must then do some arithmetic to find the optimum price. It could be said that it has the power to set the price; alternatively it could be said that it is powerless to avoid setting the price, because business cannot be conducted unless the buyers know what terms are being offered.

PRICE THEORY REVISITED

The foregoing is, I believe, a fair representation of what would be learned about power and competition from a standard text on economic analysis. Shortly, we shall consider the power-competition relationship from the behavioural point of view. Before doing so, however, we should be aware that quite a different perspective on competition and power can be obtained even from price theory if the analysis is approached in a slightly different way. In order to understand this different perspective, we shall consider trade-at-set-terms and then bargaining.

Trade-At-Set-Terms

The first case to be considered is the marginal firm in a perfectly competitive market, illustrated in Figure 25:

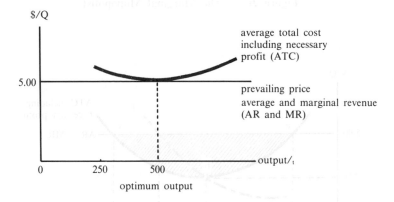

Figure 25 — The Perfectly Competitive Marginal Firm

If the firm chooses its optimum output of 500 units (and only if it does) it will cover its full costs including the cost of capital. The price of $5.00 per unit has been determined by the market. The firm can sell nothing at a higher price, and will not cover full costs if it charges less. The firm in this example can be referred to as a "perfectly competitive tangency case" because the ATC is tangent to the AR.

The second case is also a tangency case, but this time the firm faces a sloped demand or average revenue curve (Figure 26). Since the ATC (which includes necessary profit) touches the price-sales curve at only one point, there is only one price, $4.00, and only one quantity, 1,000 units, at which the firm can survive.

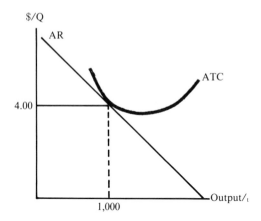

Figure 26 — The Marginal Monopolist

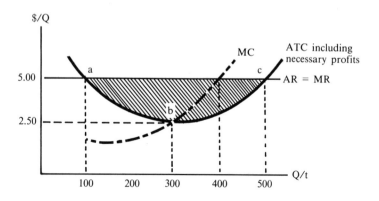

Figure 27 — The Perfectly Competitive Supra-Marginal Firm

The third case (Figure 27) describes the position of a supra-marginal, prosperous, perfectly competitive firm. Here, the average cost curve over much of its range falls well below the prevailing market price of $5.00. If the firm chooses to maximize profits then it will produce 400 units, because that is the quantity which equates MC and MR.

It is no longer a question of survival, however. For if the firm chose to do so, it could charge a price of $2.50. At an output of 300 units, it would still realize normal profits. Or the firm could be lazy and offer only 100 units, or it could go on an ego trip and maximize size (as measured by volume) and sell 500 units. The firm could also alter price and output together, so long as it picked a price-output combination within the shaded area abc.

Big wheel

The fourth case is that of the supra-marginal, prosperous monopolist

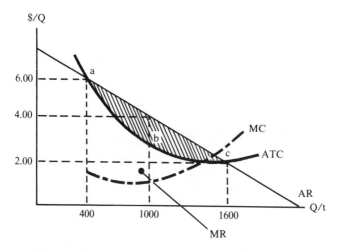

Figure 28 — The Supra-Marginal Monopolist

(Figure 28). If the firm chooses to maximize profits then the correct price is $4.00, at which point 1,000 units can be sold. As with the previous firm, however, this one has a range of choice: it can if it wishes charge as high as $6.00 and sell as little as 400 units, or charge as little as $2.00 and at that price sell as much as 1,600 units. The shaded area abc again represents the area of choice from which the monopolist is free to pick a price-sales combination.

An examination of these cases puts the matter of power in a completely different perspective. The *marginal* monopolist has not one erg more power than the *marginal*, perfectly competitive firm in the range of choice or the severe-sanction sense. The only difference is that the perfectly competitive firm finds the price in the newspaper (price taker), while the marginal monopolistic firm discovers its own price-sales relationship; then it *must* find and pick the only viable price-output combination (price maker). By contrast the perfectly competitive firm has the somewhat simpler task of calculating and then choosing the only viable quantity.

Special note should be made of the fact that *neither* marginal firm has the power to raise the price by withholding supplies. Should they try to do so, the only difference would be that the perfectly competitive firm would die quickly and from an obvious cause. Indeed it would appear to the outside world as a case of suicide. The death of the marginal monopolistic firm would be slower, and the cause of death more difficult to determine.[41]

All in the same boat

The supra-marginal firms are also in the same position with respect to power. Both firms have a range of prices and quantities within which they are able to choose. One might argue that the perfectly competitive firm would be unlikely to choose a price-output combination other than the $5.00 and 400 units in Figure 26, for to do so would be stupid, that is, non-profit-maximizing.

But exactly the same can be said of the supra-marginal monopolist. Its profit-maximizing, price-sales combination is also a single point ($4.00 and 1,000 units in Figure 27). The point is that both firms have the power to select from a variety of possible price-sales points. If for some reason they are both constrained by a requirement to choose the profit-maximizing combination, then both firms must obviously accept the one and only optimum position.

Our simple price-theory models should demonstrate one matter very clearly: it is *not* the steepness or flatness of the demand curves and it is *not* the label of monopoly or perfect competition that determine the power of a firm. Instead, it is what we shall designate as "competitive advantage." Later on we shall argue that in the absence of government regulations or constraints, which may give sheltered positions to government bodies, private companies, or unions, the main explanation of competitive advantage and the power that goes with it is above-average competitive performance.

Bargaining

In the foregoing cases we assumed that all exchanges involving perfectly competitive, marginal firms took place on terms set by the intersection of supply and demand curves. In the case of marginal monopolistic firms we assumed that trade took place on the terms set by a monopolist who simply picked the only viable point on the industry's price-sales demand curve. In the case of supra-marginal firms whether "perfectly competitive" or monopolistic terms were set by the manager. As we have seen, however, there are many markets in which the terms of the offer are determined by bargaining, and an analysis of such a market will throw additional light on the relationship between power and competitive advantage. As before, we shall continue to assume that price and volume are the only variables that matter — quality in each market being a "given."

Let us begin our analysis in a very small hamlet with only one small general store and only one person who is at all suited to the profession of sales clerk. Suppose the proprietor of the store has calculated or guessed that the potential clerk might add $250 a week to his net revenue: this figure, therefore, is the maximum that he would be willing to pay. On the other hand, given his humanity, his reputation, and the fact that the clerk's salary is likely to become known to his friends and customers, and that the clerk must work unsupervised for some part of each day, he might be unwilling to pay less than $100 a week.

The potential clerk, for his part, may have some other source of income — perhaps another job, or unemployment insurance — that would pay him $150 a week, and therefore he would be unwilling to work for less. On the other hand, he may be honest, modest, and realistic enough to recognize that he would look foolish if he asked for more than $400.

The range of offers

The exchange surplus, or the bargaining range for the market, (that is, the range in which a deal can be made) is obviously somewhere between $150 and $250 a week, and is shown diagrammatically in Figure 29.

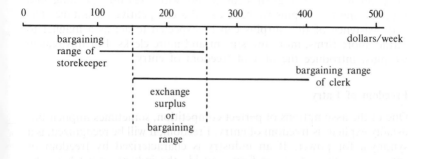

Figure 29 — The Bargaining Range

In this example, both the storekeeper and the clerk could present a claim for the available surplus. By stipulating the availability of only one suitable person as clerk, we implied that the next best candidate made such a bad clerking offer that he promised to add more to costs than to revenues. The best clerk can claim it was only because he stayed in school, developed his social skills and so on that the merchant is in a position to earn the extra $250.

On the other side of the bargaining table, the merchant can sing a similar song about incurring risks and working hard. He too will no doubt argue that it is only through his efforts that the situation has been created allowing the clerk the possibility of a better job. The interesting thing to note about this example is that it is the superiority of both the storekeeper and the clerk that has created the surplus which is the subject of the bargaining between them.

The no-surplus case

Let us rework the arithmetic of the foregoing example in such a way that there is no surplus. Suppose that the business of the single (monopolistic)[42] storekeeper has grown only to the point where he can afford to pay the one possible (monopolistic) clerk $150. Suppose further that the clerk is already earning $150 as a farm worker. What power do monopolists have over price? None at all.

On the other hand, let us suppose that the storekeeper changes his general store into a quaint frontier outpost and is able by appropriate billboards to divert 0.1 per cent of the motorists passing on a neighbouring throughway to detour via "frontier village." Because of the success of the innovation, the value of the clerk to the monopolist may rise to $500 a week. The minimum that has to be paid the clerk is $150. But to whom does the extra $350 properly belong?

Competition and power, even in the context of conventional price theory, have a great deal to do with creating, dividing and rationalizing the surplus we have called a competitive advantage. The very existence of this surplus can be expected to act as a magnet to attract more firms, more investment and more clerks. For this reason we must introduce the idea of freedom of entry.

Freedom of Entry

One of the assumptions of perfect competition, sometimes implicit but usually explicit, is freedom of entry. Freedom, it will be recognized, is a synonym for power. If an industry is characterized by freedom of entry, some individuals or firms outside the industry must have the power to set up a new firm within the industry.

It seems logical to assume that if there are many small firms in an industry, it must have been relatively easy to enter in the first place. The capital requirements, the scale of operations, the number of employees, the complexity of the product and the processes, must all be modest and within the competence of quite a large number of firms or households. This must have been the case in the past at least, and presumably it will continue to be so in the future.[43]

One of the questions arising from this concept is whether supramarginal firms with competitive advantages can persist in a perfectly competitive industry. The answer depends on how much "perfection" is assumed. If knowledge is perfect, and all factors are perfectly mobile then the answer is "No." Whatever factor is responsible for the superior performance of any firm will soon be recognized for its superiority. If there is a perfect factor market, then open bidding for these superior services will pass all excess profits on to the owners of those superior productive factors. It can be shown that in time all firms (as opposed to the owners of all basic factors of production) will end up as perfectly competitive tangency cases of the kind illustrated in Figure 25. This should not be taken to mean that all incomes in this perfectly competitive world will be the same. Far from it: the good managers and the good workers will be paid according to their contribution to production; poor workers and poor managers will also be paid what they are worth, which may not be very much. The working poor may be simply poor workers.

Reality, once again

Since perfection in factor and resource markets is not and cannot be possible, superior labour, management, and resources are associated with some firms and not with others. Thus there are always above-average and below-average firms. No doubt new entrants hope to emulate the most successful firms, but many are continually doomed to disappointment. Given the mortality of human factors, and a realistically long period of adjustment, all that can be guaranteed by freedom of entry is a flow of average, above-average and below-average firms in and out of the industry. We can be sure that at any one time half the firms, even in industries characterized by many firms and homogeneous products, will be above average. As any farm boy knows, some farmers drive Continentals and some drive beat up tin lizzies, and relatively speaking, 'twill always be so.

The monopolists — the makers of unique offers — cover a much wider spectrum of size of firm and complexity of product than do firms in multi-firm industries producing homogeneous products. For this reason it is more difficult to make generalizations about ease of entry. In Chapter 5 it will be argued that in the absence of government laws preventing entry, no successful firm can enjoy any significant amount of competitive advantage that will not be joined in hot pursuit. But as any B.Com. student should know, fortunes wax and wane. Some monopolists ride first class and others, economy; relatively speaking, 'twill always be so.

Conclusions to be Drawn from Conventional Price Theory

Whether we approach the connection between competition and power through bargaining or through trade-at-set-terms, we do not arrive at the conclusion that monopoly, in the sense of a single seller or buyer, automatically conveys power in the sense of (a) having a wide range of discretion; (b) being able to set price (at any level except the only one that is viable); (c) being able to earn above-average profits; (d) being able to invoke severe sanctions; (e) being able to direct production or even (f) enjoying discretionary power. Before a monopolistic firm can acquire power in any of the above senses, it must first create, or be lucky enough to stumble across, a competitive advantage or surplus of some sort. Only when the monopoly becomes supra-marginal can it attain power beyond that level which *all* buyers and sellers have to affect the economic destinies of everyone else. (Morgenthau-Dahl type power)

The same is true of firms in "perfect competition." The marginal firm has very little power except in the Morgenthau-Dahl sense. The supra-marginal firm has more; how much more depends on the extent of its competitive advantage.

Even conventional price theory leads to the conclusion that the *creation* and/or *holding* of competitive advantage, not the number of firms in an industry or a sloped rather than horizontal price-sales relationship, lies at the heart of power.

A BEHAVIOURAL VIEW OF POWER AND COMPETITION

In the previous chapter we considered six different activities, or in some cases groups of activities, which we called dimensions of competition. As we pointed out, they all implied that the competitor had at least enough power to perform the appropriate actions. The possession of power is a prerequisite to the performance of a competitive act. This is so self evident in most cases that we need do little more at this stage than summarize the obvious.

First of all, it is clear that innovation requires the existence and not the absence of power.

Being able to choose and being able to offer a choice, along with all of the other activities that are subsumed such as searching and bargaining, all bespeak the existence of power. Clearly, the "assertiveness" part of "independent assertiveness" is associated with power and its use. But even "independence" suggests enough power to "stand on one's own feet," or "buck the trend." Energy and expertness are also closely associated with the acquisition and exercise of power.

The only dimension not obviously dependent on the existence of power is the observance of fair and equitable rules; indeed it could be argued that the imposition of rules is designed by the weak to protect themselves against the competition of the more powerful. If we accept this proposition it might be argued that rules, at least those that shackle power, are anti-competitive. It was primarily this problem that led to the suggestion that a useful distinction could be made between rivalry and competition. The use of rivalrous power without the constraint of rules would have to include murder and mayhem. But it is presumably not our intention to include such behaviour in a category of activities that are endorsed by the state and by society under the heading of "competition."

Fundamental disagreement

We saw earlier that many respected economists have said or implied that when there is "perfect", "real" or "adequate" competition, there is no power. Other economists have argued the reverse: if there is no power then there can be no competition.[44] How can there be such a complete divergence of views on such a fundamental issue? One possibility is that the meaning of power has not been explored or made explicit. Another explanation is the grip (recognized or unrecognized) of neoclassical price theory on the thinking of most of the economic fraternity. The "ideal" of perfect competition in long-run equilibrium with perfect knowledge and perfect factor markets is a static world in which there is no need for change and, one might assume, no need for anyone to have the power to change. Only if we abandon this static, perfectly competitive concept as an ideal, and accept instead an ideal of progress, can change and power become an essential ingredient of our economy.

In the nirvana of perfect competition there is no need for rivalrous activities to direct the path of the economy, because the economy is already "there." In a world that seeks progress and change, however, competitive behaviour and the power that makes it possible are necessary to guide our steps in the never-ending quest for something better.

POWER AND SIZE

There is all too often an uncritical acceptance of the proposition that power and size are closely correlated. That there may be *some* correlation in *some* circumstances cannot be denied, but size is at best only one explanatory variable. It may have zero effect, and, in some circumstances, the relationship between power and size may be negative.

The ease with which size and power can be confused was made evident in the quotation from Dewey on market and discretionary power.[45] By implication this made power a function of size. Extended to its illogical conclusion it would suggest that since there is, undoubtedly, more discretionary power in Ontario than in New Brunswick, those wishing to reduce the power others hold over them should move to New Brunswick!

The bigger they are, the harder they fall

Berle provided something of a rationale for "big is powerful" when he devised his "five natural laws of power".[46] The fourth of these is: "Power is exercised through, and depends on, institutions." When he introduces the subject of economic power he says, "Most individuals have a fragment of this power, if only microscopic."[47] However, the decisions of single persons, have little appreciable effect. To bring about common action, organization is needed, be it a co-operative or a corporation, a labour union or a consumers' boycott.[48] This absence of power of the unorganized individual, however, is at complete variance with his description of the switch from silk to nylon stockings only a few pages later.

> In economic life, every decision made affects, in some way, every life in the modern world. This is the peculiar quality of economics. The impact of economic-power decisions may be imperceptible or great, but it is always there. The women who chose nylon stockings instead of silk (a choice she still has [in 1967], though nylon has clearly won the campaign) affected the lives of silk growers in Japan, China and Southeast Asia. Because the effects are often not immediately visible, economic power is still considered mysterious, though the mystery steadily grows less.[49]

We can safely assume that each woman made the choice of nylon over silk on an individual, what-is-best-for-me, basis. There was no institution apart from the market mechanism, which Berle does not seem to consider as an institution, and yet the silk-stocking industry was injured as surely as if a great stocking-buying syndicate had been organized. Indeed, it is very doubtful whether such a syndicate or a boycott could have affected the lives of silk growers any more decisively.

Silk and cotton

Berle's emphasis on the organizational or institutional basis for power seems to suggest that if an organized set of sellers faced a disorganized array of buyers *all* of the power must reside with the sellers. Yet a monolithic organization of the silk producers would have been unlikely to have had the power to change the results to which we have just referred. Had a silk monopoly raised price and restricted output (the response that is presumed to be typical of a monopolist), it would only have speeded its own demise. On the other hand, had the production of silk stockings been in the hands of a monopolist who rationalized, cut costs, and tried to find ways of improving the product, the monopoly might have preserved some fraction of its market. When cotton producers were confronted by a similar challenge by synthetic fibres they responded by producing blends, easy-care and no iron cottons that did much to preserve their market share.

From this it must be concluded that a monolithic organization of stocking buyers would have been irrelevant, and an organization of silk producers would have changed the course of economic history only if it had used whatever power it had to provide a better product. There is surely no doubt in this case that power resided with the unorganized consumers, who were not represented by any kind of an institution save that of a free market, and not with the silk producers who were. The conclusion would not be different had we chosen any other successful innovation.[50]

What the foregoing discussion indicates is that in the case of producers and ultimate consumers, the power rests in the hands of the small unorganized households, not producers, whether big or small. Since this is just another example of consumer sovereignty, we shall look at a more difficult case in which consumer sovereignty plays a less significant role.

David and Goliath

Consider the case of a big firm and a small firm selling a very similar product in the same market. Conventional wisdom holds that a match between a heavyweight company and a bantam competitor is uneven and probably unfair. A reader of balance sheets knows otherwise. Anyone who has been near a price war knows that the power to survive is a matter of efficiency and ratios, not absolute amounts. If the bantam-weight firm is making a profit of 50 cents per unit and its heavyweight competitor is earning 25 cents, it is obvious that with a price reduction of 35 cents the small firm could stay in business indefinitely, whereas the large firm would eventually have to go out of business, or smarten up.

Let us assume that the large firm was misguided enough to think that it could "throw its weight around" and drive its competitor out of business with a predatory price reduction of 75 cents. The small firm would lose 25 cents per unit sold; the large firm would lose 50 cents. Which firm would survive would depend on the size of liquid reserves relative to monthly losses. If the large firm was four times the size of its small competitor then, with the cost figures assumed, it would need reserves eight times as large in order to last out the consequences of its predatory price cut and not be the first to go bankrupt.[51]

Suppose that the large firm was not only large in its own industry but also a member of a conglomerate. Would this not change the relative power? If it did so at all, it would presumably be because the large subsidiary could call on the reserves of the whole conglomerate. It would be rather fun to be there when the "call" was being made: "Dear members of the finance committee: I am engaged in a predatory price war in which I can inflict a loss of one million dollars on a small competitor at a cost to our conglomerate of only eight million". One can imagine several different scenarios developing at this point!

The power to survive, the power to grow, and the power to prosper depend on the ability of the firm to make an attractive set of interrelated offers to customers, workers, managers, investors and suppliers. The company that can devise the best set of offers will be a worthy opponent, regardless of its size. If it can continue to make the best set of offers over an extended period of time, it need fear no company, regardless of size.

BALANCING OF POWER

An analysis of power and competition would be incomplete if it ignored the idea that competition might be enhanced by a balancing of power. The widespread urge to organize countervailing power which was a principal thesis of Galbraith's book, *American Capitalism, The Concept of Countervailing Power*,[52] seems to lend support to the popular preference for a balance of power. The appeal of perfect competition may be found, at least in part, in the fact that buyers and sellers are assumed to have equal powers. Few economists would object to a monopoly-versus-a-monopsony market (single seller versus single buyer) replacing a monopoly-versus-a-large-number-of-small-buyers' market.

Support for a balancing of power undoubtedly comes to us subconsciously from our attitude towards competition in sports. In contests of individual against individual, the rules are very carefully drawn to produce a balance of power and thus produce a narrow range of possible outcomes. This increases the uncertainty of the outcome within that range. If one team in the mosquito house league keeps beating all its rivals by margins of ten goals, there will undoubtedly be a rearrangement of players in the interests of "better competition." Juniors cannot play against mosquitoes; professionals are prohibited from playing in amateur sports; and "'ceptin' on special occasions" boys do not play with girls.

A balancing act

The idea that the balancing of forces enhances competition is implied even in situations in which man is pitting his strength against nature. A person is expected to choose a mountain or a body of water worthy of his mettle. Leander swims the Hellespont at night in storms; small boys swim in the local creek on sunny afternoons. The contest of man against beast is also expected to be a toss-up. Young lads ride yearlings; their cow-punching daddies are expected to ride Brahma bulls.

The balancing of opposing forces is one of the principal ideas of a pluralistic society. Since the existence of power is inevitable, let it be divided among consumers, governments, unions, churches, companies, and so on.

Those who defend the market system usually do so in part, at least, because it is an alternative to the concentration of power in the hands of government. The market system distributes economic power very widely among consumers, unions, suppliers, companies, and even includes foreign buyers and sellers. A command system, on the other hand, concentrates economic power in the hands of the commander, be he prince of church or state — a Richelieu or a Stalin.[53]

The analogies of sports and politics, apt as they may be, should not lead us to the conclusion that we ought to have an outside referee bent on achieving the same balance of power in the market place. To see why this is so, let us reconsider the sport analogy. From the point of view of both the participants and spectators, uncertainty is a major factor in explaining the pleasure derived from the activity. There is no point in attending a game in which a junior double A team has been pitted against a team from the mosquito house-league. The outcome would not be in doubt, and neither the spectators nor the players would enjoy the game much. Some balancing in sports makes sense, but even here it must not be overdone.

A dead heat

Suppose that we grew so skilful at balancing the weight being carried by race horses that every race ended with all of the horses crossing the finish line at the same time. Again, ticket sales would drop. Why? Once again, the perfect balancing of power would remove uncertainty. More to the point, in the long run it would remove any advantage to the trainer, breeder, and jockey of working extra hard to improve their "product." The undernourished, badly trained cart-horse would cross the finish line at the same time as the best thoroughbred.

An exact balancing of power in horse racing would remove any incentive to breed better horses. A similar attempt to balance power in business could remove all incentives to create better products. When a firm produces a better product, it enhances competition by widening choice and enabling some people at least to satisfy their needs more effectively. At the same time, however, the firm increases its power *vis-à-vis* its competitors. If we are foolish enough to pass a law that insists on an immediate rebalancing of power by forcing the innovating firm to share its knowledge with its competitors, there will be little incentive to innovate.

We need better food, clothing and shelter much more than we need faster horses. Presumably, therefore, we should be even more willing to accept and reward business firms that create surpluses, even though in doing so they acquire a competitive advantage which in fact gives them more power.

CONCLUSION

If by competition one means behaviour consistent with the verb to rival or to compete, there can be no doubt whatsoever that power is a necessary ingredient of the competitive process. Those who would compete must first have, or acquire, power. They must use that power to frame the best possible selling and buying offers. If in the opinion of their suppliers and buyers they succeed, they may be rewarded with a surplus that can be taken as a measure of their past competitive performance. This surplus will attract the attention of those who would like to take it for themselves; but if those who won the surplus can invest it wisely in even better offers, they may retain and even increase their advantage and power.

What kind of companies or individuals are likely to win this advantage or power? In exercising their free choice as consumers, workers and investors it can only be the households that determine the winners and the losers. If we are prepared to accept the proposition that households are themselves the best judges of their own welfare, then we must also accept the proposition that in awarding power to, or in increasing the power of, the winners, they are at the same time increasing their own welfare. After the fact, the power that accrues to the various producers may be called by some, monopoly power. It could more accurately be called competitive power.

A typical view

This is not the relationship between competition and power that is presented in most college texts. A more typical statement reads as follows:

> Market power gives the firm (or cooperating group of firms) a degree of discretion in controlling the price, the quantity and the nature of the products that it sells. *Competition* is the reverse condition. It removes discretion. . . .[54]

This statement may be meaningful to a student who has been schooled in the mysteries of perfect-competition equilibrium; it will make no sense at all to a firm that is trying to change "the price, the quantity and the nature of the product it sells," as well as its wages and dividends, in order to arrive at a better set of offers. This is only to say that the textbook treatment of competition and market power will make no sense to a firm that is trying "to compete."

In 1968 P.J. McNulty wrote, "it is one of the great paradoxes of economic science that every *act* of competition on the part of the businessman is evidence, in economic theory, of some degree of monopoly power."[55] Surely it is time that we stopped speaking in paradoxes and riddles. Riddles for which there are no answers belong in *Alice in Wonderland*, and paradoxes do not provide a sound basis for legislation.

Chapter 5

Monopoly

INTRODUCTION

There is a tradition in economics that competition and monopoly are opposites. If the world were black and white, we would need only to define competition as white to know that monopoly is all black. Joan Robinson encouraged this view of the world when we proclaimed all firms to be monopolists.[1] Since then, textbook writers in the neo-classical tradition have been pleased to cast the world into outer blackness, leaving us to look to the chapters on perfect competition in their good books to see the white.

Unfortunately, neither competition nor monopoly is a single concept to which an identifying colour can be attached. Competition turns out to be a *set* of behaviours or, according to structural tests, a *set* of market conditions. In the economic literature there are no corresponding *sets* of conditions that have been spelled out for monopoly, perfect or otherwise. It is, therefore, necessary to consider the meaning of monopoly quite separately.

The discussion of monopoly is complicated by the fact that, like competition, it has been referred to in the literature as both a condition and as behaviour. Furthermore, because monopoly is so closely associated with power we shall see that some, though not all, of the meanings of power can be reworded slightly and reintroduced as possible meanings of monopoly.

In this chapter we shall begin by considering four different meanings that might be applied to monopoly when the term is used to describe a market condition. We shall then consider, very briefly, monopolization as behaviour. The remaining task will be to consider the effect of monopoly on price. As we have seen, the standard position is that the monopolistic price is higher than the price that would be charged under perfectly competitive conditions. We shall argue the exact opposite, first in terms of the simple price-theory model, and then in the real world of multidimensional needs and multiple market participants.

MONOPOLY AS A CONDITION

Single Seller, Unique Offer

Of all the possible meanings of monopoly, the one that comes closest to its etymological meaning is simply a "single seller." This indeed is the meaning that is most often implied when the word is used in common parlance and in most economic studies (including this one) when words are being used rather loosely.

It seems very straightforward to define a monopolist as the single and only seller of a product; the problem is that every firm is the single and only seller of its *own* product.[2] If, therefore, we are to get beyond the point where "monopolist" is just a synonym for a firm, we must explain what is meant by "product."

The problem of definition can be delayed one more sentence by saying that a product refers to all of the offers made by a single industry. Now all we have to do is define an industry!

If an industry is defined to include all firms making an identical offer, we are not really any further ahead. By this reckoning all firms are monopolists, except those textbook firms that belong to perfectly competitive industries — and then only when those industries are in a state of equilibrium. In fact, almost all firms make more than one unique offer. Many firms in bargaining situations, moreover, or in industries with complex products, may almost never make exactly the same offer twice. Insisting on complete homogeneity of offers must mean, therefore, that there are many more industries in the world than there are firms, and that each firm is not just a monopoly but a whole group of monopolies.

Let your fingers do the walking

Despite the foregoing conceptual difficulty we do, for practical reasons, combine firms into groups so that we can find them in the yellow pages or in classified ads. We also combine firms in industries or sectors in government statistics to avoid national accounts that are simply a list of all unique transactions. Our question, therefore, becomes this: is there any objective or scientific way to group similar but non-identical offers into industries? If there is, we can embark on a firm-counting exercise, and whenever we find an industry with only one firm, that firm can be pronounced a monopoly.

Unfortunately there is no objective way in which industry boundaries can be drawn. In theory, and sometimes even in practice, cross elasticities, which measure the changes in the quantity sold of one product against the changes of price of another, can be calculated. By accepting some arbitrary cut-off point we can express an opinion on what products are close enough substitutes to be put into the same industry.[3]

Star wars

We can go beyond price theory and picture all firms as making a cluster of offers, each of which represents a point in n-dimensional space. We might imagine measuring the distance between the clusters of selling offers of different firms. We would then inspect our universe in the manner of an astronomer, and group the clusters into galaxies — each of which would be given a separate industry name. If, perchance, we found a galaxy that contained selling offers of only one firm, and the buying offers of many firms or households, and if judgement told us it was located an appropriate number of light years away from the next closest galaxy, we would then pronounce that seller to be isolated in space and therefore a monopolist.

There are several problems with such an approach. The first and most obvious is that the identification of industries and, therefore, of monopolies, can never be more than an expression of opinion once we try to apply the "monopoly" label to any subset of firms narrower than "all non-perfectly competitive firms." An "appropriate" intergalactic space differential is necessarily arbitrary. Indeed the critical concept of distance between offers must be a matter of individual judgement. As such it will vary from person to person. One person insists on Brand A and would rather fight than switch. Another person would rather go without, if Brand B is not available. Yet another is sometimes observed to choose A, sometimes B. Are A and B in the same industry? For one person presumably yes, for two people presumably no.

Second, what measurements we can perform must of necessity be historical. In a world of evolving offers, yesterday's monopolist may not be a monopolist today or tomorrow. Third, our analysis of this issue to date has been confined almost entirely to a consideration of price. How easily one product can be substituted for another depends on all their dimensions, not just price. Cotton producers for example recaptured some of their market from man-made fibers not by lowering price, but by raising it and at the same time greatly improving their product.

Finally, monopoly, as we have been discussing it, has been implicitly cast in a static or comparative-static mold. In a free market it is inevitable that changes will occur and that they will occur unevenly. The successful innovator will, by definition, be a monopolist as judged by point-of-time analysis. But can the innovating firm that is being hotly pursued by other innovators and imitators really be considered a monopoly?

We're all monopolists, now

When we described competition as a process, we saw that in some circumstances, at least, it involved a struggle to be number one. Is first prize to be the label "monopolist," with all of that word's connotations? "Damned if you don't compete; damned if you do compete successfully."

Monopoly as Prohibited Entry

The fastest racehorse in the world makes a unique offer; one could even imagine a fan claiming it had, in effect, a monopoly on all the racing trophies in the world. Not even the enthusiasts, however, would seriously insist that an actual monopoly existed, for the simple reason that others — *some* others at least — are free to try to breed and train an even faster horse. The only circumstance that would be likely to earn the owner the title "monopolist" would be a silly law that prevented anyone else from engaging in the horse-racing business. Protection from rivalry, therefore, is the second possible meaning that might be given to monopoly.

At first glance this second structuralist definition might appear to provide us with a much less ambiguous test of what a monopoly is. Such is not the case, however. In the first place it does not solve, or in any way clarify, the question of what an industry is. A prohibition of entry must presumably specify what field would-be entrants must not enter. The order that no one should compete against the horses from the stables of the King's mistress might just be the greatest thing ever to hit dog racing. And who knows, with such a law we might see the development of super-fast cows, chuckwagons, sulkies, humans, bicycles, cars, cockroaches and boats representing Oxford and Cambridge.

Even if we define the area into which entry should not be made, there is a second problem: what constitutes a prohibition or barrier to entry? Let us pose the problem as a multiple-choice question. Would a firm making a unique offer qualify as a monopolist if any would-be competitors:

1.   Would be harassed and probably shot if they competed?
2.   Would be fined or imprisoned by the government?
3.   Would be fined or imprisoned unless they agreed to delay entry until a specific licence or permit expired, at which time they would be provided with some free "know-how?"
4.   Must comply with a long list of tests and requirements concerning the environment, native rights, Canadian content, etc.?

5.   Required an exceptionally high degree of intelligence, persuasiveness and hard work in order to amass an appropriate team of people and resources?
6.   Would have to overcome a significant amount of goodwill or loyalty that customers felt towards the firm or firms already in the industry because of a long history of good and improving offers?
7.   Would be more likely to succeed if they spent considerable money on advertising, quality control, and research and development?
8.   Would be at a disadvantage if they were shiftless, badly educated and lazy.

It is easy to identify a gun or a prison as a barrier or a severe sanction, but start at the bottom of the list. Are we really going to worry about a barrier that keeps out the shiftless and the lazy? Should we be disturbed that entry requires intelligence, persuasiveness and hard work?

The third and final problem concerns the number of people or firms covered by the prohibition of entry. Because we are discussing monopoly it is at least arguable that we would have to accept the proposition that so long as there is at least one would-be entrant to whom the prohibition does not apply, the single firm, protected by only a partial prohibition, cannot be considered a monopolist. A horse-racing queen and the queen's mother might give the King's mistress a good run for her money, and provide adequate entertainment for the fans, the gamblers, and the gossips, even if everyone else is prohibited from taking part.

"Free" Entry

There is no doubt that freedom to buy and sell, to wheel and deal, to invest or disinvest in a new industry or an old industry according to one's own self-interest is what a free market is all about. It is also what competition is all about. Brozen began his discussion of the subject with the heading, "Open entry is the necessary and sufficient condition to maintain competition."[4]

It would be unwise for anyone running for public office to speak out against either motherhood or freedom of entry. On the other hand, it is not inconsistent with supporting motherhood to appreciate it most when it does not sneak up unawares. Thus there are those who praise motherhood but practise birth control.

We must be equally on our guard against those who are promiscuous in their advocacy of freedom of entry. The need to be on guard is suggested by the fact that the same folks who brought us the "perfect" in perfect competition also brought us the "free" in freedom of entry.[5] If everyone does not enjoy a God-given right to manufacture cars in competition with General Motors, it is apparent that it is idle to talk about freedom of entry. It follows, of course, that if freedom of entry is not absolutely free, the existing businesses must be monopolistic. As Rothbard said,

> Some critics charge that there is no "real" free entry or free competition in a free market. For how can anyone compete or enter a field when an enormous amount of money is needed. . . ?
>
> This argument is but another variant of the prevailing confusion between freedom and abundance. . . .Every man is perfectly free to become a baseball player; but this freedom does not imply that he will be as good a baseball player as the next man.[6]

This matter is worth pursuing in some depth. Barriers to entry are, within a structuralist framework, quite obviously barriers to competition. They are widely held to foster "monopolistic" rather than "competitive" prices. With few exceptions economists have generally regarded all such barriers as undesirable and anti-competitive. Let us consider a sample of these barriers in order to see what role they play in competition and whether they are impediments that should be swept away by enlightened policy.

"Control" is the word

The first is "control of production techniques by established firms, via patents or secrecy, which permits exclusion of entrants from optimal techniques or the levying of a royalty charge for their use."[7]

The use of the word "control" is interesting. Why not "the development of," or "investment in" or "discovery of," production techniques? It matters greatly to someone studying competition how a firm acquires its production techniques. Indeed, it is probably true that almost nothing else matters. In a melodrama, the villain can keep a scientist in his dungeon lab because he holds the scientist's daughter in a high tower — where he threatens to do unspeakable things to her fresh young body. In this way he may gain "control" of both a production technique and a highly motivated scientist.

If dungeons and daughters are not available, then the firm may have to use other techniques. It might consider hiring and motivating skilful and imaginative employees, spending money on research and development, being prepared to take risks, having the sense to relate buyers' needs to technology that is within the company's grasp. Above all, the firm should be astute enough to know that its prosperity and security does not come from having control of *a* production technique, but comes instead from mobilizing a team of people who can produce a *stream* of superior production techniques. A given production technique, even one which is temporarily superior and protected by a patent and a secret, will not be superior for very long.

Control, according to Bain, is maintained by patents or by secrecy.[8] Patents, it is true, prevent would-be competitors from using a specific technology for a limited amount of time; that is what they are designed to do. The whole purpose of a patent is to provide an opportunity for the investor to recover the investment in research and development before his intellectual property can be used by anyone else. A patent would be of no use unless the firm's profit during the period of protection was sufficient to compensate it for the research costs and risk. Even so it is stretching things a bit to call a patent a barrier to entry. Patents delay the use of intellectual property, they do not prohibit a firm from entering an industry. They compel the new entrant to do what the patent holder did: innovate. The new firm may even have to innovate its way around someone else's innovation.

Blabber mouths

As for secrecy, it is an economist's "Catch 22." Are we to understand that for the sake of competition, managers are supposed to tell their secrets to their competitors? If so, future managers must be warned: if they reveal their secrets to other managers, indeed even if they exchange pleasantries with other managers, they are likely to be visited by the combines sleuths, who may not believe that telling secrets promotes competition. In any event, the issue of secrecy cannot be taken too seriously. A corporation has no mind, no voice and no secrets; people in the corporation do have them, and their memories and their voices can be hired away.[9] Furthermore, commercial intelligence is an important product line of the consulting industry, and what Macy's doesn't tell Gimbel's, Gimbel's can find out.

The firm that can maintain a stream of production techniques superior to those of other firms is competing successfully. It would seem strange indeed to say that its behaviour, so clearly competitive, is instead monopolistic. No doubt its success will be an inspiration to some and a deterrent to others, in exactly the same way that a superior athlete or artist may inspire some people to try harder and discourage others from trying at all. And one must not forget that companies, the artists and the athletes that succeed are examples showing what can be done. In that way they make it easier for others to improve their performance.

The rich get richer

Our next sample of a barrier is "imperfections in the markets for hired factors (including materials) which favour established firms, or ownership or control by agreement of strategic factor supplies by such firms."[10]

Let us deal first with management and labour. It seems strange to argue that managers and workers would go to work for a successful, established firm on terms less favourable than those being offered by a new firm. Everything else being equal, a winning company is usually more successful in recruiting the top students in the graduating class. This is surely because the prospective employees anticipate they will obtain *more* favourable, not less favourable, terms in the long run. Indeed on the basis of common sense one would expect a winning company to prosper because it is able to put together, motivate, and keep happy a winning team of workers and managers who will be paid more, not less, than members of new or less successful companies.

At the same time, new firms begin every day, and if their dreams hold promise and their plans make sense, they will be able to sell "challenges," and "hopes" and "opportunities." My experience in the establishment of new companies in such diverse fields as mining and computer software suggests that companies with only dreams often find it *easier* to attract money and people than companies with dreams and some real-world experience.

The benefits of being well-established

When it comes to supplies of equipment and of materials the story is a little different. Successful, established firms that also happen to be large will have achieved over time a winning team of suppliers who are loyal, well rewarded and who see their fortunes tied in some way to the fortunes of their customers. A new, unknown company will have to make the same kind of appeal to the suppliers of cotton waste or metal plate that it makes to a new manager or worker. If the account shows promise of becoming profitable and important, the new firm will be shown every consideration.

Bain also includes ownership or control of strategic factor supplies in this particular barrier.[11] Even the Austrians seemed to accord special significance to "exclusive ownership."[12] Yet in this age of substitutability, it seems difficult to see why it is any more of a problem for a firm to innovate its way around a resource constraint than around a product or technological constraint. To find and develop a good resource or stream of resources takes the same kind of competitive activity as to find and develop a stream of good production techniques, or products.

Credit-worthiness and goodwill

The third barrier we will consider is "Money-market conditions imposing higher interest rates or more severe rationing of investable funds on potential entrant firms."[13] This barrier is no different than the one we have just considered. Companies that have obviously been successful in maintaining a stream of superior offers to all the groups that contribute to its well-being will have a good credit rating. Would-be rivals are going to have to be very persuasive indeed to convince factor owners and lenders they will be able to do as well.

But let us clear up a misunderstanding at this point. Established companies are *not* treated more favourably by suppliers, or lenders, than new companies. It is only the *successful* established companies whose business is sought by suppliers. Old established companies that have proven their incompetence will have no special advantages at all. A credible new company will have little trouble taking over the customers and suppliers from an old, established company that has not been able to maintain an improving stream of compatible offers.

Bain sites a number of other barriers, but they seem of either less importance (an entering firm might cause factor prices to rise) or to be covered by the analysis we have already made (patent control of superior product design). The fourth and last barrier that we will consider is therefore "The possible accumulative preference of buyers for established brand names and company reputations."[14]

Again it must be pointed out that there is no inherent advantage to being an old established company. Such companies disappear every day of the week. The only old established companies that can count on goodwill are those that have maintained a stream of improving compatible offers. The ease with which the new can compete with the old is a function of the performance of the old (as compared with the promise of the new), and this is as it should be, whether in sports, romance, or business.

Why be a winner

What, then, has Bain told us? He has told us that fast runners may discourage so-so runners from getting into the race. This is true — one might almost say self evident — but he has not told the whole story. Moreover, the slant is wrong. Society benefits in four ways from the success of the competitive winners. First, winners make superior offers. The benefits that winners confer on customers, shareholders, workers and investors is so obvious they are usually overlooked. Second, the winners and their winnings act as an inspiration to those who would also like to be winners. Third, by their example, winners show the field how the race should be run. Fourth, the very success of the winners acts as a reminder that by and large the industry is being well served and that there are no such things as free lunches or entries. Nor should there be. Entry uses scarce resources, and before they are dedicated to a new venture the investors, suppliers and workers, who are invariably called on to make important commitments to the new firm, would like to be as sure as possible that their commitment will not lead to disappointment.

Satisfied customers should constitute a warning to would-be entrants to avoid wasting resources in new facilities that are unneeded and unwanted. Dissatisfied customers make entry easy, if not free.

Bain's barriers turn out to be nothing more than manifestations of successful competitive activities. At most, they are economically useful hurdles to discourage the waste of resources that are not free. The economy does not need or want complete freedom of entry any more than it wants perfect competition. If those who undertake feasibility studies do their job well, they should find that entry into industries that are being badly served is rather easy; by contrast they should find entry difficult and inadvisable in industries that are being well served.

Monopoly as Exclusive Resource Ownership

In a book published in 1836, Senior suggested that if everyone has free and equal access to the factors of production, there is no monopoly.[15] It is the exclusive ownership of the means of production by the capitalist class that provides Marxists with their *bête-noire* of monopoly,[16] and it is the fencing off of the only waterhole in Arizona that causes the bullets and the arrows to fly and the cameras to roll.

This particular resource-ownership brand of monopoly was most recently elaborated on by I.M. Kirzner. His position on monopoly[17] can be summarized in this way. The market is not in equilibrium, but is full of unexploited opportunities which, if seized, would move buyers and sellers towards positions where they would be better off. The persons who are aware of these opportunities and who do the seizing are entrepreneurs. They can operate without owning any resources except their own powers of perception and persuasiveness. The entrepreneurs' activities are wholly competitive, by which Kirzner appears to mean they are moving toward a closer approximation of equilibrium.

The question Professor Kirzner poses for himself is this: what obstacles or impediments can there be in a free market to prevent the competition of these entrepreneurs? The first, of course, is government monopoly, which, by decree, can prevent crops from being sown, pipelines from being laid, or plants from being built. The second could arise if a resource owner succeeded in obtaining ownership or control of 100 per cent of the available supply of an essential resource.

The question I would put is whether a unique offer by a resource owner is conceptually or practically any different from the unique offer of a producer. Let us examine this problem with the aid of a few simple cases which will begin by putting Professor Kirzner's argument in the strongest possible way.

Case 1: A monopolistic land owner

Suppose that a shipwrecked sailor takes possession of an entire small island and shortly thereafter a second sailor is washed ashore. Provided the first sailor can establish his ownership, which presumably would have to be done by having superior strength (and needing little sleep), his offer of food, or of the land to produce food, might be made on terms that passed the test of being "a severe sanction." This case seems to confirm Kirzner's argument. The absence of other islands or of other resources puts the second sailor at the mercy of a monopolist.

Case 2: Two sailors: monopoly-monopsony

Suppose that two sailors land together on two halves of an island and that they immediately agree on a division of the land. Only after the division is agreed to is it discovered that one sailor has ownership of the only source of fresh water and the other the only source of food. They are no less monopolists according to the resource-ownership test than the sole owner in Case 1, but now it is no longer clear that one could gain much advantage over the other.

Case 3: The blueberry-strawberry monopolies

In case three the island is divided between two sailors as before except that both halves of the island have an abundance of everything — save that one has the only strawberry patch, and the other the only blueberry bushes.

As in the previous cases we have two monopolistic resource owners, neither of them having much of what might be called monopoly power.

Case 4: Doctor-patient

In case four there are two land-owning individuals as in Case 3, with lots of food and drink on both sides of the island, but this time one of the owners used to be the ship's doctor while the other was a simple sailor. A deadly disease hits the island against which the doctor can prepare a medicine. The sailor possesses nothing of comparable value.

Is not Case 4 exactly like Case 1? Yet the resources, or at least the natural resources to prepare the medicine, are not subject to monopolistic control. What gives the Doctor in Case 4 and the first sailor in Case 1 their power is the fact that they can make a unique offer which is of life-or-death importance, and for which there is no substitute that will save the life of the buyer. *And they themselves are not subject to any countervailing power.* These two cases come about as close as one can get to a "perfect" monopoly provided, as we said, that the sailor and the doctor are powerful men and don't need any sleep.[18] Let us hasten to rescue our sailors and bring them back to North America. Desert-island economics should make us about as nervous as should the economics of perfect competition — nice places to visit provided we remember to set our alarm clocks.

The purpose of these primitive cases was to help us to decide whether there is any conceptual difference between a unique offer based on exclusive resource ownership and a unique offer based on an invention or, simply, on superior knowledge or management. Cases 1 and 4 seem to suggest that if any difference exists it must be a difference of degree, not of kind.

The importance of resources

The feeling that resources are of special importance might be based on a number of considerations. It may be argued that resources are more basic, more fundamental — lower on the production chain, as it were. This very fact, however, can be used to argue that resources are *less* important than end products. It is the end product that is needed, not the resource. Given time, why should it be any more difficult to innovate one's way around a shortage of natural resources than a shortage of any product higher on the production chain? My own experience in industrial marketing leads me to believe it is very difficult to find any narrowly-defined natural resource that does not face competition in all its end uses.

The popular designation of monopolist derives from this uniqueness of the offer, its importance and the absence of countervailing power. Whether the unique offer is for a processed or unprocessed product does not seem to make much of a conceptual difference. The usefulness of making a distinction has to rest on the proposition that unique resource offers have fewer or less satisfactory alternatives than unique product offers. This seems, to me at least, to be a difficult position to maintain.

Monopoly as any Departure from Perfect Competition

We have already referred to Joan Robinson's proposal to call all firms monopolies, and we have already quoted a current textbook to the effect that all firms outside of perfect competition enjoy monopoly power. Kenneth Arrow has gone further: "In disequilibrium, the market consists of a number of monopolists facing a number of monopsonists."[19] The most general picture, according to Arrow, is that of a shifting set of bilateral monopolies. Since the perfect competition in equilibrium belongs exclusively to the textbook rather than to the real world, we must conclude that all firms are monopolistic.

Such a use of terms might be acceptable if monopoly were a neutral word; if it did not almost automatically invite public disapproval and government regulation. Unfortunately, managers who enjoy elements of so-called monopoly because of the uniqueness of their offers but who, at the same time, are highly competitive earn opprobrium of being monopolists not laurels of being competitors. Twenty economists looked out of their ivory tower. One saw free markets, nineteen saw just power. Yet all of them claimed that they were realists. But only one saw competitors, the others just monopolists.

MONOPOLIZATION AS BEHAVIOUR

Our search for the behavioural meaning of monopoly is complicated by two facts. First, as Rosenbluth has said, "The verb 'to monopolize' does not have a well-defined meaning in economic or legal usage."[20] The second is that in both law and everyday speech, monopoly is a pejorative term. It is a serious matter to call a firm a monopoly, and it is particularly damaging to "accuse" it of monopolistic activities.

The foregoing quotation by Rosenbluth continues with: "the most common uses of the term can be summarized by saying that to monopolize means to pursue policies that create, protect, entrench, or extend a monopoly position."[21] Rosenbluth has indeed given us the "most common uses" of the term, but not an adequate definition.

The world's fastest runner may win a gold medal in every contest he enters. Are we to understand that it would constitute monopolization if he were to undertake further training, study new techniques, and try even harder to increase his lead over his rivals?

Assume that for a particular computational purpose, there is one calculator that is far superior to any other now available, so much so that most of its users would pay double the price rather than make do with the next best machine. In other words, the company has a monopoly in the popular sense of the word. Is it our understanding that if this firm continues to undertake development and research work to improve its already good product that it would be engaging in an act of monopolization?[22] Certainly if its plans and its R and D are successful it will be pursuing policies "that create, protect, entrench, or extend" its monopolistic position.

Competitive behaviour vs competitive conditions

Our analysis made it clear that competition in the behavioural sense has nothing at all to do with perfect competition as a condition. Indeed, economists have caused themselves a good deal of confusion by trying to infer ideal competitive behaviour from a condition that is not ideal to begin with. The same thing is happening with monopoly. But monopoly as behaviour need have nothing at all to do with monopoly as a condition. Further, just as real world structures approaching the "ideal" of perfect competition are not necessarily beneficial, the real world conditions approaching the "ideal" of monopoly (a one-firm industry) are far from being necessarily harmful. On the contrary monopoly as a condition may be desirable, inevitable and the result of activities that are wholly beneficial. Behaviour that can lead a firm to make a unique offer and discourage other firms from staying in, or entering the same industry, can be wholly competitive and very much in the public interest.

THE EFFECT OF MONOPOLY ON PRICE

As we noted earlier, there is hardly a textbook on economic theory that does not say, or at least give the student a strong impression, that the monopolistic price is higher than the price charged by firms in perfect competition. In defence of textbooks, it must be added that in holding to this view they are following a very old tradition. Adam Smith, for example, wrote:

> The price of monopoly is upon every occasion the highest which can be got. The natural price, or the price of free competition, on the contrary, is the lowest which can be taken, not upon every occasion indeed, but for any considerable time together.[23]

It is customary for textbook writers to lead their readers through a series of simple diagrammatic exercises demonstrating that monopoly price is higher than competitive price. This conclusion may be qualified and the reader may be warned about falling long run costs, learning curves, innovation and even about the possibility of competition in an industry with only a few firms. Notwithstanding these caveats the impression left by the geometry is a general rule stating that monopoly price exceeds the competitive price. Let us, therefore, take a careful look at the conventional geometry.

A Flat Long-run Average-cost Curve: The Raspberry Scenario

Figure 30 is a reasonable facsimile of a set of cost and demand curves that appear with minor variations in a number of leading textbooks. The product, let us say, is raspberries. The total market demand is AB. The industry supply curve under perfectly competitive conditions is EF, which as we noted in Chapter 4 is roughly the horizontal summation of a segment of the marginal cost curves of all firms in the industry. An example of one such firm, Firm X, is shown in Figure 30B.

It is assumed that however many raspberries are wanted in the market, the most efficient way of producing them is to add small units, the size of Firm X. It is also assumed that average costs do not change as more production units are added or deleted. These conditions give us the flat long-run average-cost curve shown by the line P_cJLH, which is also the long-run marginal-cost curve and the long-run industry supply curve.

The perfectly competitive price of raspberries is P_c or $1.00 a box, which is determined by the intersection of AB, the market demand, and EF, the short-run market supply.

Enter the villain

Now let us suppose that a monopolist succeeds in buying up all the raspberry-producing farms and begins to operate the whole industry as a single firm. The demand curve for the monopolist would be the old industry demand curve AB. Since it slopes downward to the right the monopolist would derive the marginal revenue curve, AG. As a profit maximizer he equates marginal cost and marginal revenue. While this is exactly what each individual farmer does, the results are quite different. The farmer sees only a flat demand curve for his product — the line marked "$P_cAR = MR$" in Figure 30B. In effect this line tells him he can sell all the product he wants at $1.00. He chooses to produce q_c or 10,000 boxes because at that output his marginal cost MC_x ($1.00) equals his marginal revenue ($P_cAR = MR$, also $1.00).

For his part, the monopolist finds the intersection of his marginal revenue, AG, and his long-run marginal cost, P_cJH, at J (again $1.00). Point J corresponds to point K on the industry's (now the firm's) price-sales relationship (demand curve). The price corresponding to K is P_m, or $3.00, and the quantity is Q_m or 25 million boxes.

Higher price, less quantity sold

The monopoly price of $3.00 is higher than the perfectly competitive price of $1.00, the amount the monopolistic supplier is willing to sell

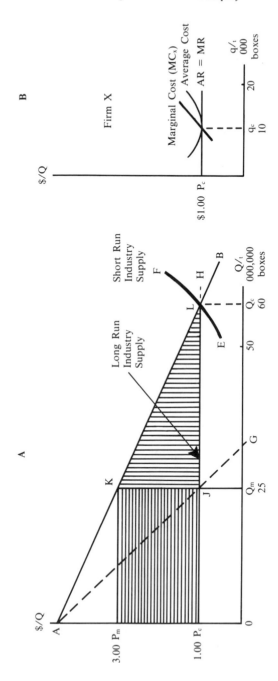

Figure 30 — Monopoly and Competition: A Contrast

(or, rather the amount that customers are willing to buy at $3.00) is only 25 million boxes, whereas at the competitive price of $1.00 consumers would have bought 60 million boxes. The geometry of this case thus "demonstrates" that the monopolist has raised price and restricted supply.

More bad news

When the price was $1.00 consumers enjoyed a "surplus" (called, appropriately, consumers' surplus) equal to the triangle P_cAL. This is the difference in the utility between what the consumers must pay for raspberries (OP_cLQ_c) and what they would pay (roughly $OALQ_c$) rather than go without.

The consumers' surplus occurs because consumers generally pay the same price for all of the units of a product they buy, but because of diminishing marginal utility they value the first units purchased more highly than they value the later units. What the monopolization of the raspberry industry has done in effect is reduce the surplus going to consumers from P_cAL to P_mAK. The area P_cP_mKJ is, in effect, captured by the monopolist (who no doubt would have to use some of it to defray the costs of creating the monopoly — and for legal fees). The area KJL is simply lost to both producers and consumers. This is sometimes called the "dead weight loss" attributable to monopoly though it would be more accurate to say that it is simply a bit of space in the diagram that is the inevitable result of a sloped demand curve.

To students impressed by geometry, this exercise must be impressive, even if the results are later modified, as they usually are, by qualifications in the text. Let us now look at the modifications that are made, or should be, in the text that accompanies the picture.

Qualifications

The first thing the textbook should say is that it is virtually impossible to think of circumstances outside the ivory tower in which this monopolization could really happen — unless the scheme was put into effect by, or with the support of, the government. This kind of monopolization could not take place without the use of physical force or the threat of physical force (jail) to keep out new entrants. Freedom of entry may be a much misunderstood concept, but if the long run cost curve really is as shown by P_cH, the capital and technology required must be minimal. There must be many firms or individuals with the means to enter the industry, and the incentive to do so, should the price go above $1.00 a box. No sooner would the monopolist raise the price to $3.00 than other raspberry patches would start to receive

tender loving care. Unless the monopolist enjoyed a ban on all raspberry production but his own, there is no way the price could remain
at $3.00.

There is more

Nor does this tell the whole story. It is doubtful whether the demand
curve was calculated in such a way as to cover the situation we have
just been exploring. According to Figure 30, when the price of raspberries tripled, the amount of land devoted to raspberry production
was cut in half. Agricultural resources suitable for the production of
this sort of product are now "on the market" looking for new employment and investment opportunities. Would not loganberries, blue-
berries, chokecherries, gooseberries, thimbleberries, huckleberries,
dewberries, blackberries, boysenberries, lingonberries, saskatoons,
strawberries and black-market raspberries begin to look like golden
opportunities? And once these raspberry substitutes start coming on
the market in increased supply, what will happen to the demand curve
for the monopolist's raspberries?

Students subjected to the geometry of this case are hearing the
wrong message. The story should be told the other way around. In the
beginning, somebody invented raspberries or at least discovered that
despite the seeds they were edible. For a while the inventor or discoverer
developed his business as a "monopoly" in competition with other
fruits and berries. As output expanded and raspberries "caught on",
the monopolist came to realize that any farmer could quite easily
enter the raspberry business. Then he began to ask himself, "What can
I do to perpetuate my raspberry monopoly?"

Monopolization

There are five possible ways in which the raspberry producer might
preserve his monopoly.
(a)   He could hire his own special police force to terrorize those who
       would like to compete with him. This is likely to work, however,
       only if he can persuade the government that all raspberry pro-
       duction (including his own) should be illegal. This will deny his
       competitors the protection of the law, and he could maintain
       his monopoly position provided he had the biggest private army
       and the appropriate arrangements with government officials.
(b)   He could try to get a government law or license that prevented
       anyone else from producing raspberries.
(c)   He could buy up all the raspberry farms as they prepared to
       come into production. This method was tried by Standard Oil,
       and all that happened was that there grew up a new, profitable

industry of building refineries for the purpose of selling them to Standard Oil.[24] Raspberry farms are much cheaper to produce than oil refineries.

(d)   He could apply for a patent, but raspberries are not patentable, and even if they were it would be only a temporary solution.

(d)   *He could make an offer that is more attractive than the offers that could be made by perfectly competitive firms.*

Within the strict limiting assumptions of the model, a would-be monopolist will not be able to charge more than $1.00 a box. Even at *that* price it is unlikely he could discourage other firms from entering. If we take one step closer to the real world, we can see that the monopolist has only one real hope of preventing other firms from coming into the industry. This is to find an innovation that changes the cost curve in such a way so that he can produce bigger, better raspberries at a price of less than $1.00 per box.

The conclusion to be drawn is *not* that the single-firm-monopoly price is higher than the many-firm competitive price. It is rather that if the raspberry producer has any hope at all of becoming large in raspberry production, he must find a way of bettering the perfectly competitive offer. The many-firm competitive price is the *ceiling*, not the floor, of the one-firm-monopoly price. This is not the message that the reader usually gets.

A Falling Long-run Average-cost Curve: The Widget Scenario

Figure 31 shows a falling long-run average-cost curve (LRAC) and two short-run curves. The LRAC shows the minimum average cost of producing any desired quantity when the firm has time to adjust its plant to the optimum size for producing that quantity. The long-run curve must therefore be made up of short-run average-cost curves (SRAC), only two of which are shown. The one on the left, $SRAC_c$, illustrates the case of a small plant with a very limited output. The one on the right, $SRAC_m$, would apply to a large plant.

Assume that in the beginning someone invented a widget, and since there had been no widgets before, and customers had survived quite nicely without them, the demand was very limited. So the first firm — the monopolist — developed an appropriate technology for producing a small number of widgets. Now the demand curve shifts to the right, as more and more people discover the joys of widgeting, and two developments become possible. The industry can take the path of perfect competition, as shown by Scenario A in Figure 32, or it can follow the path of monopoly, as illustrated in Scenario B.

Scenario A makes the not-necessarily unreasonable assumption that there is a technology available that can efficiently produce quite

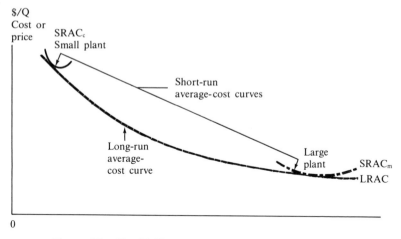

Figure 31 - The Falling Long-run Average-cost Curve

small quantities of widgets. This being so, it is theoretically possible for many new small firms to duplicate the efforts of the first. The horizontal summation of these average cost curves (one of which is shown as $SRAC_c$) would produce horizontal LRAC curve (shown as the dashed line in Scenario A — just like the one in the raspberry scenario. Assume that the industry demand curve finally shifts out to DE. The industry supply curve in the short run is GH. The intersection of supply and demand occurs at J; the perfectly competitive price is P_c or $12.00; and the perfectly competitive output is OQ_c.

Enter the monopolist again

In Scenario B it is assumed that economies of scale exist, which would permit an aggressive firm to expand and build an ever-larger firm enjoying ever-lower costs. So long as the LRAC continues to fall, a larger firm will always be able to undersell a smaller one. The industry demand curve, DE, is the same as in Scenario A, but in Scenario B one firm has expanded to become a monopolist, with a short run average cost curve, shown as $SRAC_m$, a marginal cost curve, GH, and a marginal revenue curve KL, which intersects marginal cost at R. The monopolist recognizes that profits will be maximized if he operates at the price and output indicated by the intersection of marginal cost and marginal revenue, $13.00 ($P_m$) and Q_m respectively.

The intersection of marginal cost and marginal revenue again lies to the left of Q_c, the competitive output. Have we once more demonstrated that the monopolist's price will be higher than the

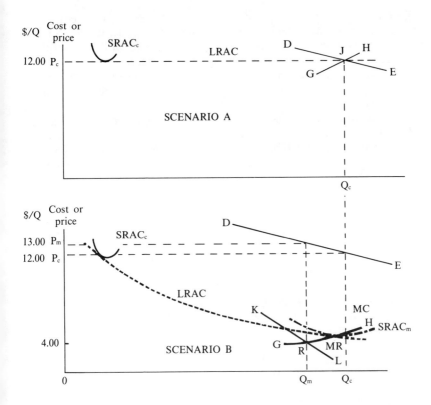

Figure 32 — Two Scenarios: Competition and Monopoly

perfectly competitive price, and his output, lower? It should be apparent that we have done no such thing. Unless the monopolist has been able to arrange with the government a ban on entry, a price above P_c will bring in some of the small firms using the appropriate small-firm technology; the monopolist will lose sales, and indeed, he will no longer be a monopolist.

As before, the perfectly competitive price puts a *ceiling* on what the monopolist can charge. But the monopolist would not even be safe charging P_c because a somewhat larger firm using a different technology could come in at a still lower cost, and take business away from him.

What must be of greater practical concern to the would-be monopolist is the possibility of segmentation. Price-theory analysis generally assumes that a product is given, but in reality it never is. The offer made by the seller is always capable of some variation. A high price might invite a new entrant to come in, not with just another widget, but with a marvelous new widget that serves at least some of the customers better. As a result of such an entry, the monopolist may not be able to retain his customers solely on the basis of a somewhat lower price.

Of one thing we can be sure. The monopoly price will be no higher than the price in an industry with many small firms and a homogeneous product unless there is an absolute ban on all other would-be widget-makers, or makers of things that look like widgets, or of devices that do the work of widgets.

Rising Long-run Average-Cost Curves

So far we have considered the possibility of long-run average-cost curves that are flat or falling. The remaining possibility is that the long-run curve rises. This situation poses no problem, however, because a large monopolist could always be undersold by a small firm. Our conclusion does not change, however. If, by any chance, a firm was determined to operate as a monopolist (until it ran out of money) it still would not be able to charge more than the perfectly competitive price.

A MONOPOLISTIC (UNIQUE) OFFER IN A WORLD OF PERFECT COMPETITION

Without A Surplus

In all of the cases presented so far, we have been asking whether, on the basis of the tools of price theory, we can conclude that the monopolist's price will be higher than the perfectly competitive price *for the same product*. We have seen that even within the limitations of price theory, it cannot be claimed that the monopolist's price will be above the perfectly competitive price so long as there is freedom of entry. Our problem now is to determine whether this conclusion can be generalized into a world in which there are multi-dimensional needs of many different consumers; a world in which there are not just a few standard products, but rather millions of different offers.[25]

In the last chapter we considered the case of a perfectly competitive world of five industries, A, B, C, D and E. Into this Garden of Eden crept an innovator who acquired control of one of the small firms, and used the power of his position, his intelligence and his persuasiveness to introduce a totally new product, F. Let us now extend our analysis, and suppose that enough consumers liked the new offer so that it was accepted with gratitude and sufficient enthusiasm to make the reconstituted, and now monopolistic, firm viable. At the same time the consumers were not quite enthusiastic enough to buy the quantities necessary to earn the innovator a fortune. What can be said about the attractiveness of the terms of the monopolistic offer *vis-à-vis* those in the perfectly competitive industries? Are consumers generally better or worse off because of the arrival of this monopolist in a world of perfect competition?

Before we can answer these questions, there are two assumptions that should be made explicit. The first is that consumers know better than anyone else what is best for them, and that in general, their welfare cannot be improved by forcing on them products or policies they have not freely chosen. The second follows from the first: if an individual rearranges his or her spending pattern by withdrawing a dollar from the purchase of X and using it instead to buy some, or some more, Y, the transfer of spending must be taken as indicating an increase in welfare.

The monopolist as hero

If these propositions are accepted then it must follow that if dollars are switched from the consumption of products A, B, C, D and E to the new monopolistic product, F, total welfare must have been increased. The innovator has enlarged the area of choice, and some households at least have been able to obtain more satisfaction from their given incomes. We can conclude, therefore, that the offer of the monopolist is better (for some people, of course) than the rejected offers made by the perfectly competitive firms. Can we now generalize and say that monopolistic offers (prices) have to be better (lower) than perfectly competitive offers (prices)? Before we can make such a statement, there are some matters that need to be clarified.

Since we have assumed that our monopolist was successful in earning only an average return, his firm in price-theory terms is analogous to the monopolistic tangency case presented in Figure 26. Since we explicitly recognize the multiplicity of the dimensions of the offer, we should point out that the innovator has had to optimize not only price, but also warranties, credit terms, quality control and scores or even hundreds of other aspects of his offer in order to be viable. As a "multidimensional tangency case" he achieves his best possible position only after choosing the best position with regard to *all* dimensions. Needless to add, the offer to consumers must be consistent with the offers to all other participants in the firm's activities.

Getting blood out of a stone

The analogy to the tangency case of price theory allows us to see more clearly (price theory does have its uses) that there is no practical way of imposing on the monopolist a requirement that he improve his offer (lower his price) so that it becomes, in effect, a perfectly competitive offer (price). In price-theory terms, a purist might argue that while the monopolist may have made consumers better off, he would have improved their position even more if the government forced him to do what perfectly competitive firms do, i.e., equate price and marginal cost. But our monopolist is a "tangency case." Such a regulation would place him in a loss position, and if he is to remain in production he will have to receive a subsidy. Equity suggests that those who consume the product are the logical ones to pay the subsidy. If they do so in proportion to their consumption levels, the monopolist's customers will end up paying a price plus a subsidy — which is about what the monopolist was charging in the first place. It does not make practical sense to argue that resource allocation can be improved by trying to abolish or in some way regulate those monopolists who make unique offers but cover only their costs including the cost of capital.

A second matter of clarification concerns the long-term costs and structure of the monopolistic industry. Can a better offer be brought about by breaking up the monopoly into a large number of small firms? The answer to this question hinges on the nature of the long-run average-cost curves, and on the demand for product F. If, for example, the monopolist, in ignorance, builds a large plant using large-plant technology when there are, or are about to be discovered, technologies that allow smaller firms to make superior offers, industry F will not be a monopoly for very long. Our general conclusion still holds. The only way the monopolist in industry F can maintain his monopoly (unique offer) position is to make an offer more attractive than offers that can be made by the many small firms. It cannot be otherwise. If he is so foolish as to believe that his monopolistic label permits him to shift benefits from consumers to himself as a manager, or to his shareholders, then he will simply make insufficient sales to remain in business.

With A Surplus

By introducing a marginal monopolist have we stacked the deck in favour of the proposition that monopolistic offers have to be superior to perfectly competitive offers? This is not the case. Suppose the monopolist who created industry F succeeded in producing so superior a product that it caused enthusiasm, queues, and vast profits. It should be even more obvious that his offer is superior to those in industries A to E. The only difference is that the innovative success of the monopolist will now produce a surplus that will keep imitators, tax collectors, regulators, academics and other rogues tossing and turning in their beds. For it turns out that the creation, division, and the rationalization for that division, of the surplus are the liveliest and most emotionally charged issues in economics, politics and in society in general.

The previous analysis of the no-surplus case stands with one exception. Now the regulator will be able to make a better case that good though the innovator's performance may have been, he, the regulator, can improve things even more by forcing the monopolist to lower his price until all the surplus has disappeared. Whether such a policy is fair and equitable, and whether it will produce more growth and more innovation are questions that we will leave for the reader to consider. For the moment we simply claim that it is valid to generalize the conclusion that so long as there are no prohibitions on entry, a monopolistic position cannot be maintained unless it involves making a better offer than can be made by firms operating under conditions of perfect competition. The monopolistic price must be lower than the perfectly competitive price; the monopolistic offer must be better than its perfectly competitive counterpart.

Chapter 6

Competition and the Number of Firms

INTRODUCTION

It is the purpose of this chapter to consider the optimum number of firms in an industry. The question presupposes that we have already settled on a definition of an industry. This we have not done, and cannot do on any objective basis. The drawing of industry boundaries is, and always will be, a matter of judgement. In practice, however, industry boundaries are recognized, and for now we shall simply assume that a panel of reasonable practitioners has divided up heavenly space into constellations of firms and that each constellation has been given the name of an industry. It will, of course, be borne in mind that the inter-constellation boundaries:

(a) are matters of judgement;
(b) are historical and may not apply to the future;
(c) may separate two firms with respect to one product or use or buyer, and combine them with respect to some other product, use or buyer;
(d) recognize competition among *all* constellations for purchasing power; and
(e) leave room for a good deal of direct inter-constellation rivalry that will vary from product to product, from customer to customer and from time to time.

The industry-boundary question can never be off our agenda. It can never escape from being a *caveat* on all our conclusions. Be that as it may, we shall still pretend that reasonable boundaries have been agreed to and proceed to consider the number of sellers we might like to see in each industrial constellation.

If we begin our analysis by observing competitive behaviour in the real world, the first thing that would probably strike us is the unevenness of the amount of rivalrous behaviour in different industries. Paradoxically, in those industries that come as close as possible to the perfectly competitive "ideal", there is virtually no rivalrous activity at all. Whatever offer-improvement takes place over time generally originates from outside the industry itself: man-hour productivity on the farm goes up not primarily because farmers are trying to outdo each other, but because oligopolistic farm implement companies and fertilizer companies are vying with each other to produce and market better farm implements and more efficient fertilizers.[1]

When we come to organizations that are at the other extreme — as close to monopoly as possible — we get a mixed picture. Government monopolies such as the post office,[2] provincial liquor boards, and other government departments do not give an impression of much progress or offer-improvement over time. On the other hand some near monopolies such as Bell Canada, and a number of utilities have a creditable record of offer-improvement. Telephone and communication services have improved, and the real cost of service has declined.[3]

It is readily apparent, however, that it is in the middle of the number-of-firms spectrum that rivalry flourishes. This was the picture of rivalry that we tried to capture in Figure 1 and again in Figure 22.

INNOVATION — IMITATION

Our discussion of the process of innovation and imitation must begin with two initial caveats. First is the reminder that we tend to associate innovation with laboratories, white coats, and Research and Development departments. This kind of innovation is very important, to be sure, but it is only part of the process of change. The machines and systems that emerge from the R and D lab and that may look like "great leaps forward" usually capture the most attention, but they generally require many more little steps by people who do not wear white coats, and whose salaries are not charged to R and D, before the change can be pronounced a success. The second *caveat*, which is closely related to the first, is that the data and the measurements available for a statistical study of the innovation process are, understandably, quite unsatisfactory.

In the most general terms the relevant question at this stage of our analysis is this: in any given industry, what is the probable relationship between the number of firms and the rate of offer-improvement to all participants in the market process? In more specific terms, the question might be framed in this way: if the size of the Canadian market warrants the employment of 5,000 employees in the steel industry, for example, are consumers, workers and shareholders likely to enjoy a faster rate of offer-improvement if these employees are organized into two firms of 2,500, five firms of 1,000, or 50 firms of 100 each? Of course, the answer will depend on the judgement and experience of the person providing the opinion (and the answer is never likely to be more than an opinion) and on the technical and market characteristics of the industry past, present and future. Let us consider some of the relevant factors.

In many cases, bigger is better

There are several reasons for expecting a positive relationship between offer-improvement and company size, at least up to a certain point. This point will depend on the nature and scope of the innovation and of the industry. Obviously the design and development of a new aircraft or a new computer system or an arctic pipeline will require the backing of a large company.[4] At the same time, it must be the case that smaller projects can be undertaken by smaller companies, although the advantages of size must never be overlooked.[5]

The specialization of personnel that comes with increased size should promote increased innovation. The one-man marketing department must deal with advertising, layout, packaging, salesmen, point-of-purchase materials, warranties and so on. It is not likely to have the time or the expertise to invent a new computerized routing schedule for faster deliveries. It is self-evident that a firm that is large enough to have one or two specialists in transportation, information systems and operations research should do somewhat better.

Most changes involve some risk. Even if a given innovation involved exactly the same absolute potential gain or loss, and the same probability of success or failure for a large or small company, it would be more likely to be undertaken by the larger firm. The loss to a small company would mean bankruptcy. The same loss to a large company contemplating many such changes would involve no such risk.

Equally important, the payoff promised by an already existing large volume of sales, or by a large distribution network unquestionably stimulates research and development. In the course of a survey of corporate practices of American firms operating in Canada, I was surprised to find one small Canadian chemical company that was spending more on R and D than most of its larger competitors. The explanation was that the small company had traded a minority interest in its common stock for the right to market all new products in the U.S. through its large American affiliate.[6]

Small is beautiful, too

While there are a number of good reasons to expect a significant correlation between size and innovation, this is not to say that small companies cannot survive or innovate. The small Canadian company just mentioned is a case in point. Around the colossus of I.B.M., a goodly number of software companies and hardware manufacturers have flourished. Some of them have filled in gaps on the periphery of big systems; some provide special-purpose machines for particular customers or users; some compete head-on with alternative software or hardware packages.[7]

Small companies sometimes develop a strategy of avoiding major innovations until they are developed and proven by their larger competitors.[8] In the meantime, they pursue innovative activities of a more modest, customer-oriented nature that appeal to only a limited segment of the market that may be overlooked by the larger companies. In some industries, especially those concerned with fashion, small flexible companies do much of the innovating for a particular market segment. Large companies enter only when it has been demonstrated that the product is suitable for mass production and mass marketing.

Co-operation between large and small companies

In some industries there is an intimate interplay between innovation in large and small companies. Many small companies are formed by breakaways from large companies. These breakaways are sometimes explained (or rationalized) by the frustration caused by large-organization bureaucracy;[9] sometimes they occur because the innovating employees of a large company see the possibility of a very big payoff to themselves. Big companies spawn and, in many circumstances, unwittingly subsidize, small innovative firms. It is not uncommon in the electronics and computer business to see a team of managers break away from one or more large companies, develop a product or a system to the point at which the superiority of the product can be demonstrated, and then sell themselves back to become a division of a big company in order to market their new product on a large scale.[10]

While experience suggests that for many industries a size-innovation relationship undoubtedly exists, it will not lend itself easily to statistical validation.[11] The optimum size of a company will be different for different industries and for different times in the same industry. A firm with a size, history and expertise that give it a competitive advantage in the design of a new, more energy-efficient, paper-making machine is unlikely to have any advantage at all in the design of a more energy-efficient fractional-horse-power motor. Furthermore, the innovative relationship between large and small companies can be wonderfully varied, and there is no reason why all of the innovative companies in the same industry need to work on the same problems or be the same size. A couple of large companies and a few small ones may together produce a path of product improvement and a mix of product offers, especially in a segmented market, that is better than what could be accomplished by an industry made up only of large companies or only of small ones.

In Scherer's words:

> One conclusion relevant to public policy follows immediately. No
> single firm size is uniquely conducive to technological progress.
> There is room for firms of all sizes. What we want, therefore, may
> be a diversity of sizes, each with its own special advantages and
> disadvantages.[12]

The foregoing considerations suggest that, on balance, larger
firms generally have an advantage over small firms in the rate of
innovation and offer-improvement. Despite all of the conceptual and
measurement problems involved it is comforting to find that the data
and the available studies generally support the thrust of our *a priori*
reasoning. Jesse W. Markham, after a review of studies by Hamberg,[13]
Horowitz[14], Scherer,[15][16] Comanor,[17] Grabowski and Baxter,[18]
Worley[19] and Mansfield,[20][21] concluded

> If technological change and innovational activity are, as we
> generally assume, in some important way a product of organized
> R and D activities financed and executed by business companies,
> it is clear that the welfare payoffs that flow from these can to
> some measurable extent be traced to the doorsteps of large
> firms operating in oligopolistic markets.[22]

This is essentially a confirmation of the Schumpeterian
hypothesis which Markham restates by saying that

> the traditional practice of drawing inferences concerning the state
> of competition from such parameters as indexes of industrial
> concentration and business size is logically indefensible. Since
> such statistical measurements apply only to a given point in time,
> they provide no basis for interpreting the dynamic forces that
> shaped them, or those they in turn set in motion in the future.[23]

Is smaller better?

Both *a priori* reasoning, and empirical evidence suggest that there is
undoubtedly a positive correlation between company size or industry
concentration, and innovative activity. But both *a priori* reasoning
and empirical evidence also suggests that size is not such an advantage, and not such an advantage in *all* industries, that there is no
room left for the small firm. Can the case for the small firm be so
strong as to suggest that innovation could be *inversely* related to size?

One of the areas of research that might suggest that small is not
only beautiful but better is that concerning the history of innovative
ideas. Perhaps the most famous study in this regard was by Jewkes,
Sawers and Silberman.[24] They present case studies on 71 important
inventions and trace over half of them to individual inventors. Only
about one in four can be said to have come out of a big company. Care

must be taken, however to interpret such results. Corporations do not invent or think or eat smoked meat sandwiches. People do. There is but a tiny fraction of one per cent of these people in the research labs of large companies and perhaps what should surprise us is not how few original inventions they make but, per capita, how many.

In any event a reading of Jewkes *et al* hardly leads to the conclusion that large corporations are not in many cases essential to the innovative process even if the original idea occurred to someone "off the premises." An invention of any significance hardly ever presents itself as a marketable product. It was brilliant of Fleming to note that the mould, *Penicillium notatum*, destroyed certain bacteria, but much more work had to be done and many more inventions had to be made to extract, stabilize the product and bring its cost down to present levels.[25]

Chester Carlson's invention of a Xerographing process was again an example of a single perceptive individual starting a new product, but before anything useful emerged, the product was developed by organizations and companies of ever-increasing size. There is nothing in the case history to suggest that Xerography could have been developed as a cottage industry or that the product would have been improved faster if it had.[26]

A second argument against the size-innovation thesis does not deny the likelihood of the relationship, but instead questions whether the innovations generated by larger scale are likely to provide a net benefit to society or customers. We made the point earlier that only a miscalculation on the part of management would lead it to undertake a change that made one or more parties worse off and no one better off. The kind of innovations most likely to ensure the peace, harmony and prosperity of a company are those that enable management to improve the offers to everyone involved, or at least to improve some offers without making other offers any worse. Of course it may be necessary from time to time to transfer benefits from one party to another. This, however, is unlikely to be the kind of change management can continue to make for very long, and still stay in business. It is for this reason that we have associated innovation with a net improvement in all offers taken together.

Innovation is not always viewed so favourably, however. "Product differentiation, which we have found to be a natural aspect of competitive activity, has come to be almost synonymous with the *absence* of competition."[27] From what has been said about conventional price theory, it should come as no surprise that those who think of competition as demanding the conditions of perfect competition associate innovation, or product differentiation, not with offer-improvement, but with monopoly.[28] There can be little doubt that product innovation in a world of perfect competition must, in practical terms, create a monopoly in the unique-offer sense. An innovation creates something new. By definition, the new product must be different from the homogeneous products that existed before. Furthermore, monopoly is associated in most textbooks with raising prices, withholding supply and misallocating resources, which surely must involve a net reduction in human welfare. If (a) an innovation makes a difference and (b) a difference is equated to a monopoly and (c) monopoly leads to inefficiency, then it follows, through this tortured chain of logic that (d) innovations engender inefficiency.[29]

Let's kill the golden goose anyway

Herein lies a dilemma for those who distrust differentiation and concentration. Certain types of innovations appear as economies of scale and result in larger firms. These are in a position to undertake even more innovation, which could mean more progress and more benefits to society. At the same time, however, it may be argued that economies of scale and large firms are monopolistic, which means a loss to society. Are large-scale enterprises, therefore, good or bad?

This issue troubled the Royal Commission on Corporate Concentration. Referring to the theory associated with J.A. Schumpeter and J.K. Galbraith which suggested that oligopoly (relatively large-scale firms) provides the best climate for innovation it said,

> The Schumpeter-Galbraith hypothesis implies that there may be a conflict between two measures of performance — efficiency of resource allocation and progress — thus raising an issue that has perplexed policy-makers and troubled this Commission.[30]

As further evidence of their dilemma, the Commission quoted Scherer and Markham to the effect that:

> a misallocation of resources *stemming from oligopoly* may be quickly *overcome* by rapid technological change from innovation.[31]

Let us call the Commission-Scherer-Markham position dilemma number one. Like many economic problems it is two-handed. On the one hand, innovations result in long-run falling costs and learning functions, in large firms and oligopolistic industries. Because of their scale of operation, the oligopolies are admirably suited to continue the innovation-imitation process responsible for their creation in the first place. On the other hand, oligopolies are monopolistic (since they are not perfectly competitive) and therefore do not give us the optimum allocation of resources described in Appendix A to Chapter 2.

One solution to this problem was given in Appendix A. There it was shown that the optimum allocation achievable in the world of perfect competition could be closely approximated in a world where the same average degree of monopoly was maintained — the world of the second best. Strictly on the grounds of the theory of static resource allocation, therefore, there is no reason to shy away from a world made up of competing oligopolistic industries. They are as likely to approximate the world of the second best as closely as any government-regulation-produced world is likely to approximate the resource allocation of perfect competition.

The progress-resources allocation trade-off

Let us suppose that the resource allocation problem is serious, and try to fashion a simple price theory type model illustrating the trade-off between allocation efficiency and progress. Assume a two-industry economy. One industry is made up of many small firms and approximates the conditions and resource allocation of perfect competition; the second is an oligopoly, made up of a few large firms. Assume further that the oligopoly is successful in obtaining double the mark-up of the perfect competitive industry, namely 10 per cent on sales as compared with 5 per cent. Suppose that this higher rate of profit of the oligopolistic industry constitutes a misallocation of resources and that if the large firms were shattered into small bits the mark-up would fall to 5 per cent. We further assume the large-firm-more-innovation relationship, and that the larger oligopolistic firms are able to obtain a 3 per cent increase in productivity each year while the small firms can average only 1 per cent. If we make the further simplifying assumption that all innovations decrease costs (rather than change the product) we shall be able to set out, in tabular form, the progress of the two industries over time. In Table 1, we have assumed a cost per unit in each industry equal to 100 in year zero.

Table 1 — Innovation and Decreasing Cost

	Year	0	1	2	3	4	5
Oligopoly	Cost	100	97	94	91	89	86
	Price	110	107	103	100	98	95
Perfect Competition	Price	105	104	103	102	101	100
	Cost	100	99	98	97	96	95
Advantage of oligopoly over perfect competition	For buyer	-5	-3	0	+2	+3	+5
	For seller	+5	+5	+4	+4	+4	+4

Table 1 suggests that the buyers of the oligopolistic product in year zero are being overcharged by five index points, while the sellers are gaining a like amount. To avoid argument, let us stipulate that this initial position constitutes an undeserved allocation from consumers to the suppliers of services in the oligopolistic industry. Is the solution to break up the oligopoly and thereby to achieve a 5 per cent reduction in price and settle for a 1 per cent increase in productivity? Or is it to leave well enough alone? The table tells us that even if there was a misallocation of resources to begin with (a proposition that in a dynamic world would have to be proven not assumed), Scherer and Markham are still right: "a misallocation of resources stemming from oligopoly may be quickly overcome by rapid technological changes from innovation."[32] By period three, consumers are getting a better deal from the oligopoly, warts, misallocation of resources, and all. Note that this will be true even if the oligopolists are able to maintain double the rate of profit of the perfectly competitive firms.

The lazy and shiftless capitalist

Dilemma number two of the Royal Commission concerns another aspect of the size-innovation relationship. The Commission cites the view of Carl Kaysen and Donald F. Turner that:

> competition is an important, if not essential, condition for technological change in an industry and that market power is detrimental rather than helpful. Competition gives firms the incentive to innovate to defend their market positions through new products and more efficient production.[33]

These words obviously had considerable influence on the Commission because they are echoed in its own concern, that in "highly concentrated Canadian industries in which price competition is low, there is less incentive to introduce new products or processes."[34]

The first thing that needs to be pointed out about the Kaysen-Turner-Commission thesis is the unflattering X-inefficiency bias of the remarks. Managers are inherently lazy and, unlike civil servants and academics who can do their best work only when they have security of tenure, they must have the threat of bankruptcy constantly hanging over their heads in order to stay awake. The second thing to note is that the Commission-Kaysen-Turner concern does not deny that innovations may be easier for larger firms; it simply introduces the probability that large firms will not face enough competition (which must mean enough competitors) to force them to put up with the fuss and bother of innovating.

What are the implications of the Commission-Kaysen-Turner concern? Let us suppose that our scenario began, not unrealistically, with a number of small firms constituting an industry. Some of these firms innovated by building larger, more efficient plants in order to make better offers to customers, workers and investors, and to entice them away from the smaller, higher-cost operations. So far, progress has been made and welfare improved. What the Commission-Kaysen-Turner thesis seems to suggest is that as surviving companies grow and as their numbers decline, a point is reached at which the firms are sufficiently large and few enough in number that they can henceforth arrange among themselves to cease trying to improve their offers.

Will success spoil XYZ Ltd.?

It is conceivable that a single firm sheltered from the rivalry of others might adopt a policy of making no changes and leaving all its offers as they are. But such a policy is by no means inevitable or even likely. As we noted earlier, "One," even a protected and needed one, must still compete with past ones, one's past, one's dreams and with zero; and one's innovation and imitation may be substantial and, conceivably, close to optimum.[35]

If a firm alone in its industry may choose to innovate, what is the likelihood that a few will stop the innovation-imitation process? According to the Royal Commission on Corporate Concentration, the probabilities are high enough to cause concern.

> In those highly concentrated Canadian industries in which price competition is low, there is less incentive to introduce new products and processes. . .the adoption of new production process technology often makes capital plant and equipment obsolete. Firms in highly concentrated industries may attempt to prolong the life of their fixed assets by slowing the rate of adoption of new technology. This strategy will be successful only in a highly coordinated oligopoly with little import competition, in which all competitors openly or tacitly refrain from introducing innovations.

> Canada may therefore be caught between the necessity of having large firms in order to have large, successful R and D programmes and the fact that large firms in general imply the existence of concentrated industries. At high levels of concentration, however, firms may become insulated from competitive pressures and hence. . .engage in less innovative activity.[36]

There are two problems with this analysis. In the first place, it does not make it sufficiently clear that a conspiracy to stop innovating — which is what we must be talking about — can work *only* if entry is blocked. There is absolutely no point in three restaurants or copper producers or ice cream manufacturers agreeing not to make any improvements in their offers if they cannot prevent an interloper from making a better offer and winning away their customers. The Commission does give some recognition to this problem when it states that the conspiracy will be successful only if there is little import competition. But surely the conspiracy would be unwise if there was *any* import competition or any danger of import competition. Unless foreign producers also agree to stop innovating, the tariff or transportation barriers that protect the domestic industry will steadily shrink as the foreign products improve *vis-à-vis* those of the Canadian cartel. A *little* import competition would soon become quite a lot of import competition.

The conspiring companies could hardly limit their concern to imports. New domestic suppliers would be even more threatening. One must not overlook the fact that a conspiracy to stop innovation is necessary only if an innovation is sufficiently well known to be the subject of an agreement. It is hard to believe that an agreement, once made could be kept secret, and that the self-inflicted backwardness of the domestic industry would not be an open invitation for new domestic firms. The marriage of the people who know about the banned innovation with entrepreneurs or companies looking for investment opportunities would seem to anyone familiar with venture capital to be almost inevitable.

Mr. Chairman, Mr. Chairman

The second problem of the analysis is that it assumes that a conspiracy to arrest innovation is practical and possible. Let us try to imagine the agenda for a meeting of conspirators desiring to ban all further offer-improving innovations in their industry. To make things simple, let us suppose that the meeting is concerned only with offers to buyers, and that there are only thirty dimensions considered to be of major significance to the majority of customers. Since every dimension is capable of being used to transfer value to the buyers, the agreement will have to cover all thirty of them.

Suppose, now, that all dimensions are not uniform at the present time: One firm has just introduced a component that will give it a real advantage in the future. Are other firms to be given the opportunity to catch up? And if they have been holding their position by making a better offer in some other dimension, should those dimensions now be standardized, or should they be standardized only after the new component has been adopted by all?

Point of information

What happens if one firm finds a cost-saving production technique that makes absolutely no difference to the buyer but cuts production costs in half? Is this innovation to be allowed? If only one firm adopts the technique it may put itself in a position to withdraw from the agreement and puts its "friends" out of business.

Order, order

There are many more such questions that can be asked: What if a supplier offers some firms a better material at no extra cost? Is the training of salesmen permitted? What about faster deliveries? What qualifies as an innovation anyway? The most difficult question, however, is "Why?" Why on earth would oligopolists want to get together to eliminate innovation? The *Report* follows Fellner[37] in arguing that firms might resist innovation to prolong the life of their fixed assets. This judgement probably arises from the subconscious use of a simplistic model of the firm that makes no provision for competition as a process. Technological change is an integral part of the competitive process. It is not external to the market, like the weather, requiring only a reaction by managers. *A plant becomes obsolete because an innovator makes it obsolete!*

Perhaps the management of a particular company might be embarrassed about building a plant and planning to write it off over a ten-year period if its useful life turns out to be only eight years. But its embarrassment is likely to be much greater if it is slow to seize the opportunities presented by those developments that made the write-off necessary.

In any event surely the life of managers is much more pleasant if they can arrange to improve offers to all participants on a fairly regular basis. Unions are likely to insist on it, and if the unions' rewards are always at the expense of shareholders and consumers, the long-run prospects for the industry will not look very bright. It is hard to see why managers would find it in their interest to avoid or delay innovations for the sake of economic bygones Perhaps this is why the Commission did not provide us with any examples of such agreements.[38]

Innovation and size thresholds

On both *a priori* and empirical grounds it is universally accepted that larger scale promotes innovation, at least up to a substantial size of company. This proposition is accepted by the Royal Commission when it states:

> There is a general consensus among other studies that concentration aids innovation within the firm up to a threshold level, after which there is no further positive relationship.[39]

It is somewhat disappointing that the Royal Commission did not point out two problems, however. The first is the low quality of the data and the serious limitations of the research methodology. Statistical studies of innovation and change that try to arrive at an optimum size for companies that would apply to all industries are not very useful. Innovative opportunities vary greatly from industry to industry and from innovation to innovation. One must, therefore, remain very sceptical about rules of thumb concerning either company size or concentration level that are put forward as a guide to either merger or divestiture policy.[40]

The second disappointment is that the Commission did not spell out more clearly the differences that exist between Canada and the United States. In the United States, there has been an active divestiture lobby of academics and civil servants intent on breaking up some of the largest American companies. The intellectual battle lines have been drawn, and the conflicts show up in the research. If one reads John M. Blair's *Economic Concentration*,[41] one must also read John S. McGee, *In Defence of Industrial Concentration*.[42]

It is all very well for the Americans to break up their large companies. Indeed it is an activity that Canadian, German and Japanese competitors should encourage. (Generous research grants to an approved list of academic economists should do the trick.) Canadians should be applauding quietly on the sidelines when it is pointed out to the U.S. Congress that the oxygen steel-making process was developed by a small Austrian steel-making company (Voest) that was less than one-third the size of a single plant of U.S. Steel.[43] And if this information leads the American government to break up U.S. Steel a group of academics and all the steel makers around the world will, no doubt, be most pleased.

Canada, however, is in a somewhat different position. The small Austrian steel maker is a significant company. It was, and is, about the same size in steel making capacity as the largest Canadian company and is, in addition, more diversified. The Austrian company was both a manufacturer of machinery and a supplier of engineering services.[44]

At most, those who champion the cause of divestiture in the United States are able to point to some evidence that the amount of research would probably not be reduced if a few companies were broken up into smaller (but still very large) units. The point at issue is that research efforts (let us say, research expenditures per sales dollar) continue to increase with the size of the firm up to a certain threshold, at which point the amount of research effort levels off — but it does not decline.

Evidence from Canada

The Royal Commission noted that in 1964 only 40 companies in Canada would have exceeded the upper threshold of Scherer's estimate of the point at which R and D expenditures might be expected to level off.[45] The point, of course, is not how many companies in Canada are at the threshold but rather how many exceed it by a margin that makes due allowance for the low quality of the data and the conceptual problems of the research.

But if one takes seriously the charge that Canadian companies are too large, one must be sure that each of the companies in each of its industries is looked at individually — by experts who know a great about the present and future of all aspects of *each* industry. Such experts may not just be hard to find they may not exist.

Besides, knowing the industry very well our experts will have to take account of some general principles. For example it must be remembered that the potential payoff of research in a market of 25 million is very different from the potential payoff of the same research in a market ten times that size. Our experts could not, of course, look only at the overall size of a Canadian company. What matters most is the size of the *product division* for which a research program is designed. If Canadian companies are more diversified than their American counterparts, they will have to be bigger if they are to be expected to make the same research effort.

To be more specific: Scherer is quoted by the Commission as having concluded "that 'technological vigor' increased to the point at which the four-firm concentration ratio (CR4) reached 50-55%, after which increasing concentration had a depressing effect on innovation."[46] CAE Electronics is Canada's only manufacturer of flight simulators. To achieve a 50 per cent concentration ratio at the four-firm level would require breaking the company into at least eight parts. Are we to believe that CAE would be even more innovative and more able to compete on the world markets if we broke it up into smaller companies? It is a proposal that would appeal only to someone who knew nothing about the industry.[47]

Innovation and the number of firms in Canada

On *a priori* grounds, and even on empirical grounds (such as they are and to the extent that they apply to Canada), we should be safe in assuming that innovative activity for most Canadian manufacturing and resource-based industries is likely to be at a maximum if we have relatively few large companies in each industry. For exports, and for companies facing import competition, or the threat of import competition or new entrants, the optimum number could quite easily be one.[48]

For Canada, a graph relating number of firms to innovative activity for some industries might look like "A" in Figure 33. For other industries the appropriate graph might be "B" and for still others the graph would be a single point "C." All that we can be sure of is that different industries have quite different profiles and that the same industries probably have different profiles at different points in their history. There may also be industries that cannot be described on such a graph because an optimum innovation-imitation process is produced with some combination of large and small firms.

One conclusion seems clear: as far as the innovative-imitation dimension of competition is concerned, there is no convincing evidence that would support a government policy for Canada that attacks or discourages concentration.

CHOICE

Introduction

We left discussion of choice in Chapter 3 with the question of whether the value of choice (range, density, etc.) at a point of time, and the value of choice over time, would be different if the Canadian economy had more or fewer firms in each industry. As has already been pointed out, there is a classical and neoclassical legacy on this matter that has led to the assumption that more is better, and an infinite number perfect. It is clear from a more careful analysis, however, that whatever perfection there is in perfect competition, it does not arise from the amount of choice offered in each industry. Strictly speaking, the only choice offered is whether to buy more or less of the same product. We cannot assume from the structure of the market, therefore, that there is or can be a simple algebraic relationship between the number of firms or offers, and the benefits that arise from choice.

Since it has already been established that choice itself is a multidimensional phenomenon, we must be prepared to examine each of its various aspects in order to determine the optimum number, if indeed, there is such a thing as an optimum number that would apply to all industries.

Factors Affecting Optimum Amount of Choice

Heterogeneity of needs and range of choice at a point of time

It seems fairly obvious that the more heterogeneous are our needs individually and collectively, the more offers we would like to have.

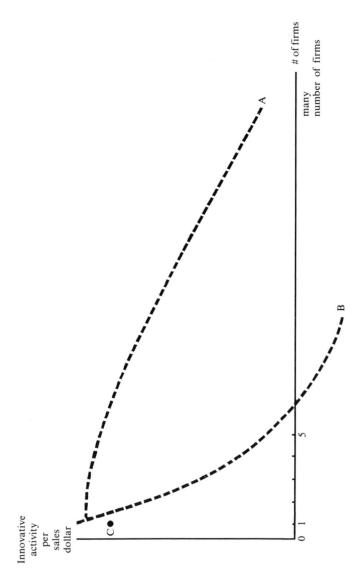

Figure 33 — Innovation and the Number of Firms

Furthermore, we would undoubtedly prefer a wider range to a narrower one. Three widely spaced offers would probably be better than ten almost identical ones. This desire for variety will be satisfied not just by the choice offered within an industry boundary, but also by having many different industries.

Even if we agree that, other things being equal, the more choice the better — a proposition that will be questioned shortly — it does not follow that we can say the more firms the better. As we have seen, firms generally make multiple offers and, often, over a very wide range.

Progress and range of choice over time

Not only do we want a range of products in the 1980s, we would also like to have a range of better products to choose from in the 1990s. The number of firms in each industry likely to produce the optimum rate of offer-improvement was the subject of the last section on innovation and number. There it was argued that the number of firms per industry most likely to optimize the rate of offer-improvement, especially in the Canadian context, was in the range of a few large firms (an oligopoly) rather than in the range of many small firms.

Suppose it happened to be true that the many small-firm industries option offered more choices than the few large-firm oligopolies. We would then have to decide whether we want more choice at a particular time, with no broadening of choices over time, or whether we prefer less choice from the oligopolistic industries at a particular time, but a more rapid rate of offer improvement and therefore a bigger range of choice cumulatively over time.

Importance of the product

We would surely expect that the importance of being able to choose is related in some way to the importance of the product. To have alternatives in religion and in politics is very important. To find that there is only one drugstore within walking distance, or that the local hardware has only one brand of nails, would normally concern us very little.

Inter-industry competition

We stated that industry boundaries can be drawn only on a judgemental basis, and can never be removed from the agenda. Nowhere is that conclusion more relevant than in determining the optimum number of firms in an industry. Normally we draw boundary lines between wood, aluminum, steel and cement, yet firms from all four industries compete vigorously to persuade utilities to string their wires on poles or towers using their products. Copper competes against aluminum for the electrical cable business. Satellites, copper, glass and sometimes the Post Office compete for the privilege of sending our messages.[49]

There can hardly be any quarrel with the proposition that the more inter-industry competition there is, the smaller the number of firms needed in each industry. One can also conclude that as knowledge and technology add more industries, and improve the versatility of our products, there can be a secular decline in the number of firms required per industry without any decrease in the utility of choice.

Control: protest and sovereignty

In describing the nature and role of choice we have already made the point that consumers need alternatives in order to direct production at any one time, and they need the alternatives of the new as well as the old to be able to control the direction of change over time. If, as most people believe, these objectives can be achieved in politics with relatively few competing political parties, it is difficult to see why satisfactory consumer control cannot be exercised over dishwashers and roller skates with relatively few competing firms.

Costs of choice

All the elements of choice we have outlined involved a cost to both buyers and sellers, and the costs would, for the most part, increase with the number of offers. Additional offers to consumers mean that more information must be collected and processed.[50] If more choice means more and smaller firms and if smaller firms mean higher costs (i.e. the industry is one in which costs fall with scale and/or learning) then more choice may also mean more expensive products. It is possible, although in most situations far from practical, to conceive of a function relating the utility of choice against the cost of choice. Presumably buyers will opt for less choice and fewer firms the higher the cost of choice and the lower the benefits.[51]

Independence

We have already noted one of the reasons Adam Smith gave for preferring that the grocery trade be divided among twenty rather than among two: there was less chance of their combining together in order to raise the price. There can be no doubt that if two or more competitors sacrifice their independence and agree to make the same offer, choice will be affected. Whether a specific agreement destroys or enhances choice and/or competition depends on the circumstances. This problem is so vast, however, that independence or aggressive assertiveness has a section to itself.

Conclusion

Now let us combine all of the relationships we have been considering — progress, control, cost, and so on. What can we conclude about the ideal number of firms? If the object of our choice is that one picture that is to highlight an already furnished room, there can hardly be too much choice. To satisfy our need for white thread, however, we seldom look beyond the first spool we find.

What happens in the range between these two extremes? First of all, we can reject "perfect competition" as a means of optimizing choice whether we are considering the amount of choice offered at a point of time or the improvement in choice over time. Second, we *cannot* reject monopoly in the unique-offer sense, because every unique offer adds to the *range* of choice available to us. Third, we can reject monopoly in the restricted-entry sense. A prohibition on entry by definition prevents a willing buyer and seller from accepting and offering a choice that otherwise would be available on a voluntary basis.

The difficult question, however, does not concern the extremes of perfect competition and monopoly; it concerns the middle ground. Will choice be adequate in a world of competing monopolies and oligopolies? Or should public policy be aimed at pushing the number of firms in the direction of the perfectly competitive structure? Should we accept the fact that Goldilocks hopped into Baby Bear's bed after trying only two others, or should we redesign our early childhood training to encourage young ladies to spend more time "playing the field"?

A self-test

Try a little introspection. How many options did you seriously consider: (a) in the purchase of your last automobile? (b) in the selection of your last house or apartment? (c) in the choice of your last job? (d) in the selection of your spouse? or (e) in the determination of your religion? If you accepted your family's religion, married the girl next door, took the job that happened to come up because it looked interesting, and bought the third house you looked at, you are unlikely to look for an infinite amount of choice on matters of less importance. You will probably not be too disturbed to find that there is only one drugstore within walking distance or that the local hardware carries only one brand of nails.

From the point of view of choice, all things considered, a world of competing monopolies and oligopolies may not be such a bad place to live. Come to think of it, this is not too far removed from the economic structure of most advanced industrialized democracies that have brought their citizens the highest standard of living ever known to humanity so far.

INDEPENDENT ASSERTIVENESS AND ENERGY

Introduction

For reasons that will become apparent as we go on, it is convenient to combine independent assertiveness and energy in this discussion of the optimum number of firms. Independent assertiveness was described in Chapter 3 as behaviour consistent with the goals of excellence, achievement, or survival: of being the best, of being better than most or than some, of doing better than last year, or simply of surviving. It does not mean pretending that rivals do not exist, or that there is no such thing as mutual interdependency. Nor does it mean atomistic behaviour that is stupid and self destructive. It does not mean avoiding any and all agreements.

The question for which we now seek an answer is whether there is likely to be any systematic relationship between the number of firms in an industry, and the spirit and behaviour consistent with independent assertiveness, and with putting forth a reasonable amount of energy. If there is such a relationship, we would like to know what range of numbers of firms might be best. We should also consider whether there is likely to be a relationship between number of firms and the possibility and probability of making an agreement or an arrangement that will materially interfere with the making of progressively better offers.

The X-theories of Competitors

X-inefficiency or laziness

The father of the X-inefficiency idea is Professor Harvey Leibenstein[52] whose oft-quoted article paints a picture of business behaviour which, while mildly stated, is not very flattering in its implications. Professor Leibenstein begins by making an equally unflattering observation about economists, or at least about those economists who have spent time worrying about the geometry of competition and monopoly. He says, "Empirical evidence has been accumulating that suggests that the problem of allocative efficiency is trivial."[53] After setting out very briefly the empirical and *a priori* grounds for believing that the welfare loss attributable to the existence of monopoly is hardly worth mentioning, he goes on at some length to review the evidence from the work of social scientists and management consultants who have been concerned with raising productivity. The burden of this evidence is that (1) estimates of the possible increases in static welfare by abolishing monopoly are generally a fraction of one percent; and (2) the estimates of gains in output or reductions in cost that could result from the application of existing knowledge or technology is very much larger.

Studies are cited indicating gains "from 20 to 50 per cent" and from "7.5 per cent to one of 291 per cent [with] about half of the cases falling between 43 per cent and 76 per cent."[54]

The fact that such large increases in efficiency are possible, leads Leibenstein to conclude: "People normally operate within the bounds of a great deal of intellectual slack,"[55] and, "The simple fact is that neither individuals nor firms work as hard, nor do they search for information as effectively as they could."[56]

The explanation for all of this apparent sloth and indolence is that:

> In situations where competitive pressure is light, many people will trade the disutility of greater effort, of search, and the control of other peoples' activities [managerial functions] for the utility of feeling less pressure and of better interpersonal relations. But in situations where competitive pressures are high, and hence the costs of such trades are also high, they will exchange less of the disutility of effort for the utility of freedom from pressure, etc.[57]

It is probably safe to say that most subsequent textbooks on industrial organization have accepted the importance of X-inefficiency[58] (though the triviality of allocative inefficiency is not usually given the same emphasis). Typical of the current acceptance of this principle is the following statement by Professor Green:

> A lack of "competitive pressure" on monopolistic firms may result in a rise in costs as well as price. That is, the average cost curve may shift upward. This so-called "X-inefficiency" may arise if the slack afforded to the protected monopolist results in his failure to adopt least-cost methods of production, or if he fails to purchase inputs at lowest available prices.[59]

Preference for monopolistic results

Lack of competitive pressure is not assumed to arise simply from the fewness of firms. It is further reinforced by a preference for monopolistic results. Professor Green provides us with four propositions that constitute his rationale for a strong competition policy. The first of these is "Firms will prefer the price and output levels that would occur under monopoly to those that would result under competitive conditions."[60]

Professor Stigler was quite explicit that this preference for the fruits of monopoly would push collusion to the limit:

> Of course any stopping point on the road to full collusion will necessarily be inconsistent with profit maximization; that is, the stopping point will be non-rational.[61]

Preference for monopolistic practices

It is one thing to argue that managers have a preference for the fruits of monopoly; it is another thing to argue that they are prepared to engage in monopolistic activities to achieve them. There are three different reasons that have been given to explain why businessmen engage in monopolistic practices, in addition to the obvious one that the path of monopoly is presumed to lead to riches. First of all, it is assumed by many writers that monopolists have security. In 1935 Hicks said that they enjoyed "a quiet life"[62] an off-handed remark that has gained credibility with its frequent reiteration by tenured professors.

The second is less obvious and is related to laziness. That collusion or co-ordination can take place without effort is suggested by Fellner when he mentions that the "proper understanding of the oligopoly problem requires placing the emphasis on the fact that on oligopolistic markets there exists a strong tendency towards the spontaneous co-ordination of business policies."[63] Nicholson suggests that competition requires vigor, while monopoly, requires only restraint:

> An oligopoly situation is typically one in which the participants can compete vigorously but to their mutual detriment or alter- natively restrain their aggressive instincts and reap a mutual profit.[64]

The third argument for supposing that businessmen will engage in monopolistic practices is that they have no regard for the law. Thus Gorecki and Stanbury tell us that:

> The effectiveness [of the] . . . legislation is a function of three factors: the probability of being caught; the remedy (i.e., fine imprisonment); and the benefit of the restraint of trade. The higher the probability of being caught, the higher the level of fines and the smaller the return to the restraint of trade, the greater the likelihood that compliance with the law will be secured. This view reflects our belief that businessmen act *as if* they were rational economic men, weighing the economic benefits and costs of engaging in restraint of trade which may result in committing an offence under the *Combines Investigation Act*. This view is consistent with the fact that the group beliefs and social mores of businessmen (and indeed the community as a whole) appear not to attach a very high, if indeed any, stigma to a prosecution under the *Combines Investigation Act*.[65]

The X-theory of managerial behaviour is now explicit. Managers are X-inefficient because they are lazy. They have an X-preference for monopoly gains, and an X-preference for engaging in monopolistic activities because of their X-laziness, their X-greed, and their X-indifference to whether or not they obey the law.

Support for an X-rating

That businessmen are often X-rated should not be too surprising. An unflattering image of executives can be drawn from a number of different sources. First is the obvious fact that not all businessmen are lovable or credible or honest or modest (but the same can be said of any other group). Second, neoclassical economists have constructed models of firms and markets which, as we have seen, almost automatically label businessmen as monopolists, and credit them with having monopolistic power. Ironically, the more successfully they compete, the stronger their monopolistic position is presumed to be.

Third, the regulation and prosecution* itself has become something of a competitive activity, if not a sport. The teams have been chosen — mostly self chosen — and as with many rivalrous situations, the audience attaches labels to the good guys and the bad guys. The players themselves, especially the good guys, can, by their emotional involvement and their public utterances, add to the stereotyping. As often happens in the hockey rink, language (and press releases) can become somewhat abusive, and charges may not always be factually correct.†

Academic bias

Finally, the serious academic literature on the matter of competitive business behaviour is biased to a degree that few academics understand or appreciate. The bias that arises from the use of over-simplified price-theory models of the firm is a recurring theme of this study, but it must also be pointed out that the investigation and trial processes themselves provide a very one-sided view of business.

---

*Some businessmen think it should be spelled with an "er."

†In the *middle* of the recent sugar trial, the then head of the New Democratic Party along with the Crown Prosecutor made headlines with a charge that the conspiracy of the companies cost Canadian consumers 75 cents per hundred weight (which happened to be about the amount that Commonwealth producers were able to retain of the $1.00 preferential tariff granted by the Canadian government to Commonwealth sugar producers.) The amount was not, however, expressed as a payment of $0.0075 per pound by Canadian consumers to our Commonwealth brothers slaving under a tropical sun, but rather as a $125 million rip-off.[66]

Despite the impropriety, inaccuracy and, probably, the illegality of the statement, the companies decided rightly or wrongly that nothing could be gained by answering the allegations. When one couples this with the impropriety of the criticism of the court, by the cabinet minister in charge of Consumer and Corporate Affairs, one begins to realize that one cannot tell the good guys from the bad guys without a program.

It sometimes happens that companies may be charged with a very specific illegal act for which Consumer and Corporate Affairs has reasonably reliable proof before a charge is laid. Charges regarding conspiracy, however, are likely to be made when there is a complaint or a suspicion, but little else. For this reason the first overt act of the government department is in most cases a simultaneous raid on the premises of all the suspects.[67] The raid is popularly known in the legal profession as a "fishing expedition." It is, of course, important for those who authorized the raid to justify their actions. The purpose of the search of the company records, therefore, is to find documents that justify the raid, show the company and its executives in a bad light and maximize the chances of having a "successful" trial. The game has been started; the teams have been chosen; and may the best team win — somehow.

Unrepresentative documents

The selection of documents that emerge from this process does not result in an unbiased sample of the company's records. Nor can those documents even pretend to demonstrate the nature and scope of the competitive process.

Of course the companies are free to produce other documents, ones that were ignored by the combines investigators. To some extent they do but, in my experience at least, the bias in the selection of documents is not corrected and for this there are several reasons. First, when a company is before the courts it must still meet its payroll. Most executives in a large company are not involved in a trial and those who are, are still trying to do their jobs. This means that those managers who are involved in a trial are the authors or recipients of only a fraction of the intra-company communication that is relevant to the competitive struggle. It is more by good luck than by good management when an executive remembers a memo that might be useful for the defence. Second, most managers have had very little exposure to neoclassical price theory and even less to criticism of that theory. Unfortunately, therefore, managers will generally have very little understanding of the economic theory that lies behind the charges and for that reason will not be likely to see how a particular document might be useful to challenge either the theory or the facts of the case.

"X" and Douglas McGregor

Those familiar with Douglas McGregor's work[68] must be struck by the similarity between the views on businessmen we have just cited and "Theory X," which McGregor used to try to capture the "popular" (and quite inaccurate) views held about the behaviour of workers. It seems most appropriate that Leibenstein should have chosen the letter X for his laziness hypothesis, for the very first X-assumption McGregor cites also alleges laziness: the average human dislikes work and will avoid it if he can.[69] His second X-assumption is that the average person must be coerced or punished to achieve organizational objectives. Finally, the average person wants to be directed, wants to avoid responsibility and wants security.[70]

McGregor points out that these generalizations do not accurately describe the state of knowledge about people and in this view he is strongly supported by Maslow,[71] Herzberg[72] and many others. He then goes on to present his "Theory Y," which conforms more closely to the empirical data about human behaviour. In his criticisms of theory X and in his development of theory Y, McGregor makes a number of observations that more accurately represent the accumulated knowledge about people. He states, for example, that man does not dislike work, that external control or the threat of punishment are not the only means of achieving organizational objectives, that man's higher needs will motivate his actions once his lower needs are satisfied and that — again apart from the satisfaction of basic needs — "emphasis on security" is not an inherent human characteristic.[73]

It is the major thesis of this study that economists have built a theory X of competitive behaviour based on an overly simplified, and, for purposes of studying competitive behaviour, an inappropriate theory of the firm. Moreover, they have an overly simplified and inaccurate theory of managers and of managerial work. In contrast to this theory X, we believe there can be constructed a theory Y of competitive behaviours that will more accurately describe managers and the firms in which they work. Our immediate objective is to develop one critical aspect of this theory Y that shows that independent assertiveness, rather than conspiracy, is the more natural and more likely state of affairs in most circumstances.

A Y-theory of Competition

Man does not dislike work

In constructing a Y-theory of competition, the first assumption that we might make happens to be the same as that of McGregor: man does not naturally dislike work; indeed, he may enjoy it.* There should, therefore, be no surprise that some professors with tenure, and some businessmen who have something close to it, should continue to work hard.

---

*Exceptions, such as small sons weeding the garden, immediately spring to mind.

Preference for competitive results

In the previous section, the second X-theory put forward the proposition that managers prefer the end results of monopoly to those of competition. In contrast the Y-assumption is that the reverse is the case. It is the end result of successful competition that is desired. Neither of these assumptions, X or Y, denies that larger baskets of goods are preferred to smaller ones. The Y-assumption suggests that successful competition must generally be relied on to increase the size of the basket.

There is, however, another more subtle and more important difference between these assumptions. As we have seen, economists who implicitly or explicitly apply static analysis are likely to assume that the end result of monopoly is a larger basket for the shareholder — and perhaps also for the manager — and a smaller more expensive basket for the consumer — and perhaps also for the employee.

If one starts with the hierarchy of higher and lower needs of the psychologists, rather than the maximizing-the-shareholders'-basket hypothesis of the economists, it is very much easier to believe that managers usually aim at achieving simultaneously the best product offer, the best worker offer, the best shareholder offer, and the best supplier offer. Achieving and maintaining these larger baskets will be closely associated with the results of competition, not monopoly. Even on economists' own terms, it should be recognized that there is nothing inconsistent with making the best offer to consumers *and* pursuing the long-run goal of profit maximization. Indeed, the idea that a firm could prosper in the long run, or even in the short run, by worsening the offers to consumers to improve offers to shareholders, would strike most businessmen as arrant nonsense.

Preference for competitive activities

The third X-theory was that monopolistic practices would be preferred to the competitive practices of independent assertiveness because not only would profits be higher, but also the pursuit of monopolistic practices would also mean less work, more security, and a clear conscience (with regard to law breaking). We have already dealt with the confusion between monopoly and competitive profits and offers. We have also discussed the laziness theory. On the basis of these two considerations alone, we might conclude that firms are more likely to prefer competitive activities.

A more difficult issue is raised by the question of security or, as McGregor prefers, safety. In the need-hierarchy of McGregor and others there is to be found a basic need for safety, which ranks just above the physiological needs of food and shelter. Even to non-psychologists this ordering of needs seems to be no more than common sense. When we are starving we are likely to be most concerned about obtaining today's dinner. After we have solved the problem of today our next order of priority will no doubt be the securing of a food supply for tomorrow. Once we have been assured that our basic needs have been secured both for today and for tomorrow, we can then take them for granted. We forget about dinners, and move on to the fulfillment of higher social, ego, and self-fulfillment needs.

When we apply this thinking to the security problem of competitors we can come up with what appears at first sight to be two quite different results. The usual assumption — an assumption that clearly applies in some situations — is that security will be sought in an agreement among competitors. Conspiracy and security can be linked together almost by definition if, in the absence of a conspiracy, competition poses a real and immediate threat to the physiological needs of the people involved. One of my early observations of the competitive process involved just such a case.[74] There were five small businesses in the industry in question, all of them were facing bankruptcy. Atomistic competition had reduced the level of prices well below costs, and losses were high. It was my impression that the businessmen would have been prepared to conspire despite the law, had they been willing to sacrifice their spirit of independent assertiveness, their bloodymindedness and their intense dislike for each other.

The ultimate security blanket

The need for security can be satisfied, however, by taking quite a different tack — one that fits into our Y-theory of competitive behaviour. Unenforceable conspiratorial agreements can never offer much security; being the best can. The businessman who sleeps easily at night is the one who knows he has the best product, the most loyal, productive and best-paid labour force, suppliers who feel nothing but goodwill towards him, and consumers who feel they are getting the best deal available.

If a firm is to have the best quality of product and *if it is to retain its lead over time*, it cannot enter into an agreement to standardize quality with all competing brands. The firm cannot have the most highly motivated labour force and also have an agreement with competitors to standardize the total offer to all workers. Real, long-term security cannot be purchased by making unenforceable agreements with competitors. Except for those periods in which a price war threatens the viability of all firms, the desire for security can best be met by independent assertiveness, not collusion.

Moreover, there are higher needs in the human need hierarchy that lead one to expect managers to struggle to improve through rivalry, rather than to be the same as everyone else through conspiracy. Self-esteem, the need for self-respect, autonomy, status, reputation, self-actualization and so on, all suggest a quest for better performance and achievement. These higher goals are difficult to reconcile with a cartel that prevents or even slows down the rate of offer-improvement, or that freezes a company's position *vis-à-vis* its competitors.

. . . by bread alone

These higher, pro-competitive needs do not conflict with the need for security that may prompt a conspiracy. The latter is activated by a physical threat to survival, and should disappear when the threat is removed. In exactly the same way, our need for air becomes paramount if we have a pillow over our face. We are unaware of our need for air when it is plentiful. As McGregor has said, "Man lives by bread alone when there is no bread."[75] An industry facing bankruptcy may have a completely different view of its need for security than it would in a different period when doing reasonably well.*

A price war may break out, threatening to drive price down to a marginal-cost level which, as is often the case, is below variable cost. Then all firms in the industry may face the threat of bankruptcy. In such circumstances, it would not be hard to believe that the firms would follow a leader who raised the price; or even that they might make an explicit agreement to end the price war and reduce the amount of short-run insecurity. At the same time, the rivalrous activities through which firms seek to obtain long-run security by outcompeting their rivals should continue unabated. Indeed, the "brush with death" is likely to heighten the resolve to continue with the long-term objective of strengthening the competitive position, i.e., the performance of the firm.

The need for security over the long run prompts firms to expend more than the average amount of energy in a quest for better-than-average performance. This independent assertiveness continues even during periods in which some limited joint action is taken in response to a serious threat, be it a price war, a new import, or an innovation in a competing industry.

---

*It is interesting that in the metal-culverts case, the Crown used the argument that the firms were facing difficult times to support the reasonableness of its suggestion that they were, therefore, probably conspiring.

The businessman as outlaw

The Gorecki-Stanbury assertion that, given any incentive to do so, businessmen will willingly conspire because they are indifferent to whether or not they break the law, says as much about the law as it does about businessmen. Provided, in the words of Charles Dickens, the law is not an ass,[76] however, it is difficult to reconcile the need-hierarchies described by the psychologists with indifference about breaking the law.

There are two additional observations that should be made in support of the Y-theory of competitive behaviour — the view that independent assertiveness is the rule and not the exception. First there seems to be a good deal of satisfaction, pleasure and utility to be derived from engaging in rivalrous activities. It is difficult to see why businessmen who try very hard to prove their competitive superiority on the golf course should not also try to prove their competitive superiority in business.

Secondly, rivalry breeds rivalry. Competition, whether in the ring or in business, is not a tea party. It is difficult to think kindly of the son-of-a-bitch who has just landed a hard right on your chin. It is equally hard to view with charity that wretched competitor who has just stolen one of your most profitable accounts. Macy's doesn't tell Gimbel's, C.P. doesn't like C.N. The McGill Faculty of Management listens attentively to someone who doesn't like Western. And executives of the Royal Bank don't tell "Newfie" jokes; they tell Bank of Montreal jokes.

The juxtaposition of the X and Y hypotheses raises quite a number of questions. The two that are most important for our study are, first, does the theory or the evidence suggest we need a large number of firms in order to make businessmen work harder? Second, do we generally need a large number of firms to ensure independent assertiveness and to stop them from conspiring?

Expenditure of Energy and the Number of Firms

It is Leibenstein's hypothesis that there must be a good deal of "competitive pressure" to get businessmen out of bed in the morning. McGregor's counter-suggestion is that they will get out of bed for no other reason than that they want to get on with the day's business. McGregor's hypothesis is based on psychological research; Leibenstein's evidence is based on productivity studies.

Unfortunately the productivity studies do not really address the question at hand; nor do they justify his conclusion. In not one of the cases that Leibenstein quotes does he show that the increase in productivity was the result of competitive pressure in the sense in which we are using the term. It is only an inference on his part that competitive pressure, unaccompanied by the setting of the experiment, the consultant, and so on, could produce the same results. In effect what Leibenstein seems to say is that it is possible to increase productivity by upwards of, let us say, 25 per cent per year. The economy achieves overall a productivity growth of, say, 2.5 per cent.[77] The difference must be explained by lack of competitive pressure.

In fact there are quite a number of factors that could explain the apparent difference between the 25 and the 2.5 per cent. Let us enumerate just a few.

• Extra care and affection given to one child, one member of the tennis team, or one group of workers can produce dramatic results, but care and affection are not free goods and in any event equal care and affection given to all would not necessarily produce the same results. (The differential input effect.)[78]

• Measuring how quickly a person can run a hundred yards is not an acceptable method of determining how many miles that person can cover in a year. (The sprinting effect.)

• The cases that get written up in the learned journals or get advertised by consultants are generally the successes, not the failures. (The selection effect.)

• Observers, consultants, executives, and others often put extra time and effort into the experiment without counting their own inputs (for supervision and encouragement if nothing else). (The extra inputs effect.)

• Controlled productivity studies work best with a measurable, unchanging product or offer, so that the entire productivity gain shows in a single dimension of a single output — usually units produced. In the real world, however, improvements have to be shared among all dimensions of all inputs and all dimensions of all outputs. Perhaps, therefore, our overall productivity is much higher, all things considered, than appears from counting simply units of output. (The diffusion effect.)

• There are good samaritans, managers and consultants, and there are so-so samaritans, managers and consultants. The former are few, the latter are many. When one of the few temporarily replaces one of the many in an experimental situation, large increases in productivity can be obtained, but there are not enough good people to produce the same results on a large scale. (The quality of input effect.)

False generalizations

We can accept the accuracy of every study quoted by Leibenstein and still question the validity of blowing up the experimental results to full economy scale. We can also question the spread between total aggregate effects and laboratory results, but even if we accepted the finding that the rate of productivity could be doubled or quadrupled, it would not follow that more competition is the key.

According to Leibenstein's data, the key could just as easily be more behavioural scientists![79] And even if we went one step further and accepted the proposition that more competition would increase productivity, we are still no further ahead in deciding the optimum number of firms. Two large firms vying for first place (and avoiding price wars) might be the combination that would produce the highest rate of productivity increase.

Let us try another approach. Suppose that Leibenstein is right and that X rather than Y describes the energy output of managers. Suppose just for the moment that not only are all managers X-types, but that they are uniformly so. All of them get out of bed at 12 noon. Adding more of these 12 o'clock risers won't help customers who want to shop early. Competition would be a slow-motion activity carried out mostly in the afternoon. Numbers could hardly matter very much.

Since it stretches the imagination to think that Leibenstein's X-theory could be 100 per cent right and McGregor's Y theory 100 per cent wrong, let us suppose that McGregor is only 50 per cent right. Let us pretend further that managers can be neatly divided into two homogeneous groups of X's and Y's, with 50 per cent of all managers falling into the early-rising, Y category.

It is, I think, implicit in Leibenstein's argument that one early riser per industry would force all managers to get out of bed in the morning. With these simple assumptions we can relate the optimum number of firms to the probability of having a whole industry with no early riser. With the X's and Y's evenly distributed in the population and with the managers drawn at random for each firm, there would be only six chances in 100 that an industry made up of only four firms would be without an early riser at its head.

With multiperson management teams in each company, one might also reason that the top persons in each team would be Y's, not X's, so that even with an equal X-Y split, it might be unusual to find a company with X's at the top. Those who have observed managers and tried to measure expenditure of time or effort, have given managers a passing grade for maintaining an unrelenting pace[80] and long hours.[81] Rothwell's study of 700 managers[82] found that a complex variable designated as effort was the second most powerful variable in explaining achievement. (The first was level of education, which itself indicates earlier effort.)

Moreover within each educational group the amount of effort explained high and low achievement. There is, thus, some statistical support for the old adage that hard work pays off. We can be reasonably sure that even with an assumed 50-50 split of X's and Y's in nature, the executive suite will be filled with Y's.

The Nature of Managerial Work Revisited

The remaining big question concerns the relationship between the number of firms in an industry and the amount of independent assertiveness (as opposed to harmful collusion). Before we proceed, however, it will help to clarify our thinking if we elaborate on the discussion in Chapter 2. There we spoke of the nature of the firm and of the industrial structure in which managers must face the choice of being independent or of seeking a collusive solution to their problems. We shall find that our understanding of the firm has a significant bearing on the judgements we are likely to make about the possibility and probability of collusion.

Anyone who has ever attended business-academic conferences on competition will be aware of the wide gulf separating the views of businessmen and economists. The main reason for these differences, it seems to me, is that the businessmen's views of competition are based on very large, experiential, open-ended models. Economists are more likely to fit experience and evidence into the price-theory models of business they have acquired in learning their trade. It is important to try to make explicit the differences that are likely to exist between the models of economists and businessmen, and to see just how these differences are likely to shape conclusions about independent assertiveness, as opposed to collusion.

Simplicity of the economist's price-theory model

It is one of the purposes of a model to simplify reality in order to make it more manageable and understandable. Both the businessmen and the economist simplify to some extent. The businessman does not review all his experience, and that of all his colleagues before making each and every decision or prediction. He does generalize, and he makes many of his decisions on the basis of quite simple generalizations. On the other hand, simplification and the overlooking of one detail may prove the undoing of a manager. Because of the risks he faces, a manager is more likely to avoid over-simplification, and to leave his models detailed, complex and as open-ended as possible.

The economist, on the other hand, especially one who needs to explain the economy to teenagers in one semester, and who in any event has had little or no experience as a manager, will find simplification much more rewarding. Nowhere is this more obvious than in the price-theory model of the firm. We are not now concerned with the question of how many grains of truth there are in the model, or how useful it is pedagogically for some purposes. Instead, the question is whether such a model is appropriate for the study of competition. Will it tell us about the process and problems of achieving a successful conspiracy? The most obvious difficulty is that the very simplicity of the model, and the fewness of the variables involved, invite the erroneous conclusion that conspiracy is easy.

The nature and importance of price

According to the usual price theory model, we might assume that the *only* item on the agenda is price.* Indeed one can think of a couple of relatively uncomplicated situations in which price might in fact be the only item on the agenda. The first might occur, for example, in a construction project where a buyer spells out (or tries to spell out) every conceivable dimension of the product and leaves only the price to be determined by bidding. In such a case price *is* the only thing that matters, in theory at least, but only because every other dimension of the product has been described and specified.

In practice, for products of any complexity, it is almost impossible to specify every dimension. This means that after the contract is signed by the buyers and the lowest credible bidder, the buyer must then bargain from a rather weak position to settle on supplementary payments (price escalations) to cover all the mistakes and the items that were overlooked in the specifications. Omissions have included such details as the flight deck on an aircraft carrier, the coffer dam on a hydro project, and partitions between the ladies' and men's washrooms in a new office building.

The second situation in which the setting of the price is equally uncomplicated occurs in those particular markets in which the products are sufficiently similar to require identical *pro forma* prices. If conditions are such that all companies *must* advertise the same price, obviously there will have to be some way in which that one price is determined. The method may be trial and error, follow the leader, leave-well-enough alone, or, over time, some combination of methods. A meeting is obviously one such method. And if the meeting limits its discussion to that one number it could in fact be quite short. Many of

---

*Lest it be thought that this is an exaggeration consider the following. Eight textbooks on *Managerial Economics* have been sent to me by publishers for adoption in an economics course for future managers in the last two years. Four have not so much as a reference to advertising as selling costs. A fifth mentions advertising but it turns out to be a reference to advertising as a product not advertising as a managerial tool. A sixth has a scant two and half pages on advertising and promotional expenses (as compared to seven pages on pure competition!) Only two, including the Canadian text by Evan Douglas, go as far as having a chapter on advertising as promotional devices. Even managerial economics has not moved far away from pure price theory!

the combine cases are concerned with whether or not such a meeting took place.[83]

A vast chasm

Even in these two special situations, however, price theory does not give an adequate description of the competitive problems or the competitive process. It is an undeniable fact that nowhere are the economist's and the manager's models of reality further apart than on the subject of price. A comparison of these models reveals three very important differences concerning the way in which price is viewed.

The first is that the economist's price model, true to its name, deals with price and little else. To a manager, price matters, of course, but it is only one of many different dimensions of the offer. The second, which follows closely from the first, is that most of the dimensions constitute a means by which benefits can be transferred from the seller to the buyer. The agenda of the meeting of the conspirators has no longer only a single item. A salesman of even a simple product who could not think of 20 different ways of making his offer to a buyer more valuable, without touching price, is not much of a salesman.[84] The agenda grows longer.

Third, on the classroom blackboard, price is almost always a single number — a point on the Y-axis. To the manager, price is almost never a unique number. It comes closest to being a single number in a take-it-or-leave-it situation, but even in that case there are usually some price-related variables that can usually be determined by the buyer, or can be the subject of negotiation. In most other situations prices are a *set* of numbers that may or may not be written down on a price list.

Pro forma price is only the tip of the iceberg

So long as there is considerable product homogeneity, there is almost bound to be a *pro forma* price. This is the most visible of all the prices. The *pro forma* prices of all brands considered to be close substitutes — as in commodity markets — are almost bound to be the same. For one firm to have a higher price would be the equivalent of placing an ad in a newspaper to tell the buyers the company was not prepared to be competitive.

The *pro forma* price will often be accompanied by discounts. The discounts may be for prompt payment, large contracts, long contracts, off-season purchases, off-standard goods, transportation allowances and promoting the product; or they may exist simply because the buyer has led the seller to believe that someone else's discount is larger.

The uninitiated might assume that the actual price would be determined by taking the *pro forma* price and deducting the discounts. It might also be thought that this number would be the one that appeared on the invoice. But such is not necessarily the case. The invoice price might be the *pro forma* price for a cash sale, whereas the goods may have been delivered two months earlier than the date shown on the invoice. The grade and the price may be shown for a lower grade than was actually shipped. The point of delivery may be shown as the seller's warehouse, whereas the actual delivery could have been the buyer's place of business, i.e., the transportation charge was absorbed and not shown on the invoice. The meeting of the conspirators on a price agreement is going to spill over into the afternoon.

Non-price dimensions

The agenda of the conspirators can hardly stop at price. The shading from price to the so-called non-price dimensions of the product is imperceptible. An agreement on price will be of little use in promoting a quiet, secure life for the conspirators if one of their members is willing to provide more credit, more service, free delivery, better-grade material, overly generous trade-in allowances, conversion loans, and so on.

During the 1930s when the National Recovery Administration codes were in effect in the United States, firms were often under orders not to cut price. As an aid to administrators, the Division of Industrial Economics printed a list of the various ways that prices could be reduced, or sales obtained, without giving the appearance of cutting the price. The list contained about 200 practices including such items as:

- Payment becomes due only when buyers receive money from other sources.
- Guarantees against defective goods.
- Accepting return of obsolete, discontinued or unsaleable merchandise.
- Sales subject to trials.
- Resale guarantees.
- Coupons.
- Sales promotion awards.
- Engineering services.
- Assuming reversed telephone charges.
- Financing of payments owed to customers.
- Trade-in allowances.
- Cartage allowance when buyer receives goods at the factory.
- Wilful manufacture of substandard products.

- Settlement of old accounts at less than full value.
- Misdated invoices.
- Invoices omitting terms of sale.[85]

The meeting to set price is quickly turning into a one-week conference.

Offer improvement competition

None of the foregoing should be taken to mean that price is unimportant to either buyers or sellers. The problem with price-theory models is that they make price the *only* dimension that matters, and price wars the *only* kind of competition likely to benefit customers. Such a view, however, suggests a lack of understanding of the very limited scope of price competition.

The annual reduction in the real price of any article is limited by the annual improvement in productivity, which has been running, let us say, between two and three per cent per year. On a one-dollar article, in other words, management would find that each year, on average, it would be able to improve *all* its offers in aggregate only by about two and a half cents.

Before we reduce the price to consumers, however, let us consider who else has claims on this modest amount. Governments will, no doubt, want a share, and unions will want some untaxed fringe benefits and increased wages. Indeed, the unions may argue that the full two and a half cents belong to them. Suppliers may feel that they deserve more. Consumers may want some improvement in all or most of the dimensions other than price: the product should be better packaged, longer lasting, more easily serviced; it should consume less gas and so on. How much of the two and a half cents will be left for a real price reduction? Very little.

Total versus consumer offers

Consistent with the economic model's overemphasis on price is the overemphasis on consumers. Obviously managers must devote a great deal of time and attention to their buyers. But they would be foolish indeed to lose sight of the fact that it is the total set of offers made by the firm to all participants (and to the firm by all participants) that determines the viability of the organization. This implies that the interests of *all* participants have to be considered. The agenda issues become even more complicated.

Independent Assertiveness, Conspiracy and the Number of Firms

We now come to what is perhaps the most critical question of all: What is the probable relationship, if any, between the number of firms in an industry and the degree of independent assertiveness in their behaviour?

The X-theories might be summarized in this way: firms want the larger profits that come from conspiracy and they are willing to conspire to get them. They are willing to conspire, first, because they have no regard for the law and second, because with conspiracy comes security and less work. Furthermore, the X-type managers operate in firms and markets that facilitate conspiracies.

Our Y theory of competitive behaviour points in the opposite direction. While accepting the desirability of more rather than less, the Y-assumptions suggest that larger material and psychological rewards generally flow from superior competitive performance, not from the uniformity of performance required by an effective conspiracy. Moreover, the "higher" needs described by psychologists suggest behaviour more consistent with independent assertiveness than with conspiracy. Security in the long run is also more likely to be the product of superior performance. Conspiracies are most likely to be contemplated when, in their absence, the viability (the physiological needs) of all or most firms is threatened.

Even then the scope of the conspiracy is likely to be limited to the removal of the immediate threat (ending the atomistic price war) and is not likely to retard the search for better long-run performance. Indeed the threat, even if safely averted, should impress on firms the great advantage of making the best set of offers in the industry. Finally, the Y-theory of competitive behaviour can be supported by the fact that competitive activities have a utility in and of themselves, and that rivalry tends to breed more rivalry. When we consider our Y-type managers in their realistic Y-theory environments, we find that in most cases conspiracy is neither practical nor desirable.

Your choice: "X" or "Y"?

The relevance of the X- and Y-theories, just to make it explicit, is that if the X-view is essentially correct, the public's protection against conspiracy must be found in two laws: the Anti-combines law and the law of large numbers — the latter reflecting the view that conspiracies are more difficult to organize if there are many firms. If the Y-theory is essentially correct, even a single-firm monopolist is likely to devote considerable energy to making offer improvements. An industry composed of a few large firms is likely to make offer improvements at a rate that is not likely to be increased by breaking them up into a large number of smaller firms. Which theory comes closer to describing the real world?

An X-believer would, perhaps, put great reliance on the concentration literature. Since this is the subject of next chapter, we shall leave the literature aside for the moment.

One of the strongest *a priori* pillars of the X-faith is the assumption that monopoly achieved by conspiracy produces higher profits than independent assertiveness. For the uncreative, the unproductive and the unwilling, this may well be true all of the time. In periods of an atomistic-type price war, it may be partially true for all competitors part of the time. But for the strong, the ambitious and the intelligent, a conspiracy that effectively stops them from making progressively better offers will not, over the long run, produce either security or achievement.

Good "Y" drives out the "X"

Another reason for rejecting the X-theories is that a reasonable rate of offer-improvement should be expected even if the Y-characteristics apply to only a few individuals in each industry.*

Though arrived at in quite a different way, this position is consistent with that taken by Fama and Laffer. In their view, when at least two non-colluding firms are part of an industry, there is no clear-cut relationship between the member of firms and the degree of competition.[87]

Moreover, there are only certain situations in which conspiracies can be limited to a few people within each firm. When a tender is being readied for submission, it is quite possible for company personnel to work up different aspects of the contract and to submit the recommendations to, say, the president. It may be left to him alone to determine that final bid. If five companies in an industry follow the same internal procedure, then an agreement among five firms could, in fact, be effected by an agreement among five individuals.

---

*Research on third party intervention in the Western coal industry[86] turned up the intriguing fact that on two occasions government officials had tried to get the industry together to stop price wars. Since the thesis of the article was that labour unrest could be traced to underlying economic, social, and political disorders we tried, without much success, to find when there were price wars and when there were not. During one interview we asked if there had been a price agreement during a certain period. Our interviewee thought for a time and finally replied that he could not really remember, but since so-and-so had been president of the XYZ Colliery at the time, we could be sure that even if there had been a formal agreement it did not mean anything.

In those situations in which the similarity of the offers demands a uniform *pro forma* price, it is again easy to imagine an explicit agreement, knowledge of which is confined to only one or two people in each company. But an arrangement for a *pro forma* price is simplicity itself compared with an agreement to limit or even to slow down offer improvements.

Blackmail

Except in the case of tenders, a conspiracy that really attempts to control the offers to consumers, or to factor inputs, must involve a large number of people in each conspiring organization. *Any* law-abiding manager or any disgruntled and disappointed one would be in a position to expose the conspiracy. More importantly from the point of view of the internal logic of the X-hypothesis: if managers generally have a disregard for the law, surely they will disregard all laws — including the laws concerning blackmail. Were a company to commit itself to a conspiracy comprehensive enough to stop offer-improvements, it would place itself in a very vulnerable and precarious position. One is left with the conclusion that comprehensive conspiracies are unlikely to work in an industry that contains either one honest individual or one rogue. Companies that make the mistake of trying to live by theory X will perish by theory X.

But companies *do* conspire

To all of this a supporter of theory X may well reply that his theory is proven by the legal record. Companies have, after all, been found guilty of conspiring. Since the legal record in Canada has just recently been reviewed by Professor Green, let us make use of his work.

To begin with, Professor Green does not direct the same gratuitous insult at businessmen as do Gorecki and Stanbury. Specifically, Professor Green states:

> Left to themselves, firms will often attempt to achieve a monopolistic position (via collusive agreement, merger, predatory or other monopolizing or restrictive behaviour) if there are no legal prohibitions or limitations against such activities. (We may call this the "Adam Smith" postulate.)
>
> These attempts will be successful in a sufficient number of cases to warrant legal prohibition or limitation.[88]

In a sense, then, his case rests only on the proposition that conspiracies will happen only often enough to warrant a law. This is a proposition with which very few businessmen and probably no economists would disagree. Professor Green goes on to try to estimate or guesstimate the extent to which businessmen conspire. This is an important exercise, not only because it provides evidence on the relative merits of theories X and Y, but also because it is an indication of how much public policy emphasis should be placed on anti-combines legislation.

To begin with, it must be pointed out that the evidence is strongly biased in favour of the X-hypotheses. When it comes to conspiracy, the eyes of the law are, with only a few exceptions, focused on price. And the only price that is easily visible, or even looked for in most cases, is the *pro forma* price. Evidence of vigorous competition with respect to other dimensions, even including other price dimensions is all but ignored.

The conspiracy literature

Green's conclusion that "collusive behaviour. . .is still widespread, and a way of life in a number of industries"[89] is serious support for the X-hypotheses and deserves our careful attention. The authorities he quotes are Naylor;[90] Reynolds;[91] Eastman-Stykolt;[92] and the actual conspiracy cases.[93] Naylor's two-volume treatise covers the period 1867 to 1914 — the heyday of mercantilism and skullduggery — and while the book is as fascinating as it is biased, it can hardly be considered, even without the colourful adjectives and the value judgements, as a treatise on competition.

Reynolds' more serious book, *The Control of Competition in Canada*, dealt with a later, but still pre-World-War-II, period. In many respects, this book is perceptive. Without naming it, for example, he assumed a theory X. However, although the term "competition" appears in the title, the reader is left to infer its meaning. As might be expected from the date of publication, 1940, competition means almost exclusively price competition, and then, as now, the economists, the lawyers and the courts saw little need to go deeper than the visible list prices. Uniformity of list prices for reasonably homogeneous products tells us next to nothing about the state of competition.

The latest study (published in 1968), and the one that must be considered most seriously, is that of Eastman and Stykolt. Green's summary of their findings is that:

> formal collusion appears to have been important in only three of the industries, although evidence of identical price and the use of basing points is indicated in four others. Avoiding price competition, if possible, remains a major objective of business, but collusion may not be as common (or as necessary?) as it once appears to have been.[94]

In assessing this evidence we must note, once again, that the authors and the courts were dealing with identity of the list prices of relatively homogeneous products, not real prices, and certainly not with all of the dimensions of competition.

Professor Green concludes:

> Thus while public knowledge of collusive behaviour has increased, the incidence of combination may have declined somewhat. Nevertheless, the evidence of combines *reports and prosecutions, which in any event reflect only the tip of the iceberg*, suggests it is still widespread, and a way of life in a number of industries.[95]

The iceberg multiplier

Icebergs, depending on the amount of air and rock entrapped, show about 10 to 12 per cent of their volume above the water line. The implied rule of thumb, therefore, is that we should take the "reports and prosecutions" and multiply that number by nine to arrive at the true number of violations. "Reports and prosecutions", however, are hardly the appropriate statistical base, unless one is prepared to say that a man is guilty as soon as he is subjected to an investigation or a charge. Surely convictions would be preferable as a multiplicand, if one felt justified in using a multiplier.

But what is the case for having a multiplier at all? Undoubtedly the implicit justification is that since conspiracies are illegal they must be committed in secret, and only occasionally is the secret exposed. The multiplier is the reciprocal of a crime-detection rate. The theory is that when offers are reasonably homogeneous, businessmen break the law in secret by setting the same price, and then make a great public display about competing and being different.

The opposite would be closer to the truth, however. The public display is for the benefit of consumers and competitors. It is designed to promote the idea that prices are uniform across the board. The conspiracies — with the *buyers* not the competitors — result in offers that are different — "But don't tell anyone or I'll have to withdraw my offer."

Evidence from the linen supply case

Anyone who believes that the Canadian judicial record demonstrates the ease and generality of agreements, should read and reflect on the linen-supply case.[96] Here an association of small businessmen supplying essentially a laundering service openly agreed to regulate the terms on which they would make offers to their customers. The evidence in this case proves *not* the ease and naturalness of an agreement, but rather its complexity. The industry operated under the constraint that its services had to be cheaper or better than those its customers could provide for themselves. It also had to compete with paper towels, to which customers could easily convert. The industry had to face the continued emergence and re-emergence of competition.

Despite the fact that the association operated openly (no doubt in the belief that as suppliers of services, i.e. rentals of clean linen, they were right next door to being a union and were thus exempt from the law), it had to resort to the use of frequent meetings, a long and detailed set of rules, an official incorporation under the *General Corporations Act*, surveillance of members and non-members, and even the hiring of a detective agency! Yet as products go, it is hard to imagine a less complicated one.*

"Evidence" of the cases

The difficulty with using combines cases as evidence of the existence or absence of competition is that no one — not the prosecution, not the courts, not even the defence in most cases — makes any attempt to establish either the amount of competition or, its *raison d'être*, the rate of offer-improvement. It is only a slight oversimplification to say that in most conspiracy cases the prosecution is trying to prove by evidence or by inference only one thing — that the defendants met to discuss price or market shares. If it can establish that such a meeting took place, the prosecution need go no further.

In preparing a case it obviously makes no difference to the prosecution whether a price "arrangement" applies only to *pro forma* prices or whether it does nothing more than take most prices out of the range in which they were atomistic i.e., between short-run marginal cost and average total cost. But, as we have already remarked, the fact that an industry has the same *pro forma* price and is avoiding an atomistic price war no more proves it is not competing, than an agreement among belligerents not to use atomic bombs or poisonous gas proves that the countries are really at peace.

Let us consider an actual case.[97] In June of 1968, Alcan announced an increase in the price of the ingots used by aluminum extruders to fabricate a wide range of products. These included such diverse items as window frames, light standards, step ladders and lawn furniture. Alcan sells aluminum ingots to a number of extruders who have no ingot capacity and to its own extruding division.

The nub of the case lies in a classical managerial problem to which we have already referred.[98] The top management of any large company tends to be made up of executives who represent the point of

---

*It was interesting that the charges referred to a period from January 1, 1950 to September 30, 1960, and that "rental" was added to the lists of activities with respect to which it was illegal to conspire on *August 10, 1960*! You really must keep your eye on the "good" guys.

view of "their constituents." These executives do not always see eye
to eye. The Alcan case hinged on just such a difference of opinion.

The executive in charge of making satisfactory offers to customers
wanted as low a price as possible for extruded products. Aluminum
extrusions must compete with wood, fibreglass, steel, nylon, plastic —
and even cement. Sales are always easier at a lower price. The executives in charge of making satisfactory offers to workers, suppliers and
shareholders obviously and naturally viewed the world somewhat
differently.

In the course of the debate, Mr. G.K. Clement, who was
responsible for sales of extruded product, produced a memo to
support his case. Unwittingly he also supplied the Crown with the key
document on which it based its case. The memo reads:

> I have talked to everybody on basis of 1.2 cents/pound extrusion
> ingot price increase across the board and carried over into
> extrusion prices. All have agreed to implement accordingly
> . . .["U"] in favour of any increase; . . . ["V"] agrees that there
> is little point in trying for additional extrusion price increase;
> . . .["W"] feels we are brave to try to increase at this time.
> . . .["X"] is happy and will go along. . . . ["Y" (an Alcan
> employee)] will follow same.[99]

In order to make sense of this memo one has to remember that there
were those in the company who wanted a higher price for extruded
products. The salesman, Clement, was saying between the lines "I have
talked to the people who know[100] and they agree that I am right
and you are wrong. Furthermore don't blame me if your revenue from
extrusions does not respond as you expect. "W" feels we are brave to
try to increase [at all] at this time' ".

In assessing the meaning and wording of the document, one
must also take into account the fact that Alcan was both a supplier and
a competitor. As a supplier Alcan would *have* to communicate with
its buyers. In order to maintain their goodwill and their continued
patronage Alcan would *have* to assure them that they would be
treated fairly, i.e., they would not be squeezed by Alcan, the competitor. As a supplier of ingots Alcan was not a monopolist in any sense
of the word.

What is most surprising about the case is that it was brought to
trial at all. So far as we are aware, the Bureau of Competition Policy
did no analysis of the state of competition or of offer-improvement.
The Crown did not appear to feel it was necessary to prove that any
buyer had ever negotiated with two or more buyers only to find that
he was confronted with identical offers. Even if the Bureau was
suffering from a case of pernicious price myopia, one would have
expected actual prices to fall within its range of vision.

The Alcan case demonstrates one thing. Very little is to be learned about competition from reading judgements in combines cases. Let the academics beware!

One is not entitled, on the basis of cases, or multipliers or the three authorities quoted by Green, or on *a priori* grounds, to assume that today, conspiracies to limit the rate of offer-improvement to customers or suppliers are either common or practical or that they justify a stronger competition act. Independent assertiveness and the expenditure of a considerable amount of energy are likely to be the rule in the vast majority of situations. Neither the amount of energy expended nor the degree of independent assertiveness is likely to be much affected by the number of firms in any industry.

EXPERTISE

To be able to utilize or develop a complex type of equipment, an advanced technology and a specialized work force are clearly advantages that are likely to increase, especially in the Canadian context, with the size of the company. So, too, is the advantage of learning.

As a general proposition, which allows ample room for qualifications and exceptions, it must be agreed that larger firms are likely to have the advantage of more expertise. Since size and number of firms are inversely related in any industry of any given size, it follows that if public policy is not to be neutral it should lean in the direction of fewer, not more, firms.

Mention should be made of the fact that the total quantity of expertise in a country like Canada is by no means a constant. If certain types of jobs are not available, young people will stop preparing for them. And even if they do they will move to the United States or take another job for which they were not trained. In any event the stock of expertise will be less.

FAIR AND EQUITABLE RULES

In his book *Ethics in Business*, Baumhart reports that on the basis of his survey:

> One-half of the interviewees spoke at length about the relation-
> ship between competition and industry ethics. Their main theme
> was: Beyond a certain point (call it the ethical optimum of compe-
> tition), as competition increases, so do unethical practices."[101]

This is followed by a diagram, which we have reproduced as Figure 34. Except for the inversion of the scale on the Y-axis, it closely resembles Figure 1, which was used to illustrate the second approximation of competition in Chapter 2.

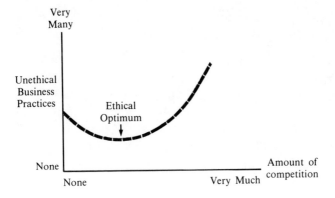

Figure 34 — Ethics and Competition

To a structuralist, who equates the amount of competition with the number of firms, this diagram might suggest that an ethical optimum was more likely to be achieved by an oligopoly than by either a monopoly or a "perfectly competitive" industry. It seems more logical, however, to suggest what the diagram illustrates is that when competition starts to threaten the physiological needs of participants, ethical standards are "relaxed."

We have already suggested that when individuals or firms are faced with the threat of bankruptcy or annihilation, they may seek desperate and even illegal remedies. Baumhart's interviewees, whose responses are illustrated in Figure 34, seemed to associate "very much" competition with just such situations. In a similar vein, the lawyer of one of the five companies involved in the atomistic price war described earlier suggested that the intense, atomistic competition had dehumanized the owner-managers. Fair dealings and honesty had become "luxuries" that no one in the industry could afford.

Death before dishonour?

But firms of any size can be confronted with the choice of death or the probability of dishonour. There is no reason to expect that the frequency of such a choice or the reaction to it should vary systematically with the number or size of firms in an industry. Such ethical problems are more likely to be related to other factors such as a high ratio of average total cost to marginal cost, extensive use of bidding, the dependence of the firm on highly volatile markets, and above all else, the danger of atomistic price competition.

Even if there is a tendency for the size of a company and its incentives to misbehave to vary together, it must be pointed out that there are two systematic factors that work in the opposite direction. First, a one-man business can keep a guilty secret more easily than can a two-man business. The more people who are involved in a company and in its wrongdoing, the harder it must be to keep it secret, and the more liable the company becomes to exposure by honest employees or to exposure and/or blackmail by employees seeking money or revenge. Laboratory simulations testing for implicit collusion should always be conducted among *teams* of players, not individuals.

The second factor is that larger companies are much more in the public eye. The larger a company, the harder it is to avoid adverse publicity and, knowing this to be true, one would expect large companies to maintain a tighter discipline among their employees.

POWER AND THE OPTIMUM NUMBER OF FIRMS

The neoclassical response to the question of the optimum number of firms was, of course, that each industry should have a large enough number of buyers and sellers to emulate as much as possible the conditions of perfect competition. One of the attractive byproducts of this type of market was held to be that it reduced power to a minimum, and divided the residual between buyers and sellers.

The desirability of perfect competition is now almost universally rejected, but the full implication of this rejection insofar as power is concerned is not always appreciated. There is something intuitively appealing about a balancing of power, and yet one of the reasons we reject perfect competition is that the rivalrous activities from which we benefit, and which are absent in perfect competition, require power. Inevitably, they require and result in unequal power.

Let us summarize those aspects of power that relate to firm size and the number of firms in an industry. First, we should note that it cannot be our objective to minimize power. The competitive process requires that competitors acquire power. Moreover, big jobs and major innovations will require large resources, which means, if nothing else, the acquisition of spending power. But even little jobs and small innovations require that each firm have the power to administer its own affairs; this means being able to do such things as set or negotiate price and the other terms of its offer to customers and to factor inputs.

Second, it cannot be our objective to balance power. The rivalrous process must result in winners and losers. It is in the interests of households that resources shift into the hands of the winners, not the losers.

Third, we cannot object to large firms (and, therefore, in Canada, at least, few firms) on the grounds that large firms have more internal or discretionary power. Power, and unequal parcels of power, will inevitably be distributed throughout all institutions regardless of size. There is no reason to believe the average worker in a small company is any more vulnerable to this kind of power than is his counterpart in a large company.

The abuse of power

Fourth, we *can* object to the *abuse* of power. As far as discretionary power is concerned, a mean, small farmer can mistreat his hired hand and his unhired wife and children. A mean president of a large company can mistreat his executive vice-president. The solution for the victims in both cases is in having recourse to alternatives. Alternatives mean mobility; this, in turn, can be translated into freedom of exit and freedom of entry.

As for external power, we should be concerned about any single institution, be it a company, government or union, that acquires monopolistic control over an essential product or service. We can afford to be less concerned if we can be sure of being able to mount an effective challenge should the need arise. Effective protest can be assured when there is freedom of entry. As consumers, if we are unhappy, we can facilitate freedom of entry: we can publicize the sins of the old product, buy the new ones, and encourage our friends to buy it.

In Canada we give one party a monopoly on the right to govern, but voters retain the extremely important right to choose an alternative within five years. Maple Leaf Mills has won the right and the power to supply a large fraction of the total flour consumed in Canada, but it faces the constant challenge that its customers have retained the right to vote for a different make of flour the next time around. The ultimate abuse of power is the unnatural blockage of the right of entry or exit. Power must always be challengeable, so that its abuse can always be punished.

What implication does this have for the optimum number of firms in an industry? It implies that provided the abuse of power and bad performance can be punished, it is quite possible for a single firm in an industry, with all the power that derives from its position, to perform satisfactorily and in the best interests of consumers. Two or three firms increase the speed with which bad performance and irresponsibility can be punished. The key, however, is freedom of entry. This does not mean that every man can challenge the position of the monopolist. It means, rather, that *someone* is able to challenge it, and that with the support of the disenchanted, the challenger can be successful.

Power *per se* presents no problems; unchallenged but challengeable power presents no problem. Unchallengeable power is the problem. Provided challengeabilty is maintained, it matters very little how many firms there are in an industry: in most circumstances there is no obvious reason why a few should not be adequate, and there are many indications that a few would be optimal.

CONCLUSION

We can summarize the argument of this chapter by answering a single question: are the various participants in an industry likely to receive the best range of offers, and the best rate of improvement if the managers and workers in the industry are organized into a few firms or into many? The sum of the behavioural considerations discussed in the chapter suggests that the answer is "a few" — with one reservation: "few" will find it easier to conspire than "many." Is this a serious reservation? The argument of this chapter is that it is not.

Chapter 7

The Concentration Doctrine

INTRODUCTION

The Issue

Perhaps the most critical issue in the structure-of-industry literature is the relationship thought to exist between the number of firms and profit rates, and more practicularly, the reason given to explain that relationship. As we have seen, many economists believe that the number of firms in an industry is of prime importance in determining the behaviour of managers. Their hypothesis is that profits gained by collusion are monopolistic and higher than competitive profits. Since profit maximization is assumed to be rational behaviour, businessmen will collude if they can (implicitly, if not explicitly) and will be able to do so more successfully when their numbers are few. The proof of this hypothetical pudding is believed to be found in an inverse correlation between the number of firms and profitability in all industries. The fewer the firms, the higher (the more monopolistic) their rates of profit will be.

Concentration Defined

The two related variables, profit rates and fewness, present all of the usual problems of statistical measurement. Of the two, fewness is by far the more difficult. The concept of fewness is usually considered under the heading of "concentration". This term refers to one of several different ways of measuring the fewness of competitors. In essence, concentration is intended to measure the extent to which economic activity, assets or, by implication, monopoly power are held, or concentrated, in the hands of the largest firms. There are two types of concentration measures. The first might be called "total corporate concentration": it purports to measure the importance of the largest companies in relation to all companies or to the total economy. The second type is industry concentration, which focuses on the importance of the biggest firms in each industry in relation to the total industry. Usually the industry-concentration studies take the firm as their unit of account without regard to the number of plants a firm may have, but plant concentrations have also been estimated; that is, an attempt has been made to answer the question: what is the importance of the largest plants (as opposed to companies) in relation to the total industry?

Relative importance can be defined using different criteria: gross or net assets, value added, shipments or employment. The concentration ratios or measures can also be calculated in different ways. Most common is the percentage of industry output accounted for by a given number of firms. If the four largest firms account for 80 per cent of output, the industry is more concentrated than if the four largest firms account for only 10 per cent. Another measure is the inverse of the foregoing: the number of firms required to account for some given percentage of the output of an industry. An industry in which 80 per cent of the output is accounted for by three firms is more concentrated than an industry in which it takes the output of the 20 largest firms to add up to this percentage.

Whatever measures are used, concentration studies provide estimates of the fewness of firms in an industry, and they are obviously inspired by a structuralist view that the number of firms is important in explaining the amount of competition.

The Data

Before going further with the analysis, it would be well to issue a warning: the statistics used to study the concentration-profit relationship are among the lowest quality data with which economists have to work. What follows are just a few of the more obvious problems.[1]

Imports and exports

The study *Concentration in the Manufacturing Industries of Canada*,[2] which was undertaken and published by the Department of Consumer and Corporate Affairs, (and which, by the way, was cited by the then-Minister to prove that Canada needed a stronger competition bill) does not even attempt to measure the effect of the openness of the Canadian economy. Production in Canada is the "universe" studied, and actual or potential foreign competition is simply ignored. Even on structuralist grounds, the number of sellers of any product must include all importers. To pretend that Chrysler Canada has only General Motors and Ford to worry about is nonsense. As for Canadian products that enter international markets, it is difficult to understand what meaning a concentration ratio of Canadian producers is supposed to convey.

Inter-industry competition

The numbers compiled in concentration studies pretend, moreover, that inter-industry competition does not exist. But a company that manufactures steel siding knows very well that it must compete with manufacturers of aluminum siding, bricks, stone (natural and artificial), wood, stucco and cement, not to mention other manufacturers of steel siding in Canada and in all exporting countries.

Seller-buyer rivalry

As we saw earlier, rivalry occurs not only among sellers but between sellers and buyers. It makes some difference whether a few sellers face many buyers, just a few buyers, or only one buyer.

Implication of dominance or control

The logic on which concentration studies are founded is that large companies with large market shares attained those shares by eliminating competition and are now in control. A few years ago the North American big-three automobile producers held over 80 per cent of the North American car market. This was generally taken to mean that they "dominated" or "controlled" the car market. Did they? In shopping for a car was a particular customer dominated by a G.M. salesman any more than by a Toyota salesman? If the individual buyer had not lost his or her power to choose, how can it be argued or implied that 80 per cent of them had?

If three companies succeed in winning 80 per cent of the market, it does not mean that 80 per cent of the buyers have lost their right to buy a car from other than the big three. Notwithstanding the fact that there is no way for the big three to decide individually or collectively that they will sell 80 per cent of the cars next year or the year after, the language of concentration implies that they control the industry. The recent decline in the market share of the big three[3] together with the huge deficits they have incurred make it somewhat easier to argue that market share means market share and little else.

The number of competing products

Probably the most serious shortcoming of the attempts to measure concentration is that they do not measure what they are supposed to measure: they do not measure the amount of choice available to an individual buyer who wants a specific product at a particular place at a particular time. By the same token, they do not even measure the number of competitors a seller faces.

If we could, in fact, measure what a concentration ratio purports to measure, it seems clear that many if not most of the so-called unconcentrated industries would have to be broken up into their product and geographical segments and would then reappear as concentrated industries. For example, according to the 1971 government report there are 42 enterprises manufacturing office equipment, making it a relatively unconcentrated industry.[4] But does this mean that if you wanted to equip an office in Edmonton with natural-wood, western-style furniture there would be 42 companies ready to seek your business? The answer is, "No." The point is that customers do not buy "office furniture" or "pharmaceuticals" or "sporting goods" (all low-concentration industries). They buy, instead, a credenza that holds liquor and looks as if it does not; they buy corn plasters that do not look like corn plasters under sheer stockings; and they buy a hockey stick that is cheap enough so that father will not get upset when it is stolen or forgotten.

The shortcomings of these measures of concentration at a given time are insignificant compared with their shortcomings when used to make comparisons over time, or between different countries or regions. It was in response to these and other difficulties concerning concentration and economies of scale that Donald J. Dewey quipped "when measurement is very difficult, economists, like other people, succumb to a very human temptation: they believe what they want to believe because there is no good reason to believe otherwise."[5]

While a great deal more could be said about the shortcomings and the built-in biases of the data on concentration, we shall not press further with the subject. In any event, a correlation between concentration and profit is consistent with the Y-theory of competition as well. The inconclusiveness of the empirical tests is one reason we have spent so much time describing competing models.

THE EVIDENCE

There are many attempts to support the view that:

Concentration → Collusion → Profits,

or that:

Many of these were limited to a search for nothing more than a simple correlation between a measure of profitability and a measure of concentration. In almost all cases such a relationship was found to exist. Therefore, it was widely accepted that the conspiracy hypothesis had been established. As thought on the subject progressed, however, researchers began to appreciate the fact that concentrated industries had other characteristics (in addition to few enough firms to make conspiracy easy) that were either unique or were not characteristic of unconcentrated industries to the same extent. Because it seemed likely that some of the profitability of concentrated industries could be explained by these other variables, researchers began to make use of multiple correlations. As might be expected, when these other factors are taken into account, part of the apparent difference between the profitability of concentrated and unconcentrated industries is explained. Indeed, sometimes the profit difference disappears altogether — during inflationary periods, for example.

A review of these studies up to 1973 is found in an article by Leonard W. Weiss[7]. On the basis of his review and his own considerable research on the subject he concludes, "altogether, there is still plenty of reason to believe on both theoretical and empirical grounds that high concentration facilitates tacit or explicit collusion."[8]

Not every one agrees. In his own survey of empirical research and methodological problems of this topic, Professor Phillips concludes,

> What do we know from the empirical studies of relations between structure and profitability? Very little, it appears. Market concentration may be the cause of high profits, or conversely market concentration and high profits may be the result of superior performance by a few firms. . . . Better theory, better data, and above all, better econometrics are needed before policy can be based on anything other than in-depth institutional studies of particular markets.[9]

For somewhat different reasons Harold Demsetz also questioned the conspiracy hypothesis. He pointed out that on the basis of the empirical evidence:

> We now confront the proposition that successful collusion is practised only during non-inflationary periods by firms that advertise or use capital intensity — unless, of course, market concentration should be less than 70 per cent.[10]

Yale Brozen extended the time frame of several previous studies which had found "a close association between high levels of concentration and persistently high rates of return on capital," and concluded: "such an examination discloses a lack of persistence of 'high' rates of return in highly concentrated industries and denies the asserted basis for the deconcentration recommendations."[11]

However this question is ultimately decided, it is possible to accept a weak correlation between concentration and profits without accepting the Concentration → Conspiracy → Profits paradigm. What we called earlier "the Y-theory of competitive behaviour," which is the subject of the last part of this chapter, also suggests the existence of a weak relationship between concentration and profits, but rejects the likelihood that conspiracy is an important explanatory variable.

The Concentration — Profit Evidence: Data and Model

Undoubtedly the strongest support for the contention that concentration produces conspiracy is the link found by many economists between concentration and profits. Assumptions made about firms and managers, moreover, led to the belief that conspiracy was both easy, and in the self-interest of managers and owners. The logical conclusion, then, was that conspiracy was the main explanation for the higher-than-average profits found more often than not in concentrated industries.

Those who do not believe in the importance of conspiracy can attack the theory-X conclusion from two different points of view. They can question the data, or they can accept the data and provide a better explanation for the relationship between concentration and profits.

Certainly the data are not very reliable. They understate the number of competitors at the concentrated, big-company end of the scale and overstate the number at the unconcentrated, small-company end. The data are next to useless for making comparisons over time.

The main quarrel of this study will not be with the data, however. An acceptance of a Y-theory of competitive behaviour would lead to the prediction that a weak relationship between concentration and profits could quite easily exist. The factors that produce higher-than-average concentration could be expected at the same time to produce higher-than-average profits.

Let us examine this issue first from a managerial point of view. What should ambitious young managers do who are intent on outperforming those in their graduating class? If we approach the problem in this way, we can perhaps see why concentration and profits may be interconnected.

A Strategy for Achieving an Above-average Stream of Profits

The first move of our upwardly mobile young managers should be to give some thought to the industry they plan to enter. It seems obvious that they should avoid a static or declining industry — unless they have an idea that will breathe new life into an old industry. For under the constant spur of the dollar vote there will be a continuous transfer of resources from industries with unchanging offers to buyers and suppliers to those that can make progressively better or more appropriate offers. This is not to say that entrepreneurs with above-average intelligence and imagination cannot prosper in a static or declining industry; they would, however, be playing in a game that would reward their talents and efforts with a lower payoff than could be achieved elsewhere.

Where's the action?

Our young managers might ask how these dynamic industries are to be identified. That is easy. The share values of companies in the industry will be high and climbing; price/earnings ratios will be high, indicating great prospects for the future. The industries will be "news-worthy." Science reporters as well as business editors will be writing stories about the new products and processes.

But our young managers would do well to look beyond the newspapers to the products and processes themselves. If the product and the process are very simple and appear to be unchanging, there may be little scope for increasing the importance of the product either by making it better or by making it cheaper. If on the other hand the product and/or the process is complex and the dimensions are numerous, the prospects for further development and for the application of superior intelligence would seem much better.

Having picked dynamic, challenging and growing industries, and having quickly achieved a position of some importance, our managers must think about a set of strategies that will make their firms prosper. The most important is undoubtedly to acquire an above-average team of workers, fellow managers and suppliers, and a group of generous and enthusiastic investors. While there is undoubtedly considerable scope for interpersonal skills, training on the job, public relations and so on, ultimately the firm that hopes to acquire superior inputs will have to make superior offers. Not only that, but it must hold out the prospect of even better offers in the future.

Who gets what?

If the strategy of making above-average returns by employing above-average inputs is successful, the question will be raised of how the benefits should be divided. It is likely that all participants will feel that part of the surplus they have helped to create belongs to them. Would it not be good strategy, therefore, to see that they *all* received a bonus? As we have already recognized, contracts cannot, in fact, be drawn up that will specify the performance of workers, or suppliers.

The good will of all participants is most important if the success of today is to be repeated tomorrow.

As part of the task of maintaining this good will, the successful manager will no doubt find it useful to devote a considerable amount of effort to showing all participants — especially workers and customers — that they are receiving a fair share of the value their loyalty has helped to create. A cynic might believe that the desire to give the appearance of fairness would generate nothing more than an advertising and public relations campaign. In the long run, however, the best way of convincing claimants that they are being treated fairly is to treat them fairly.

Experience is the best teacher

The learning curve provides an especially compelling reason for a company to grow by acquiring more customers and more resources. In those industries in which learning appears to be important, it would be good strategy to emphasize growth. Learning, it should be understood, does not come from simple repetition, or from having more workers do exactly the same thing: learning means giving talented people the opportunity to experiment, to do things differently, and to take risks.

It is evident that learning is a human and not a corporate experience. The firm that encourages learning will have an added incentive to retain its "learned" contributors. Learning, therefore, simultaneously provides the means for making better offers and the incentives to pay at least some of the additional revenue to factor inputs.

Our ambitious managers will also be on the lookout for innovations or opportunities that would give an advantage to larger rivals (or to themselves if they were larger). Sometimes these will appear almost as textbook examples, as in the case of a supplier of equipment who can demonstrate five sizes of earth-moving machines that promise a lower unit cost with each larger machine. More often, however, the opportunities to produce more at a lower per-unit cost are generated on the premises through the application of imagination and hard work.

The customer is always right

A strategy to achieve superior performance would be most unlikely to work unless the managers kept a sharp eye on the needs and wishes of their customers. Is there a customer, or, better still, a group of customers, who are not now being well served by the exciting range of products? Can a new product line be added that would have more appeal to this market segment?

Our discussion has probably gone far enough to enable us to make the important observation that *many of the strategies designed to produce superior performance will, if successful, also produce increased concentration.* Seizing new market opportunities, taking full advantages of economies of scale and of learning, adding to the dimensions and usefulness of the product are all likely to make the firm grow and by the same token reduce the number of firms in any given industry. If successful, our ambitious managers will have created larger firms and more concentrated industries, will be paying the shareholders better returns, will be making better offers to customers, workers and suppliers and will in these and other ways earn the enmity of those who hanker for a world of perfect competition.

Static Versus Dynamic Analysis

Most economists could accept the idea that rapid change, involving scale, learning and attractive products, is likely to produce a set of dynamic industries that are above average in both profitability and concentration. What is likely to cause difficulty, however, is understanding how such a situation could persist. In effect we are postulating *continuing* differentials in profitability between dynamic and static industries.

To economists, such a condition represents a condition of disequilibrium. Just as nature abhors a vacuum, so the economic system is supposed to abhor a condition of disequilibrium. The extra returns earned by the resources in the dynamic sector are supposed to attract more resources, and competition is supposed to drive all returns back to the golden mean. Let us consider more carefully this move to an equilibrium position.

In the first place, we have noted that Professor Yale Brozen found movements towards the golden mean of equilibrium have indeed tended to occur. He updated the analysis of three studies that had identified profit differences between concentrated and unconcentrated industries for an earlier period of time. He found that the profit rates of the most profitable industries tended to fall while the profit rates of the least profitable ones tended to rise.[12]

No set timetable

The second observation is that even within equilibrium analysis, there is no set timetable for the elimination of differential rates of return. In a perfectly competitive world with perfect knowledge and complete mobility, differential rates of return should not occur in the first place; but if they did, they would be quickly corrected.

The real world is not like that, nor would we want it to be. The process of innovation and change creates rewards that provide the incentive for those who successfully innovate and take risks. Instant adjustment, even if it were possible, would destroy those incentives. We must expect, therefore, that differential rates of rewards will persist, and should persist, over considerable periods of time.

Also within the framework of conventional equilibrium analysis, the operation of consumers' sovereignty is expected to direct the shifting of resources from less desired industries (which receive fewer dollar votes and are, therefore, less profitable) to more desired industries (with more such votes and hence more profits). Again, there is no set timetable for this process. There is no reason why the shift of consumer preferences could not take place over a long period of time. There is no reason, therefore, why a difference in profit rates and a corresponding steady shift of resources should not also persist. In a static world, presumably, consumers would ultimately "settle down." Profit rates would equalize, and the shifting of resources would eventually stop. There are many who do not expect that ever to happen and many more who hope that it will not. But even if it did, the differences in profit rates might be expected to persist for a long period of time.

The market is a process

The next observation is much more important. As we have stressed repeatedly, a strategy designed to achieve above-average rates of return will involve not a once-and-for-all set of superior offers, but a continual *stream* of superior offers. Equilibrium may be a useful concept in economic sciences for some purposes, but in management science it is a dreaded terminal disease.[13] It is in equilibirum, as well as in the long run, that all innovators are dead. There is no reason why an industry cannot retain its dynamic characteristics for half a century or more and why within that period it should not always be above average in both its rewards to its factors and its degree of concentration. Its offers over that period will no doubt change sufficiently such that each dynamic industry might more properly be considered to be a succession of related industries. If, by the process of maintaining a superior rate of offer-improvement, they can continue to win dollar votes there is no reason why they should not continue to maintain above-average profitability for decades on end. As Adam Smith the Second advised — never sell your I.B.M.!

A final observation is that one should expect that over time the quality of the resources that are attracted to the static and dynamic industries will become less and less homogeneous. The opportunities, the challenges, the risks and the rewards offered by the dynamic industries should attract the more productive resources — the graduate "most likely to succeed." This will help to maintain an *apparent* difference in the earnings of resources in the two different sectors. This uneven distribution of talent is surely in everyone's best interest. Our brain surgeons *should* be more skilful than our gardeners. Our system program designers need to be better educated and smarter than our store clerks.

The product and process characteristics that encourage innovation and change will also encourage growth, concentration, and higher rates of rewards to all factors. Simple product and process characteristics will encourage little growth, small-firm technology, and lower-than-average returns to all factors. Industries, or a succession of related industries, could easily remain in a relatively static or relatively dynamic state for many years. If the process of change ever ceased, we would undoubtedly see all industries converge toward the golden mean of equilibrium. But there is no good reason why this should ever happen or why we should want it to.

Other Considerations

There are several other considerations, of limited applicability, each of which will explain why certain concentrated industries earn above-average profits. Individually their effect on an overall correlation between concentration and profits of all industries in the economy may be quite small; taken together, however, they can explain part of the relationship.

An umbrella effect

The competitive opportunities inherent in the product and process technology may be such that larger firms will be more efficient than smaller ones (because of falling long-run average costs attributable to scale and learning). In such situations competition will transform a many-firm industry into a few-firm industry. Assume that the long-run average cost curve tends to flatten as company size increases, so that a very large firm has only a small cost advantage over one that is moderately large. After a period of bankruptcies, mergers and consolidations, suppose the industry is left with three large firms of unequal size, which we shall call S (relatively small), M (the middle-sized firm), and L (for large). The different firm sizes have resulted from such factors as luck, a head start and differences in managerial ability.

It is likely that, somewhere in this process of becoming members of an oligopoly, the executives become aware of anti-combines legislation, and anti-concentration, anti-big-business sentiment in the community. At this point they will have to reassess their competitive strategies. To match the cost advantages of L, perhaps S and M should merge, but this would increase the concentration ratio, and would probably not be allowed. At the same time, L may become more aware of its political and legal vulnerability and, therefore, may decide it can no longer press its competitive advantage; in particular, it may decide to limit the attractiveness of its offer to its customers in order not to increase further its own market share.

This means automatically that the added value deriving from its competitive advantage will go to participants other than customers in the large firm. In effect, the lowest-cost firm must hold an umbrella over the heads of the other two. In so doing, it ensures that the profits of the smallest firm are high enough for continued survival. As a result the profits of the other two will automatically be higher. This will lead, in all probability, to a concentrated industry with above-average profits.

Ironical results

The irony of this situation is that the concentration-profits link in this industry will have occurred *because* of competition legislation. Theoreticians campaign against oligopoly because of their fear that oligopolies will earn above-average profits, yet their campaign leads to this very result!

It must not be thought that because of the umbrella, competition and progress will cease in our three-firm industry. Far from it. The industry will henceforth show up in financial analysts' screenings of fundamental financial data as a profitable industry that merits scrutiny by companies wishing to diversify. The umbrella will do nothing to improve the position of the industry *vis-à-vis* imports or competition from other industries. Indeed, this source of competition is likely to intensify. The industry must be even more aware of the fact that research will be directed to its product lines by other industries hoping to collect some of the profits. Finally, the three firms must continue to fear each other. Managers and researchers come and go. Over time, a new team may emerge in the smallest firm that will become a real threat to the other two. Firm L must continue to make better offers even though it may "pull" its competitive punches. Firm S must be concerned that the management of firm L may decide at any time to become more aggressively competitive in spite of the combines act. The fact that one firm decides to slow down its rate of offer-improvement to consumers in order to avoid trouble with the law does not mean that its rate of offer-improvement to consumers will be slow. It may be second only to the rate that would have been possible in the presence of a less hostile economic theory and policy.

Uniqueness

If concentration studies were really done properly, average concentration ratios would be a good deal higher than they are now, and the profit-concentration link would be even stronger. Every firm that makes a unique offer should be counted as a monopoly, and we should expect these monopolistic "industries" to have above-average profits. The above-average profits can be attributed to the risk premium that should be paid for innovative activities — and to the dishonesty of data banks. Data banks have a nasty habit of dropping the failures and counting only the survivors. Investors, however, who are being asked to finance a new venture will be all too aware of the high rate of bankruptcies.

It would be virtually impossible to determine the effect of this uniqueness factor on the data that economists have to work with. On *a priori* grounds it might be assumed that unique offers are more likely to show up in the dynamic, concentrated industries, but they can show up anywhere. Where they get counted is in the lap, not so much of the gods, as of two clerks — one who fills out forms and another who receives them. Neither of them is likely to have given much thought to the needs of those who seek the deeper significance of concentration.

Investment reaction time

The growth and decline of demand for different products should cause changes in profit rates that will, in turn, cause investment and disinvestment in their respective industries. This is, indeed, what the market system is all about. If there is a surge of demand for hot dogs at a lake because it has become unexpectedly popular with tourists, the sellers lucky enough to be there will be able to charge good prices and they will make high profits. As word spreads about the crowds and the line-ups, however, other entrepreneurs can be expected to move in quickly. Prices will "soften" and profits will decline.

It is obvious that not all industries will be able to respond to increases or decreases in demand with the same speed. In general, it seems logical to believe that industries such as our hot dog sellers with simple, small-firm technology can expand rapidly in response to an increase in demand and, therefore, that scarcity-induced profit rates will decline quite quickly. By the same token it seems likely that firms using capital-intensive, large-firm, high technology will take longer to respond to an increase in demand. If a craze develops for sailing we would expect the sequence of events to parallel those we described for hot dogs. The difference is that it will take a good deal longer to get into the business of producing sail boats than of selling hot dogs. The sailboat manufacturers who were lucky enough to be in the business (and were perhaps innovative enough to develop the "craze") should be able to hang on to their profits a good deal longer than the lucky hot dog sellers.

As we have seen, size of firm, capital intensity, and complexity of product and/or process are all likely to be related to concentration[14]. Therefore some concentrated industries sometimes will benefit from the fact that it takes longer to build a factory to make large computers than it does to build a stand to sell large hot dogs.[15]

High profits explained by superior performance

The implicit assumption of concentration analysis is that average industry profit rates act as the signal for entry and exit. In unconcentrated, low-technology, small-firm industries this may well be true. We have already noted, moreover, that a high or low average profit for a few-firm industry will act as a first indication to an investor of whether that industry merits further consideration as a possible investment. We may be sure, however, that when investors with any degree of sophistication seriously consider entering an oligopoly, they look at each company in that industry very carefully. The would-be investors at that point will not be concerned with the industry's average profit rate. Instead they will want to know what the most profitable firms are doing that make them profitable and whether those profitable activities can be imitated. They will also look at the firms that are doing less well and at the firms that left the industry. Can they do better?

It may well be that when investors look at their potential rivals they will decide they cannot match the offers of the most profitable firms, perhaps because they have too many new products in the R and D pipeline or, more generally, because they are too well managed. The profits of the leading firms in the oligopoly may act as a magnet, but their satisfied customers, and the one or two firms in the industry that are not doing well will serve as warnings againt entry. High profits earned by impressive performance may attract jealousy but not necessarily entry.

Laboratory Evidence

Undoubtedly, the main empirical support for the thesis that "conspiracy is a way of life" among oligopolists comes from the studies that indicate a tendency for average profits in an industry to vary with the number of firms. There is a second body of research, however, which it is claimed, also supports the conspiracy hypothesis. These studies use laboratory games of one kind or another in order to examine the conditions that encourage or discourage co-operative, as opposed to rivalrous, behaviour on the part of the players. The research is usually conducted under the carefully controlled condition of a laboratory, which gives it an aura of scientific respectability, if not of relevance.

What these studies have proved so far is that if the conditions of theory X really did apply to the real world, then the conventional wisdom about competitive behaviour would not be far wrong. If there are many players in the same competitive game that invites and rewards conspiracy, the players will find it harder to conspire, other things equal, the more there are playing the game. This proposition is unquestionably true in a theory X world and in a theory Y world and in the real world as well. The issue, however, is not whether it is true, but whether it is important. It is probably the case that there is a relationship between the amount of golf played and the divorce rate, but even if the relationship can be established as a fact, it does not follow that it is important enough that we should have a government department to ensure that golfers remember their wedding anniversaries.

The games are even simpler than theory X

One of our principal quarrels with theory X is that it presents such a simplistic view of the firm, of the market and of the motivation of managers that it invites the conclusion that conspiracies are easy. The laboratory games appear to lend support to the conspiracy hypothesis by using competitive simulations that are even more simplistic than the theory X view of the world!

Even so, a careful reader of the literature will find warnings. Roger Sherman found that, as expected, a decrease in the number of firms increased collusion[16] but he also found that with a greater range of choice, joint maximization was harder to achieve.[17] Exactly! One person can reach an agreement with himself on a single value, for a single variable, within a limited range, very easily. A five-person team or family will find the same exercise much more difficult. Two multi-person teams trying to agree on that single value will find agreement even more difficult.

But suppose that three multi-person teams have to agree on five values for five different variables before it can be said that an agreement has been reached. By what factor have we reduced the ease of co-operation? And yet in degree of complexity, we are still far away from a typical real-world case.

As we add to the number of variables, the range of values, the number of teams, the size of the teams, the uncertainties about the relationships between the values selected and the desired results, the chances of co-operation decline. The real question is how many variables, uncertainties and imponderables must be included in the laboratory experiments before their results can be said to have any validity in the real world?

Back to basic "X" and "Y"

In order to answer that question we must go back to our theory X and our theory Y views of the competitive process. If there are only a few firms with a single number to agree on, as in the case of a bidding situation, then we might agree that conspiracy is relatively easy. We might also agree with laboratory research suggesting that conspiracy becomes more difficult as the number of firms increases. But apart from bidding or establishing a single *pro forma* price in situations in which one is required, simple games have even less validity than the theory X model of competitive behaviour.

If hungry students are presented with the opportunity to earn two cookies for co-operation and one cookie for rivalry, they will quickly learn to co-operate. They may even begin to believe that the road to riches in the real world is the same as the path to the cookie jar in the laboratory.

In a leading textbook we are told:

> In James W. Friedman's experiments the players reached and held to agreed price about four times out of every five, even though the rewards for chiseling were good.[18]

The opening paragraph of Friedman's conclusions, however, begins with the warning "The cooperative duopoly games reported here have some special characteristics in comparison with firms in real markets."[19] This is something of an understatement! The difference between the games and the real world could have occupied several pages, but Friedman lists only three; in one of them he admits that "real firms have more than one decision variable."[20]

It is to be hoped that when the students who were taught to co-operate in the laboratory finally graduate, it will not take them too long to discover that the royal road to the cookie jar is the path of successful competitive behaviour, not conspiracy.

CONCLUSION

The case rests. The theory X way of looking at the competitive process does not provide a sound basis for believing that conspiracy is a way of life among oligopolists. Neither do the laboratory simulations, or the concentration-profits research, or the cases. Nor can it be said that the theory justifies the conclusion that oligopolies or monopolies misallocate resources in any meaningful sense. More particularly, the theory X approach cannot demonstrate that conspiracies that materially retard the rate of offer improvement are either practicable or desirable for any but marginal firms. The basic problem is that theory X does not really address itself to an analysis of the competitive process in a setting realistic enough to give it any validity.

Theory Y is still a simplification of the real world, but it tries to retain the essential characteristics of the household, the firm, the manager, etc., that are necessary for the study of competitive behaviour. Theory Y leads to the conclusion that a conspiracy to slow down the process of offer-improvement in most cases is bad business, at least for the leading firms, and is impracticable to boot. At the same time, theory Y suggests that enough co-operation to stop an atomistic price war is likely when the alternative is self-destruction. It suggests that if circumstances require a uniform *pro forma* price, then somehow that price will be established. At the same time, theory Y enables us to see a uniform *pro forma* price tells next to nothing about either the state of competition or the rate of offer-improvement — points that may be overlooked by a devotee of price theory. Theory Y enables us to see the special circumstances created by the use of bidding. It forces us to recognize the quite different competitive environment faced by industries in which atomistic price wars are a constant threat and those in which they are not.

Only when we have decided whether theory X or theory Y best describes the competitive process can we hope to agree on policies relating to competition. This is the subject of our final chapter.

Chapter 8

Policy Considerations
Monopolies, Mergers, and Cartels

GOALS

Discussions of appropriate competition policies are unlikely to produce consensus unless there is a prior understanding about goals. The goals usually considered to be most relevant to competition policy are:
1. a high and rising standard of living,
2. an optimum allocation of resources,
3. an equitable distribution of income, to which is sometimes added
4. the preservation or achievement of individual freedoms.

In the analysis that follows, these goals are accepted, and, since our objective is to find sensible policies and legislation, we add two practical constraints. First, we shall follow Robert Bork in insisting that conditions are as good as they can be unless it can be shown that they can be improved by legislation or judicial degree. Second, we shall follow common sense in insisting that our point of departure must be the existing standard of living, distribution of income, freedoms and allocative efficiency. In other words, our starting point is reality, and our goal is achievable progress.

MONOPOLIES AS UNIQUE OFFERS

Section 33 of *Canadian Combines Investigation Act* states quite unequivocally that, "Every person who is a party or privy to or knowingly assists in, or in the formation of, a . . . monopoly is guilty of an indictable offence and is liable to imprisonment for two years".[1] Undoubtedly, conventional wisdom supports this prohibition because monopolies are generally held to prevent the attainment of the goals of progress, equitable distribution of income, optimum allocation of resources and even the preservation of freedom. Is this popular view correct?

Let us suppose that the term "monopoly," as used in the law, refers, as it does in common parlance, to a firm that makes a unique offer. To what extent can the making of a unique offer be said to frustrate the achievement of our agreed-upon economic goals?

The first goal on our list is a rising standard of living. When a firm makes a unique offer, can it be said to be contributing to human progress? Not necessarily. The new offer may simply be a mistake. It may happen that consumers do not want the new product or do not want it sufficiently to justify the investment or the use of scarce resources in its manufacture. In this case, the unique offer does not need to be banished by law. It will be banished by the free choice of consumers and suppliers of labour and capital.

Suppose the new, unique offer is a success in the sense that consumers are willing to stop buying old products in favour of the new one, and that resource owners are willing to withdraw their service from old products and rent or sell them to the innovator. If this transfer of resources occurs in a free market, then in the opinion of the individuals who have done the choosing, progress has been made. The economy has moved to a preferred position.

Something new has been added

The same line of argument will also lead to the conclusion that resource allocation has been improved after the launching of a new, unique offer in a free market. We have already considered the impact of an innovating serpent in a perfectly competitive Garden of Eden. If the innovation is successful, it means that enough buyers forsake perfectly competitive products, and enough factors are persuaded to leave the perfectly competitive industries to enable the innovator to continue in business. We must conclude that, in the absence of any coercion, consumers are better off, the factor owners are better off, and the innovator is better off. The successful establishment of the innovator's monopolistic firm increases welfare and produces a better allocation of productive factors, and an enriched product mix.

It might be argued by some that while the foregoing is correct, the continued presence of the monopolistic innovator destroys the particular kind of optimum resource allocation that we encountered in Chapter 2. Consumers may, indeed, be better off because of the new unique offer of the monopolist, but they would be still better off if so many more firms produced the same product that the conditions of perfect competition were restored. But this proposition, even if true, hardly concerns the monopolist, because whatever other firms may do, or may not do, is hardly the responsibility of the innovative monopolist.[2] There is no doubt that the new, unique offer has made all participants better off. Whether still further improvements can be made will be decided when imitators or other innovators begin to offer similar or identical products.

Monopoly and equity

A law prohibiting unique monopolies would obviously not increase progress or improve resource allocation. The impact of such a law on income distribution is not so obvious and must depend on judgements about equity. To take an example, suppose that the maker of a unique offer earned no more than was necessary to justify his innovative activity and the risk he took. Assume, also, that because of the innovation, consumers and factor owners were better off by a margin that rewarded their transfer of allegiance without providing them with any spectacular gain. The post-innovation distribution of income is different from the pre-innovation distribution but is the change equitable or inequitable? Since everyone directly affected by the change chose their new jobs and products without coercion, it is difficult to see how anyone could complain that the new distribution of income is in any way inferior to the old.

Suppose, however, that the innovation was somewhat more successful: it offered such an improved product that consumers were willing to buy more of it on terms very favourable to the producer. Suppose, also, that after offering adequate compensation to the factor owners shifting from the old products to the new, the innovator was left with a large income. As before, everyone who is party to the change is better off; the only difference is that one party is very much better off. A new rich person has been added to the ranks of the rich. This is not a matter of the rich getting richer and the poor, poorer (although the chances are good that it would be reported that way); instead, the relatively poor consumers and resource owners have become better off, and one innovator has become rich.

If innovation provides the main vehicle for acquiring wealth, then it is of some interest to note that the new innovator would, in effect, be challenging the position of the old innovators. It is, therefore, quite likely that inter-industry, or rather inter-monopoly, competition would have the effect of redistributing income from the old rich to the *nouveau riche*.

From this illustration it is difficult to see how a general ban on monopolies based on innovation can be defended on the grounds that they create an inequitable or socially undesirable distribution of income.

Monopoly and freedom

The final question is how a ban on innovative monopoly would affect the fourth goal, freedom. Obviously, any law prohibiting new and unique offers would impose a dramatic limitation on the freedom of all those who make or accept offers. This includes not only firms, but all sellers and buyers of services as well.

What this analysis indicates is that monopoly, in the sense of a unique offer, passes all the economic tests of desirability. A successful offer is likely to improve resource allocation, the distribution of income, and progress. Moreover, the ability to make and accept such offers is an important freedom.

It might be argued that we have set up a straw man: the courts do not, in fact, interpret monopoly to mean the making of a unique offer. If this is true, then there should be no objection to changing the law to make the words in their usual meaning correspond to intent.* Furthermore, it is not true in the United States that the monopoly is safe from prosecution (or persecution) even if it is based on innovations.† Canada has a bad habit of repeating the mistakes of its big neighbour. In any event as the law now stands it gives the appearance of making monopoly illegal and therefore attaches a stigma to the word "monopoly." If the law does not mean to prohibit or punish monopolies that are defined in the usual way, then the law should be redrafted.

UNDUE RESTRAINTS ON ENTRY

The second meaning of monopoly we explored in Chapter 5 involved prohibition against entry. It could only have been monopoly in this sense that led Freidman to say that monopoly "means a limitation on voluntary exchange through a reduction in the alternatives available to individuals".[4] Clearly, monopoly in the sense of making a unique offer can be subject to no such charge; on the contrary, it *increases* the alternatives to consumers and factor owners.

This apparent contradiction shows that the same word is used to describe two quite different activities or conditions. Making a unique offer and prohibiting someone from making an offer, unique or otherwise, are so far apart in meaning that we should all be able to agree to use different and distinct labels. Monopoly, meaning a single seller, has a well established place in our vocabulary. There is absolutely no reason to press it into service to describe a very different condition or activity. This is particularly true since prohibitions of entry do not normally attract the use of the term monopoly in everyday speech. This fact can be illustrated by a few examples. In a community that does not

---

*The section declaring that it is an offence to be "a party or privy to or knowingly assist in, or in the formation of a. . .monopoly" should simply be struck from the act.

†For an excellent summary of the Zerox, Kodak, DuPont (titanium dioxide) and I.B.M. cases, which all involve the issue of innovation, see Betty Bock.[3]

allow Sunday sports, is it appropriate to say that the government has established a Sunday sports monopoly? This is not how we would normally describe such a prohibition, especially if we happened to like Sunday sports. In a community where the government has decided that the number of radio stations will be frozen at, say, ten, has it, by so doing, made each of the existing stations into a monopoly? Again, this is not normally the way we would describe the companies. They may still compete vigorously for listeners and for advertisers.

Putting the fox in charge of the chicken coop

If the law is to deal with prohibitions to entry, it should do so by using words that can convey their ordinary meaning[5] to those who are expected to understand and obey them. If prohibition of entry is the problem then why not use "prohibition of entry" as the term in the law? In the legislation dealing with competition, perhaps a preamble could be included that underlines the desirability of a free market and declares the government's opposition in principle to all prohibitions on entry, whether those prohibitions are imposed by corporations, co-operatives, unions or governments. Governments, it might be noted, have been by far the greatest offenders. The list of government prohibitions is long and includes such items as the franchising of utilities, protective tariffs and embargoes, local purchasing requirements, patents, zoning laws, exclusive government ownership, laws that make unions unchallengeable, censorship and all manner of other restrictive laws, rules, and regulations.*

These prohibitions all deserve more critical analysis than they receive in the economic and managerial literature. It would be most appropriate to have governments declare to their many regulatory and administrative agencies that they should not pursue policies or insist on processes that unduly limit entry.

---

*A client company found it was getting nowhere in the construction of a new plant. A study revealed that serious cost overruns were being incurred because of the failure to obtain timely government approval. An analysis of the problem revealed that no less than 50 different government departments, bureaus or agencies had to give approval at least once to different aspects of the project. Each of these bodies had the power to delay the project and frequently did. Because the project had the support of the federal and the provincial government involved and because it was unopposed by an "interest" group a 51st agency was established. Its sole function was to speed up the process of obtaining approval from the other 50!

Even more interesting is the fact that when I asked permission to use the example and name the company and the project, the company refused. Management felt that its operations were too much under the control of the government bureaucracy to risk offending anyone.

Undue limitations on entry

In addition to a statement of principle and providing for the position of a competition advocate, the law should declare it to be a civil offence for any company, association, union or other organization to take actions, the intention of which is to unduly limit the freedom of others to make or accept offers. Actions that could fall under this constraint include actual or threatened physical harassment, slander, predatory geographical discrimination and the like.

The qualifications of "undueness" and "intentions" are absolutely necessary. Apart from physical harassment and the purposeful spreading of lies and slanders, it will be a matter of judgement whether a specific act is socially and economically desirable or an undue interference with the free choice of others.[6]

It should also be underlined that, apart from the possibility of physical harassment by a Mafia-type private organization or the goon squads of unions, there is really no comparison at all between a prohibition on entry by the government — and the actions of a company or an individual that may merely make entry difficult. A company that is aggressive, spends money successfully on research and development, maintains a stream of improvements to its product, tries hard to match its offers to the evolving needs of its customers, earns the loyalty of its workers and the good will of its suppliers — in short, a company that is good and tells its customers how good it is — will make the entry of potential competitors difficult. Indeed, some of those who precede investment decisions with careful feasibility studies may decide that, in the absence of some new technological innovation, entry for them is impossible.

Vigorous competition vs coercive prohibition

But there is a world of difference between the successful competitiveness of a company and a government prohibition on entry. In the former case, there is no entry because entrepreneurs cannot see the possibility of putting together a consistent set of offers to workers, shareholders and customers that will be regarded to those involved as an improvement. The door remains open for anyone to try. And periodic re-examinations of the situation as conditions change is always possible. In the meantime, it must be concluded that entries are not occurring because they are not needed. In the case of a government prohibition, in contrast, there are no reassessments, no testing, and no entry, even if better offers can be made.

A good case can be made that as long as the criminal law deals firmly with protective rackets, goon squads and other forms of harassment, a competition law *per se* does not need to deal with private prohibitions of entry. Certainly any advances toward achieving our economic goals by including provisions about private prohibitions will be as nothing compared with the great leap forward that could be made by dismantling the network of government prohibitions. Government physician: heal thyself!

MERGERS

Introduction

If the words of the law in Canada are given their ordinary meaning, a merger would be dealt with as severely as a monopoly. Section 33 of the *Combines Investigation Act* states that "every person who is a party or privy to or knowingly assists in, or in the formation of, a merger . . . is guilty of an indictable offence and is liable to imprisonment for two years".[7] It is a tribute to the good sense of Canadian courts that the above words have *not* been given their ordinary meaning; what the law has been interpreted to mean is that it is only those mergers that are a detriment to the public interest that need fear prosecution.[8] Detriment has generally not been assumed unless the merger threatens to create a monopoly in the single-seller sense, though undoubtedly, if the single-seller was unchallengeable and could somehow prevent entry, or if it involved a significant and harmful reduction in choice, it might be assumed that the courts would be even more inclined to declare the merger to be illegal.

On both practical and theoretical grounds a good case can be made for taking the government out of the merger-approval business entirely, especially in an open economy such as Canada's. Provided the government makes sure that there are no undue barriers to entry, it should not impose any undue barriers to exit, i.e., the withdrawal of an offer through merger. Entry and the threat of entry, along with imports and inter-industry competition should protect consumers against abuse by monopolists. At the same time one must recognize a difference between monopoly that is created by making a new offer and monopoly that is created by the withdrawal of an old offer. The first, if accepted by the market, must be judged as unequivocally good. The second can be judged as good or bad in the same way — by the market — but only after a considerable period of time. Does the withdrawal of an offer, because of a merger, give rise to a market opportunity (because of unhappy customers perhaps) followed by the entry of a new firm and the restoration of the market to its pre merger condition? If so, the withdrawal of the offer was a mistake and the market will have corrected it. If not, no mistake was made and no government-imposed remedy is needed.

A practical compromise

While it can be maintained that the market will make better decisions by and large than a judicial or regulatory process, there is room for compromise. Mergers that merely reduce the number of offers, but to a number greater than one, leave in the industry a company that can move almost immediately to capitalize on the dissatisfaction created by the merger (or by any other mistake of a supplier). If mergers leave only one supplier in an industry, however, the correction of consumer dissatisfaction will take somewhat longer. In this way one can rationalize the existing policy of the courts that mergers that create monopolies will be disallowed.

What is being advocated in Canada at the present time, however, is not the *status quo*, it is, rather, a "tougher" law against mergers. It is in the context of this campaign that we shall have to consider the case for and against further restrictions on mergers.

It is customary to distinguish among three types of mergers; conglomerate, vertical and horizontal. Roughly, conglomerate mergers involve the marriage of two or more companies that do not compete with each other, or buy and sell to each other, in any significant way. Vertical mergers involve the union of two or more companies that have, or could have, a significant buyer-seller relationship. "Horizontal" is the term applied to the joining of two or more competitors. It is the latter type of merger that is generally believed to have the greatest impact on competition, and we shall deal with it first.

Horizontal Mergers

Of the seven dimensions of competition, the four likely to be most affected are the innovation-imitation process, choice, independent assertiveness and freedoms. We shall consider each in turn.

The Innovation-imitation Process

A merger will, almost of necessity, create a larger company. This, in turn, should mean lower cost if learning and economies of scale are applicable to the industry or to the firms in question. Increased size is, of course, no guarantee that more dollars will be spent on research and development, but in the Canadian context, where even our large companies are small by world standards, it is reasonable to expect that general mergers will have a positive effect on R and D expenditures.

This should indicate the possibility of an increased rate of offer-improvement to all participants as a group, although, of course, not all individuals will necessarily benefit. For example, the merger may lead to greater productivity, which, in turn, may necessitate laying off some workers. The terms of the merger may benefit one group of shareholders more than another. Some managers will find that they are redundant — fired, in other words.

As far as the dynamic, innovative-imitative aspect of competition is concerned, common sense suggests that, in view of the openness and limited size of the Canadian market, the thrust of public policy in Canada should be to facilitate rather than discourage mergers. Better still, perhaps, it should remain neutral.

Choice

Mergers may affect choice in a number of ways. What follows is an enumeration of some of them.

1. It is apparent that many of the so-called horizontal mergers do affect choice because they are simply mislabeled. When a merger takes place between two newspapers in two different market areas, it does not affect the amount of choice of papers that readers have in either market. If two pharmaceutical companies producing different products merge, the amount of choice customers have for any one product does not change. Before it can be said that a merger can affect the choice of consumers or suppliers, the companies must sell the *same* product in the *same* market, not in the same type of market or in markets geographically separated.

2. Mergers cannot be said to affect choice in any important way if they are merely the occasion for withdrawing offers that were going to be withdrawn anyway*. A failing firm, or a firm with a failing division that has been unable to make or maintain a set of offers satisfactory to all participants, will have to withdraw that offer. What the merger may do is provide special advantages to one or more of the affected groups. For example, the new company may continue to service the discontinued line of products, thereby protecting the investment of consumers. The senior employees may be able to preserve the right of their seniority in the new company. The investors of the failing company may receive something rather than nothing. One could go on.

3. Mergers may unite companies that were making viable offers at the time of consolidation but whose offers may have been doomed by technological or marketing developments looming on the horizon. For example, foreign competition, or a new

---

*This is known as "the failing company doctrine" in United States jurisprudence. For a brief description of the principle and some of the early cases see Low.[9]

source of a raw material, or a technological change or yet another government regulation may pose a threat, and a merger may offer the best chance for survival. In such cases a reduction in choice occasioned by a merger may merely mean a speeding up of the process of change.

4. The merger may be a response to a threat from some other country, industry, company or government; in addition, the merged company may, itself, through a pooling of talent or an increase in R and D, be the instrument that makes old offers obsolete. If, in a free market, the new offer or set of offers is preferred to the old offers of the two merging companies, then choice will not have been adversely affected.

5. Under quite a number of different circumstances, a merger may result in reduced choice to consumers, as measured by company-counting or even by offer-counting, without causing any significant reduction in welfare. Mergers among Canadian exporters or between two companies facing intense import competition (as in the Canadian appliance industry) are obvious examples. Mergers among companies in industries with too many offers would cause little distress. If, of course the reduction of offers does cause distress, then, presumably, entry would become attractive to companies that could see a market opportunity in that distress.

6. Some mergers may not involve a significant reduction in offers because it may be the philosophy of the management to encourage inter-division rivalry. All offers may continue to be made.

7. In all of the preceding cases, the effect on choice of a merger is either minimal or beneficial. Now let us consider the worst possible case. Let us supose that a merger takes place between two healthy competitors making attractive offers to all participants, and that, after the merger, one set of offers is withdrawn, with a subsequent loss of choice to consumers.

The example immediately raises the question of why the offer would be withdrawn, because it seems evident that the reduction in choice could only be permanent if it was accompanied by a prohibition on entry. Everyday companies, bent on expansion, diversification or increasing their investment, scan their environment looking for investment opportunities. For a new company that results from a merger to withdraw from the market, a set of offers that are acceptable to workers, customers, suppliers and investors would seem like an open invitation to other firms to enter. It is hard to believe that mergers are likely to result in the removal from the market of sets of offers that are satisfactory to all concerned. On the grounds of reduced choice, we might regret the results of the merger, so long as there is freedom of entry, there is no reason to suppose, however, that the market will not correct what looks, on the face of it, to be an error of judgement.[10]

One of the merger cases which was a *cause célèbre* in its day (and still is in official and academic circles) was the 1960 beer case[11]. Canadian Breweries Limited was accused of buying out 37 competitors, giving it 66 per cent of the Ontario market.[12] In his judgement Chief Justice McRuer said:

> The acquisition of plants did not have the effect of giving the accused a monopoly or a substantial monopoly in the market. I think it is also clear that the accused has not, by acquiring control over competitors, put itself in such a position that it can control the sources of supply of the consuming market. . .[13]

The good sense of this judgement was amply demonstrated by the fact that 66 per cent of the beer drinkers in Ontario did not lose their right to vote with their dollars. Despite the "dominant", "controlling" position of Canadian Breweries the even more dominant and controlling power of the Ontario beer drinkers decreed that Canadian Breweries would over the next decade lose approximately half of its market shares.

Looked at from the broader, historical perspective the merger program of Canadian Breweries was but an incident in the evolution of an industry from a structure of local oligopolies of small firms to a national oligopoly of large firms.[14]

Taken together, these considerations of the impact of a horizontal merger suggest that such a merger will indeed reduce choice in some circumstances. In a free market, however, a reduction in choice that matters to consumers will increase the likelihood that another firm will appear to fill the void.

Independent Assertiveness

Presumably the main reason for the campaign against mergers on economic grounds is that they are likely to increase concentration ratios and thereby raise the chances of explicit or implicit collusion. In such cases, the commonly assumed result is an unwarranted transfer of value from consumers to owners.

There are two main points to be made in rebuttal. The first and most important is that, as we have already seen, the concentration = conspiracy = profit theory is not strong enough to support any policy or legislative thrust concerning mergers. The second is that mergers are often nothing more than an adaptation to a set of circumstances that would change the concentration ratio in any event.

Freedom

Freedom to buy and sell is a fundamental ingredient of the market process for both consumers and producers. We must assume that consumers know their needs and wants better than a government planning bureau. We must also assume that companies are in the best position to know their customers, their own available resources, the relevant technology, the capabilities and limitations of their managers and the changes on the horizon. With all this information, managers must try to plot a strategy that will maintain an attractive and viable set of offers to all participants. Whether this strategy should or should not include mergers is a question more likely to be answered intelligently, in the light of all available facts, by managers rather than by either a judicial or government planning process. If so, the freedom to act should rest with managers.

Policy with Regard to Horizontal Mergers

Where do all of these considerations lead us when it comes to proposing a sensible public policy with respect to horizontal mergers? There are, I believe, four proposals worth considering.

First, the language of the law should be made to conform to its intent, using words in their ordinary meaning. No one has ever seriously proposed a prohibition on all mergers, and there seems little value in a law that holds that all mergers are illegal and punishable, even by imprisonment.

Second, it is quite obvious that merging is not in any sense a criminal activity, and, therefore, if mergers are to be subject to judicial review, the process should be civil and not criminal.

Third, mergers that have the effect of prohibiting entry are without merit and should be prohibited. This prohibition should apply whether the merger creates a monopoly in the single-seller sense or not.

Fourth, mergers that change, or threaten to change, oligopolies or duopolies into monopolies in the single-seller sense may be justified or unjustified, depending on a wide variety of considerations such as the definitions of the product, the market and the industry and, in particular, the conditions of entry. The most practical way of dealing with this matter is probably to declare that mergers threatening to lessen competition unduly by creating a monopoly in the single-seller sense are illegal. This would allow the merging companies to use the "undueness" provision to argue their case. Presumably monopolies (via mergers) that unite Canadian companies selling in world markets, or Canadian companies struggling to survive against foreign competition, or companies operating in a field in which entry is easy and in which inter-industry competition is intense would be able to persuade a judge or a tribunal that their merging does not unduly lessen competition. This would be so even though, by using a narrow definition of markets or products, the merger produces a single seller.

Application of the law

It is to be expected, however, that mergers that reduce the number of effective competitors from two to one would be disallowed by the courts in most cases, as indeed they are now[15]. The possibility would exist, however, that narrowly (and unrealistically) defined single-seller mergers might be permitted.

By including such words as "create or *threaten to create* a monopoly," the door would be left open for Consumer and Corporate Affairs to intervene in cases where mergers come close to establishing, or threatening to establish, single-seller situations. Hence, mergers that reduce the number of effective competitors from, say, three to two, may be attacked because they threaten to evolve into single-seller situations. On the other hand, mergers that reduce the number of sellers from 20 to 10 or from six to five or even from four to three would not be subject to the law, and there seems to be no good reason why they should be.

For those who are familiar with the merger cases in Canada it will be clear that the foregoing analysis amounts to an endorsation of the way the courts have actually handled horizontal mergers.* Consumer and Corporate Affairs should in the future monitor only those mergers that threaten to produce single firm industries or that might have the effect of unduly discouraging entry.

It is absolutely wrong for Stanbury and Waverman to say that "in 1976, the Supreme Court of Canada, in the *K.C. Irving Case*, formally buried the remains of the merger policy."[17] In the first place the Irving case[18] concerned the combining of businesses in *different* markets. Second, the newspaper-news-communication industry is obviously in the middle of a reorganization in which the role of the local newspaper will continue to become less important. The Irving case, like the Breweries case, is but an incident in a reorganization and

---

*There have not been many cases in Canada involving the merging of competitors in the *same* market areas. (Both the Irving newspaper case and the Western sugar case involved the merging of companies selling primarily in different areas.) Action by the Bureau of Competition Policy clearly caused the divestiture of Anthes' 20 per cent share ownership of its competitor, Associated.[16] The Erco case, already cited (footnote 15) demonstrates the point that mergers that practise monopoly are not permitted.

restructuring of an industry along national (or international) as opposed to local lines.

In 1976 the Supreme Court of Canada did nothing more than reconfirm a sensible merger policy for Canada. By and large Canadian companies are not too large, they are too small. Lower concentration levels are by no means in the interests of Canadians. In Canada the merger policy we have makes sense.

Vertical and Conglomerate Mergers

The case for increased administrative control over horizontal mergers is not soundly based. The economic case against vertical and conglomerate mergers is even weaker. The most legitimate concern is that vertical mergers might be used to prevent entry. To the extent that this is a problem, we have proposed that it be covered by a general prohibition against actions taken by private firms to prevent entry. If the device used involves a vertical merger, then that merger and whatever other practices are involved, would be disallowed. That consideration apart, any criticism of vertical and conglomerate mergers must be based on the fact they increase the size of firms.

There is no general economic case that can be made against bigness in the Canadian context of the 1980s. That means that the basis left for criticism by those who dislike large companies is political or social. This is a book about competition, not politics. To deal with the realities of the political power of big companies, as opposed to the myths of that power or, perhaps, the history of that power, would require a book of equal length. In passing, however, one might reflect on the extreme sanctions a large company can impose on politicians, on governments or on citizens, and consider how limited they are as compared with the extreme sanctions that governments and politicians can impose on large companies or on citizens, especially those who do not happen to be members of the ruling coalition.

Bigness and people-alienation

A more serious concern is the impact large organizations may have on their own managers and employees. Shepherd concludes "there is enough evidence that worker satisfaction is reduced by size to make this a general rule.[19] But when one looks into it further, one finds that the evidence is contradictory. The conceptual and measurement problems are much more difficult than may at first appear. Of all of the factors related to job satisfaction, size of organization is relatively unimportant. John W. Gartwell, in his study for the Bryce Commission, *Organization Size and Alienation*, 1976, concludes:

The linkage between organization size and alienation probably is both complicated and relatively weak. The total magnitude of these effects in the working population is probably very small not only because of the weakness of this relationship, but also because most of the labour force does not work in large organizations.[20]

Since each individual is free to seek jobs in a variety of organizations of different sizes, or to be self-employed, there does not seem to be a case for discouraging large-scale firms because of possible employee alienation. Those workers or managers who do not like large organizations can look for jobs elsewhere.

Policy with Regard to Vertical and Conglomerate Mergers

In conclusion, it cannot possibly be argued that every merger is going to work, that it will achieve its objectives, or that it will increase welfare. The same can be said for the investment process or the household purchase of consumer goods. On the other hand, the grounds on which the government can justify intervention are shaky, and, all things considered, it is impossible to believe that increased government prohibition or regulation of mergers in Canada will produce better results. Certainly, the increased powers that officials in Consumer and Corporate Affairs have been requesting for the past ten years,[21] would make mergers more expensive. If this branch of government is successful in obtaining the legislation it wants, fewer mergers will be completed, and the average size of Canadian companies will be smaller than otherwise. It is unlikely that such a policy will increase the welfare of Canadians.

The law respecting mergers in Canada may require a few adjustments to its wording. It does not require sweeping changes.

AGREEMENTS AMONG FIRMS

Classifications

Agreements among firms can be classified in several different ways. A critical distinction is between explicit agreements and what are sometimes called implicit or tacit agreements. Explicit agreements may be further subdivided according to their degree of formality and whether or not they are enforceable. All agreements, explicit or implicit, can also be grouped according to the *number* of agreeing firms or, more likely, according to the *proportion* of agreeing firms in a single industry. Next, agreements can be classified according to the number and importance of the items covered, where "importance" in turn can be judged according to different criteria.

The enumeration of the classificatory divisions is sufficient to indicate that explicit agreements can vary over a considerable range. At one extreme, we could have an explicit, formal, enforceable agreement covering all dimensions and all firms in an industry. At the other extreme, we could have an inconsequential agreement in which one company agreed to make one sale of excess raw materials to another company that happened to be a competitor. In between, there could be an agreement covering all dimensions of competition but involving only a fraction of the firms in the industry, or an agreement including all of the firms but only a few dimensions of competition.

Explicit Agreements

Of all the distinctions that can be made among different agreements, the most important, from the legal or policy point of view, is between explicit, and so-called implicit, agreements. We shall deal first only with explicit agreements. An explicit agreement is arrived at by discussions that result in a meeting of the minds. The agreement does not have to be written, it may not be enforceable and it may not be kept, but at the time of its making there has to be an understanding of what had been agreed to and which parties had agreed.

Agreements to prohibit entry

The law should declare that actions that produce or threaten to produce an *undue* restraint on entry are illegal, whether those actions are carried out by one firm or a group of firms acting under an agreement. The offence, however, would be the undue restraint on entry rather than the agreement. The qualification of undueness is absolutely necessary. As we have seen, almost any economic activity can be said to exclude someone else. If a family buys a loaf of bread or if the breadwinner takes a job, *that* loaf of bread and *that* job are no longer available to anyone else. Moreover our analysis of competitive activities makes it clear that successful and socially useful acts of rivals may make it both unnecessary and undesirable for other firms to enter a particular industry.

Agreements covering all firms in an industry and all dimensions

The most comprehensive agreement imaginable would be one made by all competing firms and covering every possible dimension of competition. Such an agreement is neither likely nor practicable. Still, we should expect the law to declare agreements illegal if they produce or threaten to produce monopolies in the single-seller sense that will unduly lessen competition. This provision of the law has the same *raison d'être* as the declaration that mergers that create or threaten to create single-seller monopolies would generally be illegal. At the same time, there are circumstances in which an industry could argue that, for example, a specialization agreement was the only way for a Canadian industry to survive in the face of foreign competition or, perhaps, inter-industry competition.[22] The use of "unduly" would prevent an ardent Crown prosecutor from trying to obtain a conviction by establishing a narrow definition of a market and thereby preventing the court from looking at the total competition facing the firms.

Agreements covering all dimensions but only a fraction of the firms in one industry

A comprehensive agreement between two or more firms in an industry should in all logic be looked at as something less than a merger between or among the same firms. Unless the agreement threatens to approach monopoly in the single-seller sense, there is no good reason for government intervention—provided, as always, that the agreement does not unduly limit freedom of entry.

Agreements covering all firms in an industry but only a few dimensions

The following discussion of partial agreements assumes that actions or agreements preventing entry have already been made illegal. This provision of the law would obviously strike down one particular type of partial agreement, namely an attempt to divide up markets.

Market-sharing agreements are of two kinds. The first and most restrictive is a division of customers among sellers. This division can be made on the basis of geography or some other means so that, in effect, each seller is a monopolist in his own market protected by an agreement with all other sellers in the industry that they will not enter. Such arrangements, clearly, would be disallowed under the general provision of the law that there should be no undue limitation of entry.

The second type of market-sharing agreement is less injurious to competition, although it should still undoubtedly be disallowed. If all companies in an industry agree that each will take a certain percentage of the market, but at the same time they do not allocate customers or areas, there will still be rivalry among the sellers for the most profitable accounts. Because of this rivalry it will be in the interest of competitors to maintain the pace of offer improvement, despite the agreement.

This having been said, however, we should anticipate that, in order to honour the market-sharing agreement, the most successful companies with the most attractive offers will have to withdraw from the market periodically in order to allow competitively weaker firms to catch up. At such times buyers in the market would find that only one seller was allowed to seek their business. That seller would, in effect, be protected during the catch-up period by an agreement that other firms would not enter the market at that particular time.

Relative stability of market shares must not be confused with a market-sharing agreement any more than uniformity of *pro forma* prices should be confused with a price agreement. The charges by the Crown against the Eastern Sugar Refiners[23] is a case in point.

In order to understand the issue it would really be necessary to have some experience in the industry. As a minimum, one should read the transcript of the trial, especially the evidence of the buyers. This evidence reveals two things. First it shows that the companies *fought* to maintain their market position (i.e. their market share) with the same kind of competitive fervour that one finds in Ardrey's "The Territorial Imperative"[24]. Holding a market share is no tea party.

One buyer in search of a better offer looked for the seller who "was weak"[25] or "who was hungry."[26] "It may be that he may want some business to supplant some business he lost."[27]

> **Q.** The information that you would get, speaking to these different people, would allow you to know that, for example, one of the refiners was off its target of sales and was interested in giving discounts to make up for the loss; right?
> **A.** That could be part of it.[28]

What is bad about a market-sharing agreement is that it would, periodically, prohibit entry of all but one supplier in order to allow the lagging supplier to catch up. Temporarily and periodically some buyers would be confronted by a monopolist — a single seller. This was obviously not the situation as described by the buyers. *

The second matter that is revealed by the transcript is just a few of the logistic and business considerations that tend in their particular industry at least to smooth out market shares. To give but one example: a refiner could get "oversold" — "maybe they had futures purchased but maybe not enough to cover some of the sales that they made."[29] More sales for such a company would mean more risk and presumably would be made with more reluctance i.e. a smaller discount.

Spokesman for Consumer and Corporate Affairs have used their loss of this and other cases as indicating the need for a "stronger" law, i.e. one that ensures that the Crown will never lose another case. On the other hand what is perhaps needed is "stronger" screening so

---

*It was also obviously not the situation as described in the internal company documents seized by the Crown. For a particularly devastating attack on the position of the prosecution on this point see the Supreme Court decision (mimeo).

that bad cases are not brought before the courts in the first place. The Western Fertilizer case,[30] which was supposed to deal with a conspiracy to set common prices, revealed that the Crown had not even bothered to collect data on real prices. Instead they wasted the court's time proving the obvious: *pro forma* prices for a homogeneous product do tend to be quite similar. But as the trial judge remarked, the Crown's expert "had made certain assumptions which were not supported by or were not in accord with the evidence. It was also brought out in cross-examination that . . . [the expert] had no information available to her which gave any indication of the actual prices of fertilizer[!]. . . ."[31]

Increased vulnerability

If either type of market-sharing agreement led sellers to slow down the rate of offer improvement, they would have to realize that they were increasing their vulnerability to imports, and inter-industry competition as well as the entry for new firms. A market-sharing agreement would not be a good policy for an industry in the long run and it would appear to run counter to the interests of the best firms in the short run. From this we may conclude that market-sharing agreements are not very likely to occur, and for that reason, at least, not very important.

Lack of importance can also be ascribed to agreements covering only one dimension of an offer. Such agreements are unlikely to have much impact on the value received by one group of participants or on the distribution of the total value among participants. The reason is not hard to find. Offers are almost invariably multidimensional, and, apart from bidding situations, there are ample opportunities for transferring value from one participant to another. Even if companies made a solemn agreement to charge the same actual price, each firm would find it quite easy to reduce the cost to any buyers and to continue to make increasingly attractive offers.

Partial agreements cannot be very important

A critic might ask at this point why partial agreements would be made if they are not important to managers. The answer is that we have no evidence that they are made in any significant numbers or that they do anything more than make a modest reduction in the risk of price wars in certain types of industries. For those who fear that partial agreement may nevertheless be used to exploit unorganized consumers, it must be pointed out that any partial agreement — or complete agreement, for that matter — that seriously injured consumers would by the same token encourage the entry of other firms.

Since partial agreements on certain matters are now permitted under the law, it may be assumed that some net social advantages were foreseen. For example, sellers are permitted to agree on package sizes or shapes.[32] Presumably, such an agreement may reduce the costs of handling, shipping and inventories by discouraging the undue proliferation of package sizes. Consumers may find the comparison of competing products a little easier, and the real costs of choice, somewhat reduced. At the same time, if an agreement prevents customers from getting the size of package that they really want, it is likely that a new firm will take advantage of this fact. Alternatively, an existing firm will withdraw from the agreement to take advantage of this unfulfilled need. Why, one may ask, would the same set of considerations not apply to virtually every dimension of the offer?

Patching up the law

As the law now stands, partial agreements concerning packaging and a few other matters are either explicitly legal or are ignored, while partial agreements concerning price and a few other matters are illegal and are not ignored. These provisions of the law result from the acceptance of conventional theory X, which sees competition only in terms of price. If price competition ends, all competition ends.

This, of course, is not true. Indeed, even a *price agreement* does not mean the end of *price competition*. On this matter, Stigler, has caused much confusion in the economics profession by making a much-quoted but illogical statement. He said, "any stopping point on the road to full collusion will necessarily be inconsistent with profit maximization; that is, the stopping point will be non-rational."[33]

This statement is simply wrong. If we think of collusion as a criminal matter then what Stigler is saying is that if a woman would steal to feed a hungry child she would go on stealing until she had stolen everything in the world that was of any value to her. A man who would kill to prevent himself from being robbed would go on to kill anyone who got in his way. A company that would behave in a way that encouraged prices to rise out of a range that threatened every company in the industry with bankruptcy would not rest content until it had conspired to exploit the public to the fullest extent possible.

If we set aside the legal implications and look at Stigler's statement from the point of view of the self-interest of the parties it is even less logical. Again, we may presume that companies will try to avoid annihilation, especially from the stupid, self-inflicted wound of driving price down to marginal cost when marginal cost is below average cost. Atomistic price wars apart, however, it is difficult to think of circumstances in which the better firms would find their own self-interest furthered by committing themselves to the lock-step of "full collusion".

What is wrong with the law on this matter is that it fails to recognize, first, the need for a uniform *pro forma* price in some circumstances and, second, the fact that a uniform *pro forma* price gives *no* indication at all about the state of competition or the all-important rate of offer improvement.

It is, perhaps, too much to hope that the law will ignore partial agreements, even though a good case can be made that the costs of surveillance and intervention are likely to exceed the benefits. What we should be able to do, however, is insist that if industry-wide partial agreements are to be investigated, the courts must be instructed to look at *all* dimensions of competition. The agreements to be disallowed should be only those that threaten an undue restraint on entry, or that turn or threaten to turn the industry into a monopoly in the single-seller sense.

Implicit Agreements

That the law should attempt to treat states of recognized mutual interdependency or conscious parallelism, which, in many markets are the *sine qua non* of competition, as being indictable monopolistic offences is absurd. The preamble to the law should make this clear.

CONCLUSION

We began with a warning paraphrased from a leading textbook: "The image that you have of competition will shape your thinking on the appropriateness of different market structures and of different government policies." If the point was not obvious then, it is to be hoped that it is now. The popular views of the firm, the market, the nature of managerial work, and managerial behaviour, which we collected under the heading of theory X, lead logically to the conclusion that most firms — certainly all oligopolies, large firms and firms in concentrated industries — have monopoly power, and that they misallocate resources and retard progress. This view suggests that government policy should take upon itself the objective of pushing the structure of industry towards that set of behaviours and structures appropriate to the perfectly competitive model of competition. It must also aim at punishing any signs of collusion including conscious parallelism and recognized mutual interdependency.

On the other hand, when we try to build models of the firm, the market, managerial work, and the nature of managers more in tune with what we observe in the real world, and with what is known about people and institutions, we come to a completely different set of conclusions. It turns out that conspiracies serious enough to slow down the rate of offer improvement to consumers are difficult, and often impossible to negotiate. Nor are such agreements usually in the interests of the best firms in the industry. The process by which certain industries become concentrated oligopolies is itself highly competitive, and the grip of the "competitive imperative" does not loosen when numbers are small. Competition is alive and well and flourishing — not only *even* in oligopolies, but *especially* in oligopolies.

Even though the X-theory of competitive behaviour remained almost unchallenged until quite recently, an advocate of theory Y should be pleasantly surprised — not by the wording of the law, which reflects conventional wisdom — but by its judicial interpretation. Our Lady of the Law is no economist, X or Y, but the evidence suggests that judges, having become immersed in the facts of the case during a trial, have been guided to a theory Y, rather than to theory X, view of the universe. Monopolists in the unique-seller sense have *not* been sent to jail despite what the law says. Mergers have generally been allowed unless they have created or threatened to create a monopoly. So far, conscious parallelism has not been prosecuted (although there have been some near misses).[34]

There are many, of course, who deplore the decisions of the courts and who see the need for "strengthening" the law, which when translated, means weakening the power of the courts to depart from X-theory precepts. A concerted effort is being made to enshrine theory X even more solidly in legislative concrete. Unfortunately, this effort is inconsistent with much of the recent thinking that has started to emerge within the economics profession. It would be a pity to recast our map of the universe only to discover that some of our most vocal advisors were members of the flat-earth society. It would be especially disturbing if we were on the brink of the general acceptance of the theory that the world is round.

Notes

NOTES TO CHAPTER 1

[1] Shepherd, 1979, p. 172.
[2] Galbraith, 1967.
[3] Friedman, 1977.
[4] Roethlisberger, 1947, p. 138.
[5] McNulty, 1968, p. 639.
[6] Kilgour, 1962, p. 1.

NOTES TO CHAPTER 2

[1] In speaking of the "lack of agreement about what competition is" Massel suggests that the reason for the "serious differences among economists, lawyers, and businessmen . . . is a general desire to simplify a complex concept that has more attributes than many are willing to recognize." 1962, p. 3.
See also Skeoch, "Competition is a many faceted concept," 1974, p. 4.
[2] For an informative description of the transition of competition from a verb to a condition, see McNulty, 1968.
[3] Frank Knight has said "The 'perfect' market . . . is conventionally described as perfectly or purely 'competitive.' But use of this word is one of our worst misfortunes of terminology." 1946, p. 102.
[4] Robinson, 1964, Chapter 2.
[5] See for example, Samuelson and Scott, 1980, especially Chapters 4, 23, 25.
[6] As a "second opinion" to Samuelson-Scott see Evan Douglas, 1979: Price theory with a managerial slant.
[7] Robbins, 1948, p. 16.
[8] For another assault on the idea that a good is a good is a good see Lancaster 1971, especially Chapters 2 and 3.
[9] Cantillon described the process of rivalry between butchers and their *buyers* (not other butchers) as an "altercation" (McNulty, 1967, p. 395).
[10] Coase, 1937.
[11] Berle, 1967, pp. 371-2.
[12] Towle, 1964, p. 255. See also Elbing, 1967, pp. 110 ff., Garrett, 1966, pp. 26 ff., Sherman, 1972, pp. 32 ff.
[13] For an early recognition of the cost of the search for information see Stigler, 1961.
[14] T. Eaton, 1919.

NOTE TO APPENDIX A

[1] Hayek, 1949, p. 104.

NOTES TO CHAPTER 3

[1] Smith, 1937 Edition, p. 706.
[2] Schumpeter, 1947, pp. 84-5.
[3] Griffen, 1955, p. 387.
[4] Bladen and Stykolt, 1956, p. 52.
[5] Stigler, 1957, p. 16.

[6] Mansfield, 1968, p. 7.

[7] Economic Council of Canada, 1969, p. 12.

[8] Skeoch, 1972, p. 8.

[9] Quoted in Skeoch, 1972, p. 1.

[10] Clark, 1961, 14.

[11] For a similar view see Solo, C., 1951, "Innovation is more realistically analysed as an ordinary business activity than as the extraordinary efforts of new firms or new men." p. 417.

[12] Economic Council of Canada, 1969, p. 11.

[13] Friedman, 1962, p. 123.

[14] Tobias, 1976, p. 258.

[15] For a treatment of competition that visualizes it primarily as a *process* see Israel Kirzner, 1973.

[16] See for example Galbraith, *The Affluent Society*.

[17] Sowell, 1980, pp. 180, 81.

[18] Schumpeter, 1947, pp. 87, 106; Paton, 1973, p. 356.

[19] *Patent Act RSC* 1970, c. P-4.

[20] Arrow, 1959, p. 46.

[21] Schumpeter, 1947, p. 85.

[22] For a comparison of delivery van versus horse and carriage, De Bondt, 1970, p. 16.

[23] Manufacturers of the horse-drawn vehicles were not about to concede the superiority of the new-fangled, unsafe-at-any-speed horseless carriage. See Advertisement McLaughlin Carriage Co., Circa 1905, Lefoli, 1965, p. 87.

[24] See note 3 Chapter 6.

[25] For example see Hackman and Oldham, 1980, pp. 71 ff.

[26] The particular task involved key punching and the case was simply an illustration of the motivating potential of feedback. The unit was competing with itself not with any other unit.

[27] Knight, 1941, p. 103.

[28] Kilgour, 1962, p. 185.

[29] Smith, 1937 Edition pp. 342-343.

[30] Mill, 1929 Edition, p. 932.

[31] The actual number of employed workers in April 1981 was 10,700,000, Canadian Statistical Review, May 1981 (11-003E) p. 38.

[32] *The Fall & Winter '81 Sears Biggest Catalogue Ever* has 1000 pages.

[33] The personal expenditure on consumer goods and services totalled $160,694 million in the national accounts in 1980. (Canadian Statistical Review, May 1981 (11-003E) p. 18. Bank Clearings at $5,375,338 million (Ibid. p. 123) were larger by a factor of 33! The markets we see as consumers are but a small fraction of the total markets for all services, intermediate goods, financial paper, etc.

[34] See Appendix A, page 33.

[35] Ford's Edsel is a marvelous case in point. It shows that when *market* participants err (being human, they must do so from time to time) they are automatically penalized. The same, of course, cannot be said on behalf of error in the public sector.

[36] Schumpeter, 1947, pp. 269 ff.

[37] It would be a mistake to conclude, however, that the political and economic processes are equally efficient in providing for all consumer wants. It is only the latter that benefits from the profit and loss, "weeding-out-of-the-inefficient" system. And while they each have a voting mechanism (ballot-box voting, the "dollar" vote), the latter is far superior in supplying most consumer goods and services. Gary S. Becker shows that the market is probably superior even if the goods supplied by the private sector are produced under monopolistic conditions. Becker, 1958.

[38] This applies, unfortunately, only to consumer products, not necessarily to political platforms.

[39] Stigler, 1950, p. 64.
[40] Adam Smith apparently held somewhat the same view when he wrote: "Some of them [merchants], perhaps, may sometimes decoy a weak customer to buy what he has no occasion for. This evil, however, is of too little importance to deserve the publick attention". (1937 Edition, p. 343.)
[41] The surface of the blackboard is often referred to as two dimensional space. Length, width and height make up the usual three-dimensional space. If there are more dimensions it is customary to refer to "n" dimensional space. Since there are obviously many dimensions of even simple products, we must try to visualize product choice as occuring within multi dimensional space. Relevance defines the limits of buyers' and sellers' ability to strike bargains within that space, and density becomes density of offers in space rather than the density or distribution of offers along a single line. If for some reason we want to compare the amount of choice offered in two static and unchanging economies then as a first approximation we might imagine comparing the volume and density of the choices in the space that is relevant for both economies.
[42] Stigler and Kindahl, 1970, pp. 4-5.
[43] See in this regard Borcherding and Dorosh, 1981 and Grubel and Schwindt 1977.
[44] Regina v. Armco *et al*, 1974, p. 61.
[45] Nicholson, 1972, p. 5.
[46] Smith, 1937 edition, p. 423.
[47] Moore, H., 1906, p. 213.
[48] Knight, 1941, p. 103.
[49] Kilgour, 1972, p. 185.
[50] Low, 1968, p. 28.
[51] Clark, 1961, p. 18.
[52] Knight, in Brozen, 1975, p. 74.
[53] Kilgour, 1962, p. i.
[54] Stigler, 1950, p. 63.
[55] Hayek, 1948, pp. 77-106.
[56] Although the degree to which the unhampered market place can itself evolve rules for standardization, when such rules make sense, should not be underestimated. For an account of the standardization of railroad track gauges, see Taylor and Neu, 1956.
[57] Consultants are, of course, not free to reveal the affairs of their clients. In passing on to students or readers what one has learned as a consultant one must be very careful not to present cases in such a way that a client can be identified.
[58] Bork, 1978, p. 58.
[59] As an example of an uncompromising, and more typical, opposing view see English, 1965, pp. 47 ff.
[60] Shepherd, 1979, p. 305.
[61] Shepherd 1979, p. 301.
[62] Tobias, 1976, p. 35.
[63] Wilson, 1955, p. 262.
[64] Rothwell, 1973, pp. 67 ff.
[65] *U.S. v United Shoe Machine Corp.* 110 F, Supp. 295, D.Mass., 1953.
[66] Leibenstein, 1966, p. 413.
[67] Hobbes, n.d. p. 81.
[68] Kilgour, 1972, p. i.
[69] Hitsman, 1965, p. 173.

NOTES TO CHAPTER 4

[1] Berle, 1969, pp. 157 and 161.
[2] Dewey, 1974, p. 13.
[3] Hartle, 1979, p. 550.
[4] Seneca and Haight, 1978, p. 342.
[5] See, for example, Scherer, 1970, pp. 9 ff.
[6] Boulding, 1958, p. 111.
[7] Seneca and Haight, 1978, p. 343.
[8] Berle, 1969, p. 146.
[9] Seneca and Haight, 1978, p. 343.
[10] R. v Cominco Ltd. *et al.*, *Particulars of Indictment*, [1980] 2 W.W.R. 693. No. CR11267AD 1978, p. 4; italics added.
[11] *R. v Canadian Coat and Apron Supply Ltd. et al.*, 1967, p. 64.
[12] Smith, 1937 ed., p. 61.
[13] *Ibid.*, pp. 564-565.
[14] Block, 1977, p. 271.
[15] Scherer, 1970, p. 10.
[16] Robinson, 1948, p. 5 and pp. 307 ff.
[17] Reuber and Wilson, 1979, p. 256.
[18] Berle, 1969, p. 199.
[19] See Appendix A, page 33.
[20] Dewing, 1921, pp. 84 ff.
[21] See in this regard John McGee, 1958.
[22] Caves, 1979, pp. 506-507.
[23] *Ibid.*, p. 512.
[24] Berle, 1969, p. 144, italics added.
[25] Kaysen and Turner, 1959, p. 266.
[26] Green, 1980, pp. 63-64.
[27] Cf. Rothbard, 1970, pp. 1, 2.
[28] Some see parallels between this kind of harassment and ecclesiastical and "ring-around-the-collar" harassment!
[29] Block, 1977, p. 271.
[30] Bork, 1978, p. 61.
[31] Although see Rothbard, 1962, pp. 560-566.
[32] Galbraith, 1967, p. 110.
[33] Dewey, 1974, p. 11.
[34] See author's note on page 179.
[35] Martin and Simms, 1973, p. 273.
[36] Simon, 1957, p. 152.
[37] Galbraith, 1967, p. 11.
[38] Stogdill, 1974, p. 293.
[39] Kotter, 1977, p. 126.
[40] For the view that perfect competition and disequilibrium are basically incompatible, see Kirzner, 1976, pp. 116, 117.
[41] Indeed no one in the price-theory world, whether inside or outside the firm, would know for sure whether the price had been too high or too low or indeed if there even existed a price that would have enabled the firm to survive. In the real world there are more unknowns.
[42] Or monopsonistic, since single buyers are sometimes called monopsonists rather than monopolists.
[43] Examples include grocery stores, laundromats, bicycle-repair shops and shoe-shine shops.

44 Knight (1941, p. 103) associated competition with freedom which clearly meant the power to choose. The attack of the classical economists on monopoly can be seen as an attempt to extend the power to choose (invest, take a job etc) to those whose freedom (power) had been curtailed by the state-granted monopoly.

45 See author's note on page 100.

46 Berle, 1969, p. 37.

47 *Ibid.*, p. 143.

48 *Ibid.*, p. 144.

49 *Ibid.*, p. 146.

50 Other examples that spring readily to mind are the substitution of automobiles for horses and buggies, electricity for oil lamps, paper for papyrus scrolls, and ball-point pens for inkwells and quills.

51 See John McGee, 1958.
   D.T. Armentano, 1972, pp. 73-74, 243.

52 Galbraith, 1952.

53 See Hayek, 1944.

54 Shepherd, 1979, p. 7.

55 McNulty, 1968, p. 641.

NOTES TO CHAPTER 5

1 Robinson, 1948 Edition, p. 5.

2 See Rothbard, 1962, pp. 587-593. For a general analysis of monopoly, see his entire Chapter 9.

3 If the price of beer went up 10 per cent and sales of wine jumped 30 per cent the cross-elasticity would be +3 (30% ÷ 10%) and it would be concluded that wine is a fairly close substitute for beer. If the same change in the price of beer increased wine sales by only 5 per cent cross-elasticity would be only +.5 (5% ÷ 10%) and we would conclude beer drinkers would rather fight (or pay) than switch. Economists usually regard positive elasticities *plus* 3 or *plus* .5 as indicating substitute goods (beer and wine). Infinite positive elasticity (between brand X and brand Y) would indicate that consumers believe both brands to be the same good. See Ferguson, 1972, pp. 70-78. Goods from the same industry will presumably have cross-elasticities somewhere between zero and plus infinity, but any cut-off point for deciding whether a particular product is in a particular industry will necessarily be arbitrary.

4 Brozen, 1975, p. 8.

5 They are probably also the people who brought us the "social" in social justice — but that is another story.

6 Rothbard, 1962, p. 582.

7 Bain, 1972, p. 82.

8 *Ibid.*, p. 82.

9 A group of executives, of which I was one, once received a difficult-to-refuse offer to walk away from our old company without removing a single piece of paper. We were then to develop a better product without duplicating any of the work we had done for our former company over the previous two years.

10 Bain, 1972, p. 82.

11 *Ibid.*, p. 82.

12 Kirzner, 1973, p. 110.

13 Bain, 1973, p. 83.

14 Bain, 1973, p. 83.

15 in Haney, 1936, p. 347.

[16] See "The Communist Manifesto" in Mendel, 1977.

[17] Kirzner, 1973, pp. 101 ff.

[18] Alternatively, each participant in our little island scenario may be an extreme advocate of the private property rights doctrine — so much so that theft would be unthinkable even under the direst of straights.

[19] Arrow, 1959, p. 47.

[20] Rosenbluth, 1979, p. 336.

[21] *Ibid.*, p. 336.

[22] This is not just an idle academic fear. Several antitrust cases in the U.S. show that the government has interpreted successful innovation and competitiveness as *ipso facto* monopoly. See Bock, 1980.

[23] Smith, 1937 Edition, p. 61.

[24] Kolko, 1967, p. 40; McGee, 1958.

[25] For an explanation of the characteristics approach "which takes into account heterogeneity in consumption goods, see Lancaster, 1966a and 1966b.

NOTES TO CHAPTER 6

[1] This can be seen by the very close parallel between output performance per person-hour in agriculture and the input per person-hour of capital (e.g. machinery) and "intermediate" products (e.g. fertilizer) See Economic Council of Canada, 1980, pp. 88 ff.

[2] Myers, 1975. Fowler, 1977. Wattles, 1973. Globe and Mail, Sept. 5, 1979, November 22, 1979. Feb. 13, 1980. Vancouver Sun, Dec. 27, 1980. pA4, Jan. 31, 1981, pA3.

[3] Mili, 1977, p. 90. *Electronics & Communications*, April 1981, p. 61. Kates, 1977, p. 28. Juneau, 1980, p. 3. *Communication Statistics*, April 1980.

[4] Or a consortium of big companies. The Canadian Arctic Gas Pipeline Ltd. sponsoring the McKenzie Valley Pipeline spent "*more than $130 million*" without getting its project past the government approval stage. *The Gazette, July 5, 1977*, p. 21.

[5] The advantage of being large was made evident to me when a client company considered and then abandoned a research project to automate a warehouse. A competitor of about equal size *in Canada* went ahead with essentially the same project. The difference was that the client company was an independent Canadian company. The cost of the research had to be measured against the benefit of the possible cost savings in two warehouses. The company that went ahead with the project was part of a multinational that was in a position to realize savings in 15 warehouses in three countries.

[6] Lindeman and Armstrong, 1961, pp. 57 ff.

[7] There are, of course, only a few manufacturers of big computer systems of which I.B.M. is by far the largest. We sometimes make the mistake, therefore, of thinking that all aspects of the computing business are highly concentrated. The "Yellow Pages" for Vancouver list 171 companies under "Data Processing Service" of which I.B.M. is one. Additional companies are to be found under other headings. See B.C. Tel *Yellow Pages*, pp. 317-320.

[8] Since in 1977, 52 per cent of all R and D expenditures in Canada was accounted for by only 25 companies this must be *de facto* the strategy of the vast majority of Canadian companies (Statistics Canada, *Annual Review of Science Statistics*, 1980, p. 26.

[9] According to Scherer, 1970:
. . .inability to get ideas approved by higher management drives many of the most creative individuals out of large corporation laboratories to go it alone

in their own ventures. During the two decades following World War II thousands of research-based enterprises were founded by frustrated fugitives from the laboratories of such U.S. giants as Sperry Rand, I.B.M., Western Electric, Hughes Aircraft, Raytheon, and many others" p. 354. As explained in the text some of the fugitives may simply be profit maximizers.

[10] When two executives in the computer business meet for the first time one of the questions usually asked is "did you graduate from I.B.M." When I commented on this form of greeting to an I.B.M. executive (whom I was trying to hire away from I.B.M.) he explained that it was his understanding that I.B.M. ran a bigger graduate business education program than did Columbia University.

[11] For a perceptive, one might say devastating, discussion of the problems inherent in studying the economics of technological change see Gold, 1977, pp. 7-29.

[12] Scherer, 1970, p. 357.

[13] Hamberg, 1964.

[14] Horowitz, 1962.

[15] Scherer, 1965.

[16] Scherer, 1967.

[17] Comanor, 1967.

[18] Grabowski and Baxter, 1973.

[19] Worley, 1962.

[20] Mansfield, 1964.

[21] Mansfield, 1968a.

[22] Markham, 1974, p. 268.

[23] *Ibid.*, p. 249.

[24] Kewkes, Sawers, Stillerman, 1969.

[25] *Ibid.*, p. 278-279.

[26] *Ibid.*, p. 321-323.

[27] Kirzner, 1973, p. 116.

[28] This follows, of course, from identifying monopoly as a single seller or the maker of a unique offer or as any departure from perfect competition e.g. having a sloped demand curve.

[29] In technical terms, this argument is valid, but since there is a false premise, or premises, the conclusion is false. An analogous argument is the following:

    (a) $8 > 7$
    (b) $7 > 9$
    (c) $9 > 10$
    (d) $8 > 10$

In both cases (a) is true, (b) and (c) are false and therefore (d) is false, but (d) follows logically from (a) (b) and (c) in each case.

[30] Royal Commission on Corporate Concentration, 1978, p. 91.

[31] *Ibid.*, p. 91, italics added.

[32] *Ibid.*, p. 91.

[33] *Ibid.*, p. 91.

[34] *Ibid.*, p. 92.

[35] See Figure 22, page 63.

[36] Royal Commission on Corporate Concentration, 1978, p. 92.

[37] Fellner, 1951, especially 560-567 that deals with an unexpected innovation and blocked entry.

[38] On the other hand there are daily reminders to businessmen of the consequences of failing to keep up with technological developments. Indeed virtually every one of the 3,000 bankruptcies per year (see note 5 above) could be said by definition to result from a failure to maintain a viable rate of offer improvement to all participants.

[39] Royal Commission on Corporate Concentration, 1978, p. 1

[40] See note 13 above and McGee, 1971.

[41] Blair, 1972.

[42] McGee, 1971.

[43] In Blair, 1972, p. 234.

[44] An engineering executive of a Canadian steel company has suggested to me that the diversification of Voest may have had something to do with its development of the oxygen process. The idea of using oxygen goes back at least to Sir Henry Bessemer. The trick was not the concept, it was the production of cheap oxygen and its delivery to the appropriate location inside the furnace.

[45] Royal Commission on Corporate Concentration, 1978, p. 59.

[46] *Ibid.*, pp. 91-92.

[47] Whitaker, 1981, pp. 1556-1559.

[48] For the thousands of products we do not produce at all, one viable Canadian producer would in most cases be as many as we could reasonably expect. For the "monopolists" like C.A.E. discussed above and for many other such firms that produce everything from machines to extract honey from honeycombs to creative playgrounds, to street sweepers, data phones and long-range executive jet aircraft we should be grateful that the number of producers in Canada is one and not zero.

[49] Much of the dissatisfaction with concentration studies hinges on the impossibility of finding a satisfactory definition of an industry. See for example McGee, 1971, or Scherer, 1970, pp. 52 ff.

[50] Seitovsky recognized the cost of choice by introducing the concept of "rational inertia" (1951, p. 320.). Buyers are likely to seek information about other offers only when they believe the probable gains exceed the costs of becoming better informed. See also Stigler, 1961.

[51] Hence, I have found company purchasing guidelines that specify the minimum *and* *maximum* number of suppliers that a purchasing agent should investigate, and an apartment house in Edmonton in which the tenants had jointly decided to have only one milkman.

[52] Leibenstein, 1966.

[53] *Ibid.*, p. 392.

[54] *Ibid.*, p. 401.

[55] *Ibid.*, p. 405.

[56] *Ibid.*, p. 407.

[57] *Ibid.*, p. 413.

[58] An exception is Stigler, 1976.

[59] Green, 1980, p. 38.

[60] *Ibid.*, p. 147.

[61] Stigler, 1950, p. 63.

[62] Hicks, 1935, p. 8.

[63] Fellner, 1950, p. 54.

[64] Nicholson, 1972, pp. 29-30.

[65] Gorecki and Stanbury, 1979, p. 181.

[66] *Montreal Star*, Jan. 19, 1974.

[67] Consumer and Corporate Affairs, 1980, p. 4.

[68] McGregor, 1960, especially Chapters 3 and 4.

[69] *Ibid.*, p. 33.

[70] *Ibid.*, p. 34.

[71] Maslow, 1970.

[72] Hertzberg, 1966.

[73] McGregor, 1960, pp. 36, 48.

[74] Identification of the industry would be quite improper.

[75] McGregor, 1960, p. 36.

[76] Actually Mr. Bumble said "If the law supposes that . . . the law is *a* ass . . . (*Oliver Twist*, Chapter 47.)

[77] The actual amount will depend on the measure and time period chosen. See Statistics Canada, *Aggregate Productivity Measures*, 14, 201.

[78] This and some of the other effects discussed below are sometimes called the Hawthorne effect. See Roethlisberger, 1947.

[79] In most of the cases cited by Leibenstein the interest of the study and the expertise of the academics or consultants was in that area broadly known as organizational behaviour.

[80] Mintzberg, 1973, pp. 29 ff.

[81] Whyte, 1956.

[82] Rothwell, 1973, pp. 66-68, 112-114, 119.

[83] The law on this matter as stated by MacKay is as follows:

Seldom, if ever, do conspirators set down the object of the conspiracy in writing or can the existence of a conspiracy be proven by direct evidence. Therefore, proof of a conspiracy is generally a matter of inference deduced from acts of the parties accused: *Archbold's Criminal Pleading Evidence & Practice*, 34th ed. (1959) 1526-7; *Paradis v. The King*, 61 C.C.C. 184.

Acts which by themselves are legal and appear to be quite innocent may begin to form a sinister pattern or have a sinister tendency. Then the inferences deduced therefrom may well satisfy the trial judge beyond any reasonable doubt that in fact an agreement or arrangement has concluded between any two of the accused or between any one of the accused and a co-conspirator: *R. v. Parnell*, 14 Cox C.C. 508; *Rex v. Brissac*, 4 East 171.

Regina v. Atlantic, 1978, p. 4.

[84] See author's note on page 24.

[85] Colberg *et al*, 1964, pp. 229 ff.

[86] Armstrong & Armstrong, 1958.

[87] Fama and Laffer, 1979, p. 674.

[88] Green, 1980, p. 147.

[89] *Ibid.*, p. 99.

[90] Naylor, 1975.

[91] Reynolds, 1940.

[92] Eastman and Stykolt, 1968.

[93] For a brief description of Reports by the Registrar, the Commissioner, the Special Commissioners and by the Restrictive Trade Practices Commission and the Cases before the courts see the Annual reports of the Director of Investigation and Research. For a convenient review of reports and some cases before 1965 see Skeoch, 1966 p. 97-155.

[94] Green, 1980, p. 102.

[95] *Ibid.*, p. 99, italics added.

[96] Regina v. Canadian Coat and Apron, 1967.

[97] Regina v. Aluminum Co., 1976.

[98] See page 26.

[99] Regina v. Aluminum Co. 1976, p. 28. (Judgement).

[100] In fact he did not talk to the people he claimed to talk to and his claim to the contrary should have been suspect to the investigators.

[101] Braumhart, 1968, p. 121.

NOTES TO CHAPTER 7

[1] For a more detailed discussion of measurement problems, see McGee, 1970, especially pp. 80-123.
[2] Department of Consumer and Corporate Affairs, 1971.
[3] In 1963 imports accounted for 9.2 per cent of passenger car sales. (Statistics Canada, New Motor Vehicle Sales 1971 p. 18. In July 1981 this figure had risen to 31.7 per cent (*Globe and Mail* Aug. 31, 1981, p. 81.)
[4] Department of Consumer and Corporate Affairs, 1971, p. 42.
[5] Dewey, 1974, p. 5.
[6] As an example of this, consider the following:
"Increased concentration in Canadian industry reduces the benefits which are expected to flow to the public from free competition in terms of lower prices for goods and services, a greater range of choice for consumers, increased innovativeness on the part of firms, and a more efficient use and allocation of resources within the Canadian economy in the long run" (Bertrand, 1975, p. 2)
[7] Weiss, 1974.
[8] *Ibid.*, p. 232.
[9] Phillips, 1976, p. 248.
[10] Demsetz, 1974, p. 171.
[11] Brozen, 1970, p. 292.
[12] Brozen, 1970.
[13] This idea is well established in Austrian economics See Kirzner 1979, "Entrepreneurship and Disequilibrium," pp. 3-33; Kirzner, 1973, "Competition & Entrepreneurship," and Jackman, 1973, "Macro-Economic Thinking and the Market Economy."
[14] Capital requirements, of course, are frequently cited as a barrier to entry (Bain, 1972, p. 83). What we are saying here is that capital requirements and the other factors cited will inevitably slow down entry.
[15] Government regulation — to the extent that it hits the large, visible projects harder than it hits hot dog stands — can be counted on to delay the investment process in concentrated industries even further.
[16] Sherman, 1972, p. 52.
[17] *Ibid.*, p. 32.
[18] Shepherd, 1979, p. 282.
[19] Friedman, J., 1967, p. 397.
[20] *Ibid.*, p. 397.

NOTES TO CHAPTER 8

[1] *Combines Investigation Act*, R.S., C-23 1970 as amended, Section 33.
[2] von Mises, 1969, pp. 114-115.
[3] Bock, 1980.
[4] Friedman, 1962, p. 120.
[5] In the U.S. there is a move under the Reagan administration to simplify all laws, contracts, etc., so that they can be read by the intelligent layman. The *Combines Investigation Act* would be a good place to start in Canada.
[6] In the titanium dioxide case the Federal Trade Commission complaint is in effect that DuPont substantially reduced its cost through a new process which it patented and did not make available to its competitors. In the Alcoa case the company was thought to have expanded its output too rapidly. (See Bock, 1980.) (Yet economics students have it drilled into them that monopolists restrict output.)
[7] *Combines Investigation Act*, 1970 as amended, Section 33.

[8] This is a sore point with officials of Consumer and Corporate Affairs who complain officially (Consumer and Corporate Affairs, 1979, pp. 13-21) and unofficially (for example, "Official laments lack of merger opposition," *Globe and Mail*, January 5, 1979. [A structuralist would argue that any merger must increase concentration and therefore reduce competition. Any merger is therefore detrimental to the public interest unless it can be shown that it offers gains that will offset the loss of competition.]

[9] Low, 1968, pp. 94-95.

[10] For what would appear to be just such a case see Consumer and Corporate Affairs, 1975, p. 33.

[11] Regina v. Canadian Breweries Limited, 1960.

[12] See Skeoch, 1966 pp. 77, 84-85.

[13] *Ibid.*, p. 85.

[14] Brewers Association, 1965. "Originally there was a brewery in nearly every community of any size" (p. 92). In 1875, 164 Brewery Licences were issued (see Table p. 94).

[15] This is demonstrated by the Erco case. Consumer and Corporate Affairs, 1970, p. 51.

[16] For a summary of the case see Consumer and Corporate Affairs, 1973, pp. 76-79.

[17] Gorecki and Stanbury (Ed.) 1979, p. 129.

[18] Regina v. K.C. Irving, 1974.

[19] Shepherd, 1979, p. 357.

[20] Gartwell, 1976, p. 32.

[21] This they have done by proposing new powers in a revised competition bill and by a public speaking program. For an analysis of what the bureau wanted to be included in the most recent legislation proposal, Bill C-13, see Quinn, 1979, pp. 269-296.

[22] Back to silk stockings again; given the intensity of the threat from nylon it would probably have been advisable and desirable from everyone's point of view if the silk stocking industry had united to attempt a technological counter attack.

[23] Regina v. Atlantic Sugar, 1978.

[24] Before economists and lawyers made hasty judgements about market share they would do well to read and reflect on Ardrey, *The Territorial Imperative*, 1966. For those firms to which learning is important, market share i.e. volume, is of paramount importance. For a brief description see Stokes, 1979, pp. 179-184.

[25] Regina v. Atlantic Sugar Transcript 11, 12, 74, p. 29.

[26] *Ibid.*, p. 30.

[27] *Ibid.*, p. 80.

[28] *Ibid.*, p. 80.

[29] Regina v. Atlantic Sugar Transcript 11, 12, 74, p. 28.

[30] Regina v. Cominco *et al* (1980).

[31] *Ibid.*, p. 715.

[32] *Combines Investigation Act*, Section 32(2)g.

[33] Stigler, 1950, p. 63.

[34] The Eastern Sugar case being an example.

BIBLIOGRAPHY

Ardrey, Robert. *The Territorial Imperative.* New York: Atheneum, 1966.

Armentand, D.T. *The Myths of Antitrust.* New Rochelle, N.Y.: Arlington House, 1972.

Armstrong, D.E. and Armstrong, Muriel. "Third Party Intervention in the Alberta Coal Industry 1900-1951" in Woods, H.D. Editor, *Patterns of Industrial Dispute Settlement in Five Canadian Industries.* Montreal: Industrial Relations Centre, McGill University, 1958. 31-116.

Arrow, Kenneth J. "Toward a Theory of Price Adjustment." Abramovitz, M., *et al. The Allocation of Economic Resources.* Stanford: Stanford University Press, 1959: 41-51.

Bain, Joe S. *Essays on Price Theory and Industrial Organization.* Boston: Little, Brown and Co., 1972.

Baumhart, Raymond S.J. *Ethics in Business.* New York: Holt, Rinehart and Winston, 1968.

Becker, Gary S. "Competition and Democracy." *Journal of Law and Economics* 1, (October 1958): 105—109.

Berle, Adolf A. *Power.* New York: Harcourt Brace and World Inc., 1969.

Bertrand, Robert J. *Testimony of Mr. Robert J. Bertrand, Assistant Deputy Minister, Bureau of Competition Policy and Director of Investigation and Research, Combines Investigation Act, Before the Royal Commission on Corporate Concentration.* Ottawa: November 3, 1975. Mimeographed.

Bladen, V.W. and Stykolt, S. "Combines Policy and Public Interest: An Economist's Evaluation" in *Anti-Trust Laws: A Comparative Symposium* edited by Wolfgang Friedman. University of Toronto, Faculty of Law, Comparative Law Series, Vol. 3 (Toronto, Carswell, 1956): 45-90.

Blair, John M. *Economic Concentration, Structure, Behaviour and Public Policy.* New York: Harcourt Brace Jovanovich, 1972.

Block, Walter. "Austrian Monopoly Theory — A Critique." *Journal of Libertarian Studies* 2 No. 4 (1977): 271-279.

Bock, Betty. "The Innovator as an Antitrust Target." *Information Bulletin* 74 (1980). New York: The Conference Board, 1980.

Borcherding, Thomas with Dorosh, Gary W. *The Egg Marketing Board: A Case Study of Monopoly and its Social Costs.* Vancouver: The Fraser Institute, 1981.

Bork, Robert H. *The Antitrust Paradox: A Policy at War with Itself.* New York: Basic Books Inc., 1978.

Boulding, K.E. *Principles of Economic Policy.* Englewood Cliffs, N.J.: Prentice-Hall, 1958.

Brewers Association of Canada. *Brewing in Canada.* Montreal: Brewers Association, 1965.

Brewis, T.N.; English, H.E.; Scott, Anthony; and Jewett, Pauline. *Canadian Economic Policy.* Toronto: Macmillan Company, 1965.

Brodrick, John. "Management and Technology." *Economics and Technical Change.* Edited by E.M. Hugh-Jones. New York: Augustus M. Kelley, 1969.

Brozen, Yale. "The Antitrust Task Force Deconcentration Recommendations." *Journal of Law and Economics* XIII (2) (October 1970). Reprinted in Brozen, Yale. *The Competitive Economy Selected Readings.* Morristown, N.J.: General Learning Press, 1975: 113-123.

——————————. ed. *Advertising and Society.* New York: New York University Press, 1974.

Canada. *Communications Statistics.* Ottawa: Department of Communications, April 1980.

Canada. *Report of the Director of Investigation and Research for the Year Ending March 31, 1973.* Ottawa: Department of Consumer and Corporate Affairs, March 31, 1973.

Canada. *Annual Report: Director of Investigation and Research, Combines Investigation Act for the Year Ending March 31, 1980.* Ottawa: Department of Consumer and Corporate Affairs, 1980.

Canada. *Concentration in the Manufacturing Industries of Canada.* Ottawa: Department of Consumer and Corporate Affairs, 1971.

Canada. *Annual Report, Superintendent of Bankruptcy: for the Calendar Year 1977.* Ottawa: Department of Consumer and Corporate Affairs, 1979.

Canada. *A Climate of Uncertainty: Seventeenth Annual Review.* Economic Council of Canada. Ottawa: Department of Supply and Services, 1980.

Canada. *Interim Report on Competition Policy.* Economic Council of Canada. Ottawa: July, 1969.

Canada. *New Motor Vehicle Sales.* Ottawa: Statistics Canada, 1971.

Canada. *Annual Review of Science Statistics, 1980.* Ottawa: Statistics Canada, 1981. Cat. 13-212.

Caves, Richard E. "Industrial Concentration, Corporate Size and Market Power: Economic Evidence and Strategic Choices for Canadian Competition Policy" in Pritchard, J.R.S., *et al. Canadian Competition Policy: Essays in Law and Economics.* Toronto: Butterworth, 1979: 505-524.

Clark, John Maurice. *Competition as a Dynamic Process.* Washtington D.C.: The Brookings Institution, 1961.

Coase Ronald A. "The Nature of the Firm." *Economica*, 1937.

Comanor, W.S. "Market Structure, Product Differentiation and Industrial Research." *Quarterly Journal of Economics* 81, (November 1967): 639-657.

Combines Investigation Act, R.S., c.C-23 1970 as amended.

Cohen, Kalman J., and Cyert, Richard M. *Theory of The Firm.* 2d ed. Englewood Cliffs, N.J.: Prentice-Hall, 1975.

Colberg, M.R.; Forbush, D.R.; Whitaker, G.R. Jr.; and Bradford, W.C. *Business Economics Principles and Cases.* Homewood, Ill.: Richard D. Irwin, 1964.

DeBonot, John. *Canada on Wheels: A Portfolio of Early Canadian Cars.* Oberon Press, 1970.

Demsetz, Harold. "Two Systems of Belief about Monopoly" in Goldschmid, Harvey J., *et al. Industrial Concentration: The New Learning.* Columbia University Centre for Law and Economic Studies. Boston: Little, Brown and Co., 1974: 164-184.

Dewey, Donald J. "The New Learning: One Man's View" in Goldschmid, *et al. Industrial Concentration: The New Learning.* Columbia University Center for Law and Economic Studies. Boston: Little, Brown and Co., 1974.

Dewing, Arthur S. "A Statistical Test of the Success of Consolidations." *Quarterly Journal of Economic* 31, (1921-2): 84-101.

Douglas, Evan J. *Managerial Economics: Theory, Practice, and Problems.* Englewood Cliffs, N.J.: Prentice-Hall, 1979.

Eastman, H., and Stykolt, S. *The Tariff and Competition in Canada.* Toronto: Macmillan, 1968.

Eaton, T. Co. (The Scribe). *Golden Jubilee 1869-1919.* Toronto: The T. Eaton Co., 1919.

Elbing, A.O., and Elbing, C.J. *The Value Issue of Business.* New York: McGraw-Hill, 1967.

Electronics & Communications. "Phone Combines Voice and Data for Office of the Future." April, 1981: 61.

English, H.E. "Competition and Policy to Control Restrictive Practices" in Brewis, *et al. Canadian Economic Policy.* Toronto: Macmillan, 1965.

Fama, Eugene F., and Laffer, Arthur B. "The Number of Firms and Competition." *American Economic Review* LXII Number 4 (September 1972): 670-674.

Fellner, William. "Collusion and Its Limits under Oligopoly." *American Economic Review: Papers and Proceedings* XL Number 2 (May 1950): 54-62.

Fellner, William J. "The Influence of Market Structure on Technological Progress." *Quarterly Journal of Economics* 65 Part 4 (November 1951): 556-577.

Flink, James J. *America Adopts the Automobile 1895-1910.* Cambridge, Mass.: MIT Press, 1970.

Ferguson, C.E. *Microeconomic Theory.* Georgetown, Ontario: Irwin-Dorsey, Ltd., 1972.

Fowler, Dorothy G. *Unmailable.* Atlanta: University of Georgia Press, 1977.

Friedman, James W. "An Experimental Study of Cooperative Duopoly." *Econometric* 35 Number 3-4 (July-October 1967): 379-397.

Friedman, Milton. *Capitalism and Freedom.* Chicago: University of Chicago Press, 1962.

_____. *Friedman on Galbraith and on Curing the British Disease.* Vancouver: The Fraser Institute, 1977.

Galbraith, J.K. "Monopoly and the Concentration of Economic Power." *A Survey of Contemporary Economics.* Edited by Howard S. Ellis. Philadelphia: The Blakison Co., 1949: 99-128.

_____. *American Capitalism: The Concept of Countervailing Power.* Boston: Houghton Mifflin, 1952.

_____. *The Affluent Society.* Boston: Houghton Mifflin, 1958.

_____. *The New Industrial State.* Boston: Houghton Mifflin, 1967.

Garrett, Thomas M. *Business Ethics.* New York: Appleton Century-Crofts, 1966.

Gartrell, John W. *Organization Size and Alienation.* Royal Commission on Corporate Concentration, Study No. 27, 1976.

Gold, Bela. "Research, Technological Change, and Economic Analysis: A Critical Evaluation of Prevailing Approaches." *Quarterly Review of Economics and Business* 17:1 (1977): 7-29.

Goldschmid, Harvey J.; Mann, H. Michael; and Weston, J. Fred (ed.) *Industrial Concentration: The New Learning.* Columbia University Center for Law and Economic Studies. Boston: Little, Brown and Co., 1974.

Gorecki, Paul K., and Stanbury, W.T. "Canada's Combines Investigation Act: The Record of Public Law Enforcement 1889-1976" in Pritchard, Roberts S., *et al. Canadian Competition Policy: Essays in Law and Economics.* Toronto: Butterworth, 1979.

Gorecki, Paul K., and Stanbury, W.T., Editors. *Perspectives on the Royal Commission on Corporate Concentration.* Montreal: Institute for Research on Public Policy, 1979.

Grabowski, Henry G., and Baxter, Nevins D. "Rivalry in Industrial Research and Development: An Empirical Study." *Journal of Industrial Economics* 21, (July 1973):209-235.

Green, Christopher. *Canadian Industrial Organization and Policy.* Toronto: McGraw-Hill Ryerson, 1980.

Griffen, Clare. *A Study of the Antitrust Laws Senate Hearings.* Part 1, June 9, 1955.

Grubel, Herbert G., and Schwindt, Richard W. *The Real Cost of the B.C. Milk Board: A Case Study in Canadian Agricultural Policy.* Vancouver: The Fraser Institute, 1977.

Hackman, J. Richard, and Oldham, Greg R. *Work Redesign.* Don Mills, Ont.: Addison-Wesley, 1980.

Hamberg, D. "Size of Firm, Oligopoly, and Research: The Evidence." *Canadian Journal of Economics and Political Science* 30 (February, 1964):62-75.

Hartle, Douglas G. "Another Perspective on Competition Policy" in *Canadian Competition Policy: Essays in Law and Economics.* Pritchard, J.R.S., *et al.* Toronto: Butterworth, 1979.

Hayek, Frederich A. *The Road to Serfdom*. Chicago: University of Chicago Press, 1944.
―――――――. "The Meaning of Competition." *Individualism and Economic Order*. London: Routledge and Kegan Paul, 1949.
Herzberg, F. *Work and the Nature of Man*. New York: World Publishing Co., 1966.
Hicks, J.R. "Annual Survey of Economic Theory: The Theory of Monopoly." *Econometrica*. Jan. 1935.
Hitsman, J. Mackay. *The Incredible War of 1812*. Toronto: University of Toronto Press, 1965.
Hobbes, Thomas. *Leviathan*. Oxford: Basil Blackwell, (no date).
Horowitz, Ira. "Firm Size and Research Activity." *Southern Economic Journal* 29, (January 1962):298-301.
Jevons, H. Stanley. *The Theory of Political Economy*. New York: Augustus M. Kelley, 1965. Reprint of 5th edition. First ed. 1871.
Jewkes, John; Sawers, David; and Stillerman, Richard. *The Sources of Invention*. Second Edition. London: Macmillan and Co. 1969.
Juneau, Pierre. "Federal-Provincial Roles in the Information Society." Notes for an address, Dec. 11, 1980. Ottawa: Department of Communications.
Kates, Joseph. "Technological Sovereignty a Strategy for Canada." *Annual Statement of the Chairman, Science Council of Canada, June 1977.*
Kaysen, Carl, and Turner, Donald F. *Antitrust Policy*. Cambridge, Mass.: Harvard University Press, 1959.
Kilgour, David G. *Cases and Materials on Unfair and Restrictive Trade Practices*. Toronto: University Toronto Press, 1962.
Kirzner, Isreal. *Competition and Entrepreneurship*. Chicago: University of Chicago Press, 1973.
―――――――. "Equilibrium as Market Process" in *The Foundations of Modern Austrian Economics*, Edwin G. Dolan, ed. Kansas City: Sheed and Ward, Inc., 1976.
―――――――. *Perception, Opportunity and Profit: Studies in the Theory of Entrepreneurship*. Chicago: University of Chicago Press, 1979.
Knight, Frank H. *The Ethics of Competition and other Essays*. New York & London: Harper and Brothers, 1935.
―――――――. "The Meaning of Freedom." *Ethics* Vol. LII, (1941-42): 86-109.
―――――――. "Immutable Law in Economics: Its Reality and Limitations." *American Economic Review: Papers and Proceedings* XXXII Number 2, (May 1946).
Kolko, Gabriel. *The Triumph of Conservation: A Reinterpretation of American History 1900-1916*. Chicago: Quadrangle Books. 1967.
Kotler, Philip. *Marketing Management Fourth Edition*, Englewood Cliffs, N.J.: Prentice-Hall, 1980.
Kotter, John P. "Power, Dependence, and Effective Management." *Harvard Business Review*. July-August 1977: 125-136.
Lachmann, Ludwig. *Macro-Economic Thinking and the Market Economy*. London: Institute for Economic Affairs, 1973.
―――――――. "On the Central Concept of Austrian Economics: Market Process" in Dolan, Edwin G. *The Foundations of Modern Austrian Economics*. Kansas City: Sheed and Ward Inc., 1976.
Lancaster, Kelvin. *Consumer Demand*. New York: Columbia University Press, 1971.
―――――――. "A New Approach to Consumer Theory." *Journal of Political Economy* 74, (1966): 132-157.
―――――――. "Change and Innovation in the Technology of Consumption." *American Economic Review: Papers and Proceedings* LVI Number 2, (May 1966): 14-23.

Lefoli, Ken. *The Canadian Look: A Century of Sights and Styles*. Toronto: McClelland and Stewart, 1965.

Leibenstein, Harvey. "Allocative Efficiency vs X-Efficiency." *American Economic Review* LVI No. 3, (June 1966): 392-415.

Lerner, J. *Regina v Armco et al.* The Supreme Court of Ontario, September 19, 1974.

Lindeman, John, and Armstrong, Donald. *Policies and Practices of United States Subsidiaries in Canada*. Canada: Canadian-American Committee, 1961.

Low, Richard E. "Introduction", Low, Richard E. (Ed.) *The Economics of Antitrust: Competition and Monopoly*. Englewood Cliffs, N.J.: Prentice-Hall, 1968.

——————. "Mergers and the Courts" in *The Economics of Antitrust: Competition and Monopoly*, Englewood Cliffs, N.J.: Prentice-Hall, 1968.

Lutans, Fred, and Hodgetts, Richard M. *Readings on the Current Social Issues in Business*. New York: Macmillan Co., 1972.

Mann, H. Michael. "Advertising, Concentration, and Profitability: The State of Knowledge and Directions for Public Policy" in Goldschmid, Harvey J. *et al. Industrial Concentration: The New Learning*. Columbia University Center for Law and Economic Studies. Boston: Little, Brown and Co., 1974.

Mansfield, Edwin. *The Economics of Technological Change*. New York: W.W. Norton and Co., 1968.

——————. *Industrial Research and Technologial Innovation*. New York: W.W. Norton and Co., 1968.

——————. "Industrial Research and Development Expenditures: Determinants, Prospects, and Relation of Size of Firm and Inventive Output." *Journal of Political Economy* 72, (August 1964): 319-340.

Markham, Jesse W. "Concentration: A Stimulus or Retardant to Innovation" in Goldschmid, Harvey J. *et al. Industrial Concentration: The New Learning*. Columbia University Center for Law and Economic Studies. Boston: Little Brown and Co., 1974.

Marshall, Alfred. *Principles of Economics*. 8th ed. Reprint 1952. London: Macmillan and Co., 1952.

Martin, N., and Simms, J. "Power Tactics." Leavitt, H., Pondy, L. (Eds.) *Readings in Managerial Psychology*. Chicago: Chicago University Press 1973.

Maslow, Abraham H. *Motivation and Personality*. 2d ed. New York: Harper and Row, 1970.

Masel, Mark S. *Competition and Monopoly: Legal and Economic Issues*. Washington, D.C.; The Brookings Institution, 1962.

McGee, John S. "Predatory Price Cutting: The Standard Oil (N.J.) Case." *Journal of Law and Economics* 1, (October, 1958): 137-169.

——————. *In Defense of Industrial Concentration*. New York: Praeger Publishers, 1971.

McGregor, Douglas. *The Human Side of Enterprise*. New York: McGraw-Hill, 1960.

McNulty, Paul J. "A Note on the History of Perfect Competition." *Journal of Political Economy*. August 1967: 395-399.

——————. "Economics Theory and the Meaning of Competition." *Quarterly Journal of Economics*. 1968: 639-656.

McQueen, David. "Revising Competition Law: Overview by a Participant" in Pritchard, J.R.S. *et al. Canadian Competition Policy: Essays in Law and Economics*. Toronto: Butterworth, 1979: 3-23.

Mendal, Arthur P., ed. *The Essential Works of Marxism*. New York: Bantam Books, 1977.

Mili, M. "Telecommunications in Canada." Editorial, *Telecommunication Journal* 44 III, 1977.

Mill, John Stuart. *Principles of Political Economy*. London: Longmans, Green and Co., 1929.

Miller, Danny. "Some Comments on the Distribution of Power in Complex Organizations." A submission to the Royal Commission on Corporate Concentration, 1976.

Mintzberg, Henry. *The Nature of Managerial Work*. New York: Harper and Row, 1973.

(The) Monopolies Commission, *Parallel Pricing: A Report on the General Effect on the Public Interest of the Practice of Parallel Pricing*. London: Her Majesty's Stationery Office, July 1973.

Moore, Henry L. "Paradoxes of Competition." *Quarterly Journal of Economics* XX (February 1906): 211-230.

Moore, Milton. *How Much Price Competition? The Prerequisites of an Effective Canadian Competition Policy*. Montreal: McGill University Press, 1970.

Myers, Robert J. *The Coming Collapse of the Post Office*. Englewood Cliffs, N.J.: Prentice-Hall, 1975.

Naylor, Tom. *The History of Canadian Business 1867-1914*. Vol. II. Toronto: James Lorimer, 1975.

Nelson, Phillip. "The Economics Value of Advertising" in Brozen, Yale, ed. *Advertising and Society*. New York: New York University Press, 1974.

Nicholson, Michael. *Oligopoly and Conflict: A Dynamic Approach*. Toronto: University of Toronto Press, 1972.

Paton, W.A. "Competition What and When." *The Freeman*. June 1973: 353-365.

Phillips, A. "A Critique of Empirical Studies of Relations between Market Structure and Profitability." *Journal of Industrial Economics XXIV No. 4, (June 1976): 241-249.*

Posner, Richard A. Anti Trust Law: An Economic Perspective. Chicago: University of Chicago Press, 1976.

Pritchard, J.R.S.; Stanbury, W.T., and Wilson, Thomas A. *Canadian Economic Policy: Essays in Law and Economics*. Toronto: Butterworth, 1979.

Quinn, John J. "Institutional Design and Canadian Merger Policy" in Pritchard J.R.S., *et al. Canadian Competition Policy: Essays in Law and Economics*. Toronto: Butterworth, 1979. 269-296.

Regina v. Aluminum Co. of Canada Ltd. *et al.* (1976) C.S. 1695; 29 C.P.R. 92d) 183.

Regina v. Atlantic Sugar *et al. Transcript* December 11, 1974. Afternoon Session.

Regina v. Atlantic Sugar Refineries *et al.* (1978) 41 C.C.C. 2d 209; 91 D.L.R. (3d) 618.

Regina v. Canadian Breweries Ltd. (960) O.R. 601; 33 C.R. 1; 126 C.C.C. 133.

Regina v. Cominco Ltd. *et al.* (1980) 2W.W.R. 693.

Regina v. K.C. Irving Ltd. *et al.* (1974) 16 C.C.C. (2d) 49; 13 C.P.R. (2d) 115; N.B.R. (2d) 360; 45 D.L.R. (3d) 45. (Trial) Regina v. K.C. Irving Ltd. and 3 other corporations (No. 2); Regina v. K.C. Irving Ltd. et al. (No. 2) (1974) 22 C.C.C. (2d) 281; 19 C.P.R. (2d) 256; 61 D.L.R. (3d) 11 (Sentence).

Regina v. Canadian Coat and Apron Supply Limited *et al.* 1967 2 Ex.C.R. 53; 2 C.R.N. 62; 52 C.P.R. 189.

Restrictive Trade Practices Commission. *A Report Concerning the Production, Manufacture, Supply and Sale of Cast Iron Soil Pipe and Fittings in the Prairie Provinces and British Columbia*. October 10, 1967.

Reynolds, Lloyd. *The Control of Competition in Canada*. Cambridge, Mass.: Harvard University Press, 1940.

Reuber, G.L., and Wilson, T.A. "Merger Policy Proposals: An Evaluation." in Pritchard J.R.S. *et al. Canadian Competition Policy: Essays in Law and Economics*. Toronto: Butterworth, 1979: 255-267.

Robbins, Lionel. *An Essay on the Nature and Significance of Economic Science* London: Macmillan and Co., 1948.

Robinson, Joan. *The Economics of Imperfect Competition*. London: Macmillan and Co., 1948.

Rothbard, Murray N. *Power and Market.* Menlo Park, Cal.: Institute for Humane Studies, 1970.

———————————. *Man, Economy and State: A Treatise on Economic Principles.* Los Angeles: Nash Publishing, 1970.

———————————. "Freedom, Inequality, Primitivism and the Division of Labour." *Modern Age* 15, No. 3, Summer 1971.

Roethlisberger, F.J. *Management and Morale.* Cambridge, Mass.: Harvard University Press, 1941. 7th printing, 1947.

Rosenbluth, Gideon. "Monopoly and Monopolizaton" in Pritchard, J.R.S., *et al Canadian Competition Policy: Essays in Law and Economics.*Toronto: Butterworth, 1979.

Rothwell, Donald Stuart. "An Enquiry into the Factors that Combine to Explain Managerial Achievement." Montreal: Thesis, McGill University, 1973.

Royal Commission on Corporate Concentration. *Report of the Royal Commission on Corporate Concentration, 1978.* Ottawa: Ministry of Supply and Services, 1978.

Samuelson, Paul A., and Scott, Anthony. *Economics: Fifth Canadian Edition.* Toronto: McGraw-Hill Ryerson, 1980.

Scherer, F.M. "Firm Size, Market Structure, Opportunity, and the Output of Patented Inventions." *American Economic Review* 55, (December 1965): 1097-1125.

———————————. *Industrial Market Structure and Economic Performance.* Chicago: Rand McNally, 1970.

———————————. "Industrial Structure, Scale Economics, and Worker Alienation" in Masson, Robert T., and Qualls, P. David (eds). *Essays on Industrial Organization in Honor of Joe S. Bain.* Cambrdige, Mass.: Ballinger, 1976: 105-21 and sources that Scherer cites.

———————————. "Market Structure and the Employment of Scientists and Engineers." *American Economic Review* 57 (June 1967): 524-531.

Schumpeter, Joseph A. *Capitalism, Socialism and Democracy.* 2d ed. New York: Harper and Brothers, 1947.

Scitovsky, Tibor. *Welfare and Competition.* Chicago: Richard D. Irwin, 1951.

Seneca, Rosalind S., and Haight, David Ernest. "The Concept of Power: Antitrust as an Illustration." *Antitrust Bulletin* XXIII Number 2, (Summer 1970): 339-369.

Shepherd, William G. *The Economics of Industrial Organization.* Englewood Cliffs, N.J.: Prentice-Hall, 1979.

Sherman, Roger. *Oligopoly, Our Empirical Approach.* Lexington, Mass.: Lexington Books, 1972.

Sherman, V. Clayton. "Business Ethics: Analysis and Philosophy" in Luthans, Fred, & Hodgetts, Richard M. *Readings on the Current Social Issues in Business: Poverty, Civil Rights, Ecology, and Consumerism.* New York: Macmillan Co., 1972.

Simon, Herbert. *Models of Man.* New York: Wiley, 1957.

Skeoch, L.A. *Canadian Competition Policy* (Proceedings of a Conference held at Queens University, Kingston, Ontario. Jan. 20-21, 1972). Kingston: Industrial Relations Centre of Queens University, 1972.

———————————. *Restrictive Trade Practices in Canada: Selected Readings.* Toronto: McClelland and Stewart Limited, 1966.

Smith, Adam. *An Inquiry into the Nature and Causes of the Wealth of Nations.* New York: Modern Library, 1937 ed.

Solo, Carolyn Shaw. "Innovation in the Capitalist Process: A Critique of the Schumpeterian Theory." *Quarterly Journal of Economics* LXV No. 3 (August 1951): 417-428.

Solow, Robert M. "The New Industrial State or Son of Affluence." *The Public Interest* 9, (Fall 1967): 100-108.

Sowell, Thomas. *Knowledge and Decisions.* New York: Basic Books, 1980.

Stigler, George J. "The Economics of Information." *Journal of Political Economy* LXIX No. 3, (June 1961): 213-224.

———————. "Monopoly and Oligopoly by Merger." *American Economic Review: Papers and Proceedings* XL, Number 2 (May 1950): 23-47, 63-64.

———————. "Perfect Competition, Historically Contemplated." *Journal of Political Economy* LXV, Number 1 (February 1957): 1-17.

———————. "The Xistence of X-Efficiency." *American Economic Review* 66 (March 1976): 213-216.

Stigler, George J., and Kindahl, James K. *The Behavior of Industrial Prices*. New York: National Bureau of Economic Research, 1970.

Stogdill, R. *Handbook of Leadership*. New York: Free Press, 1974.

Stokes, Charles J. *Economics for Managers*. New York: McGraw-Hill, 1979.

Taylor, George Rogers, and Ney, Irene D. *The American Railroad Network: 1861-1890*. Cambridge, Mass.: Harvard University Press, 1956.

Tobias, Andrew. *Fire and Ice*. New York: Warner Books, 1976.

Towle, Joseph W., *et al. Ethics and Standards in American Business*. Boston: Houghton Mifflin Co. 1964.

Wattles, George M. "The Rates and Costs of the U.S. Post Office." *Journal of Law and Economics* XVI (1), (April 1973): 89-117.

Weiss, Leonard W. "The Concentration — Profits Relationship and Antitrust" in Goldschmid, Harvey J., *et al. Industrial Concentration: The New Learning*. Columbia University Center for Law and Economic Studies. Boston: Little, Brown and Co., 1974.

Whitaker, Richard. "Canada's Simulator Giant." *Flight International*, 23 May 1981.

Whyte, W.H. "How Hard do Executives Work." The Editors of *Fortune. The Executive Life*. Garden City, N.J.: Doubleday & Company, 1956.

Wilson, Sloan. *The Man in the Grey Flannel Suit*. New York: Pocket Books Inc., 1956.

Worley, James S. "The Changing Direction of Research and Development Employment Among Firms." Universities — National Bureau Conference, *The Rate and Direction of Inventive Activity: Economic and Social Factors*. Princeton: Princeton University Press, 1962.

INDEX